Pick of the Web

Make these sites your first stops for real estate information
bookmark your favorites so you can refer to them often.

Home Buying Megas...

REALTOR.COM	http://www.realtor.com
iOwn	http://www.iown.com
HomeAdvisor	http://www.homeadvisor.msn.com
CyberHomes	http://www.cyberhomes.com
Century21.com	http://www.century21.com

For Sale By Owner Sites

owners.com	http://www.owners.com
FSBO.COM	http://www.fsbo.com

Online Mortgage Lender Sites

QuickenMortgage	http://www.quickenmortgage.com
E-LOAN	http://www.eloan.com
iOwn	http://www.iown.com
LendingTree.com	http://www.lendingtree.com
mortgage.com	http://www.mortgage.com

Online Credit Report Sites

Equifax	http://www.equifax.com
Experian	http://www.experian.com
Transunion	http://www.transunion.com

Real Estate Agency Sites

REALTOR.COM	http://www.realtor.com
Century21.com	http://www.century 21
RE/MAX	http://www.remax.com
Coldwell Banker	http://coldwellbanker.com
Better Homes and Gardens	http://www.bhg-real-estate.com
ERA.com	http://www.era.com

cut here

QUe ®

Ten Things to Do After Buying a Home

1. **Start two house files with all records and documents.**

   Keep a file with all documents pertaining to your home in the house and another stored somewhere else for safekeeping.

2. **Watch your spending and try to still save money.**

   Even though it's tempting, don't go overboard spending money on your new home. Garage sales and second-hand stores are great.

3. **Build your emergency reserve funds again.**

   To be ready for major repairs or problems, work to replenish your emergency fund savings—especially if you used some or all of it for the down payment.

4. **Consider direct deposit of your mortgage payment.**

   Simplify bill paying and guarantee timely payments by having your mortgage paid electronically.

5. **Keep receipts of all improvements and repairs.**

   Receipts help you market the home when you sell and might allow you to pay less in taxes. Ask an accountant about the adjusted cost basis of your home and how receipts help support this.

6. **Consider paying principal faster with principal-only payment.**

   If you need to build equity fast, making a second payment (at $100) towards principal only will accelerate your equity build up.

7. **Ignore ads for mortgage insurance and equity credit lines.**

   Get rid of ads for mortgage life insurance, mortgage disability insurance, credit lines, homesteading, and twice-monthly payments. These solicitations aren't wise uses of your money.

8. **Appeal property taxes if values decline or the bill is wrong.**

   If your taxes seem high or homes have gone down in your area, contact the Assessor's office and request an appeal.

9. **Refinance your loan if interest rates fall.**

   Watch interest rates and refinance your mortgage to lower your payment if rates go down.

10. **Track values of homes in your area to know the market.**

    Understand your market and be knowledgeable about prices and conditions by tracking home sales while you live in your home.

    And a special bonus tip that may be the most important thing:

11. **Enjoy your home and make it your personal haven.**

    Take time to enjoy all the wonderful features that attracted you to your home in the first place and create an atmosphere of harmony in your home that makes it a special place to be.

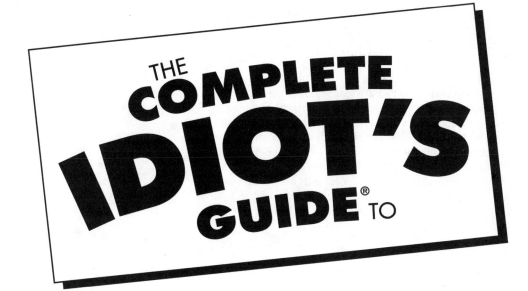

THE COMPLETE IDIOT'S GUIDE® TO

Online Buying and

Selling a Home

Matthew O'Brien

A Division of Macmillan USA
201 West 103rd Street, Indianapolis, Indiana 46290

The Complete Idiot's Guide to Online Buying and Selling a Home

Copyright © 2000 by Que®

International Standard Book Number: 0-7897-2257-7

Library of Congress Catalog Card Number: 99-65791

Printed in the United States of America

First Printing: *February 2000*

02   01   00   4   3   2   1

Trademarks

All terms mentioned in this book that are known to be trademarks or service marks have been appropriately capitalized. Que cannot attest to the accuracy of this information. Use of a term in this book should not be regarded as affecting the validity of any trademark or service mark.

Realtor is a registered trademark of the National Association of Realtors.

Warning and Disclaimer

Publisher
Greg Wiegand

Acquisitions Editor
Stephanie J. McComb

Development Editor
Gregory Harris

Managing Editor
Thomas F. Hayes

Project Editor
Casey Kenley

Copy Editor
Sossity Smith

Indexer
Heather McNeill

Proofreaders
Aaron Black
Jeanne Clark
Harvey Stanbrough
Matt Wooden

Technical Editor
Debbie Morris

Illustrator
Judd Winick

Team Coordinator
Sharry Gregory

Interior Designer
Nathan Clement

Cover Designer
Michael Freeland

Copy Writer
Eric Borgert

Production
Eric S. Miller
Louis Porter, Jr.

Contents at a Glance

Table of Contents

11 New Construction or Designing Your Own Home

12 Condominiums

13 Patio Homes/Zero Lot Lines: What Are They?

Foreword

Homeownership. It is still the great American dream. As we enter the twenty-first century, that dream is one of the few things in the real estate industry that has not changed during the past decade.

Thanks to new technology and the Internet, the home-buying experience has undergone a major transformation. In the past, real estate was basically a closed industry. Real estate professionals were the gatekeepers of information available on homes for sale through the local Multiple Listing Service. Today, the consumer has been empowered. Anyone with a computer has access to a world of real estate information, from home listings to mortgage rates.

In the new millennium, the role of the real estate professional has been redefined. No longer are real estate brokers and sales associates gatekeepers of information. In the marketplace of the twenty-first century, agents have become interpreters of data. We are service providers, leading consumers through the complexity of the real estate transaction. The real estate industry has become high-tech, but it is still a process that demands "high-touch."

While the role of the real estate agent has changed, it is more critical than ever. Today's real estate professional must act as a guide for the customer—addressing the client's needs by providing a mix of market knowledge, technological savvy, and industry insight.

Technology is a fantastic tool that can provide consumers with vast amounts of information, but buying or selling a home is still one of the largest investments most people ever make. It is more critical than ever to "do your homework" and understand all the aspects of the real estate transaction before making any decisions, and there are sure to be many.

The Complete Idiot's Guide to Online Buying and Selling a Home is a great first step in the journey to the American Dream.

Marty Rodriguez

CENTURY 21, Glendora, California

Marty Rodriguez is the CENTURY 21 System's all-time top-producing agent and arguably the top-producing residential agent in the industry. She has been the number one U.S. CENTURY 21 agent for 10 consecutive years and the number one agent in the world four times. Over the past three years, Rodriguez and her team have sold nearly $350 million in real estate.

About the Author

Matthew O'Brien has worked full-time as a real estate agent, consultant, and investor since graduating from St. Joseph's College in 1992. He has been a multi-million-dollar sales producer and quality service award winner each year in the business. He is the President of Matthew O'Brien Realty Unlimited Inc., a consulting firm that specializes in For Sale By Owner and investment property transactions. O'Brien does new agent training for Century 21 at the Crossing, a top Century 21 office in the Midwest.

A former college basketball player, O'Brien is also a published fiction writer. His sports mystery novel, *Chameleon: The March Madness Murders*, debuted in 1997. He is currently working on another sports mystery novel and finishing his first screenplay for the big screen.

Matthew welcomes any questions or comments. He can be reached via email at mattob9023@aol.com.

Dedication

In loving memory of Denny Hickey and Bernie O'Brien, my beloved mother, Kay Hickey O'Brien, and my soul mates, John, Sussan, Kevin, and Chris O'Brien. Thank you for showing me how to work like I don't need money, love like I've never been hurt, and dance like no one's watching.

Acknowledgments

Special thanks to Stephanie McComb, acquisitions editor extraordinare, for your considerable insight and help; Gregory Harris, development editor, for superbly overseeing and running this project; Casey Kenley, project editor, for your patience, assistance, and cheerful attitude; and Sossity Smith and Debbie Morris for your excellent work as copyeditor and technical editor, respectively. To my angel buddy Julie, there are not strong enough words in the English language to recognize you. Many thanks for research and data to Ted Sherfick at MNC Mortgage Co. in Indianapolis, the premier loan originator in the business because of Warren Harling. Kerry Miller gets the MVP for the regular season and the playoffs. You had the biggest assist of the year, Stroke.

Warm thanks to Mike Hasch, Liz Everidge, and my computer consultant, Ed Sherfick, one of the highest-quality people alive. Endless thanks to the owners (Steve Dec, Tim O'C, & Mr. Bill), Marsha Patrick, and the staff and agents of Century 21 at the Crossing in Indianapolis, the greatest place in the world to sell real estate. Finally, thanks a million times over to an amazing Country girl who is my best friend. The Soul Summit, it's a whole new world, and cornballishness got me through this. 498-76599......breathe.

Tell Us What You Think!

As the reader of this book, *you* are our most important critic and commentator. We value your opinion and want to know what we're doing right, what we could do better, what areas you'd like to see us publish in, and any other words of wisdom you're willing to pass our way.

As a Publisher for Que, I welcome your comments. You can fax, email, or write me directly to let me know what you did or didn't like about this book—as well as what we can do to make our books stronger.

Please note that I cannot help you with technical problems related to the topic of this book, and that due to the high volume of mail I receive, I might not be able to reply to every message.

When you write, please be sure to include this book's title and author as well as your name and phone or fax number. I will carefully review your comments and share them with the author and editors who worked on the book.

Fax: 317-581-4666

Email: consumer@mcp.com

Mail: Greg Wiegand
          Que
          201 West 103rd Street
          Indianapolis, IN 46290 USA

Introduction

Welcome to *The Complete Idiot's Guide to Online Buying and Selling a Home*. Just a few years ago, home buyers crammed into their Realtors' cars or spent Sunday afternoons walking through open houses in search of their dream home. The Internet was little more than a theory. People in academia and the military talked about an information superhighway, but most Americans had never heard of it, let alone surfed it. Even nine months ago the idea of using the Internet to buy or sell a home was unthinkable.

How times have changed! Buying a home is the biggest investment in most people's lives and an extremely complicated process. The Internet is the greatest source of information in the world. Combining the two was a natural fit, so it would seem.

Unlike the automotive and travel industries, the real estate industry was slow to embrace online buying and selling. Agents feared they would lose their jobs, others resisted simply because computer technology was new and foreign to them. Realtors were finally dragged onto the information superhighway, some kicking and screaming, by home buyers and sellers who were using the Internet for other less-important tasks.

To the delight of real estate professionals everywhere, the online phenomenon has created more educated homebuyers and sellers; made transactions quicker, easier, and more convenient; and appears to be a major factor in For Sale By Owner transactions decreasing in number the last two years.

Real estate buyers and sellers have benefited just as much, if not more. Along with having a wealth of information at their fingertips, they are able to cut time and expenses in half, make more informed decisions, and instantly accomplish tasks online that used to take hours or days.

Two years ago buyers would view twenty to thirty homes in two or three months before making a decision to write an offer to purchase. That same buyer today, using online services, would look at only eight to twelve homes in two to four weeks before writing an offer. Timing is the key ingredient in real estate transactions being consummated or falling apart. Online buyers and sellers have a huge advantage over their counterparts who are not online. Armed with more information and a higher comfort level, they are able to act more decisively and time the market to secure the best results.

Another advantage of online home shopping is the control factor. Consumers are able to house hunt in the middle of the night, on their lunch breaks, whenever they want. Pushy sales agents are less of a problem because buyers have already narrowed their selections down to a short list of around five to fifteen homes before they even contact a Realtor. The old days of agents showing you homes out of your price range or in areas you don't want to live in are history.

So, Why Do You Need This Book?

If you've picked up this book, odds are you have never bought or sold a home, never spent considerable time surfing the Internet, or never attempted to buy or sell real estate online. *The Complete Idiot's Guide to Online Buying and Selling a Home* will

➤ Walk you through all the steps of the online buying process

➤ Explain industry jargon and define key terms and concepts

➤ Instruct you on what to look for in selecting money-lending institutions, Realtors title companies, and home inspectors

➤ Compare and contrast various real estate Web sites

➤ Show you how to prepare your house to be sold by a Realtor or By Owner

Some aspects of real estate have not changed in 50 years and probably won't ever. But the online marketing of homes has caused more rapid change in the industry in the past two years than all other advancements during the last ten, and online buying and selling is still in the infancy stage! This topic is so new, real estate professionals are becoming educated at the same time their clients are, or simply learning as they go.

This book will focus on two things: where to go to perform tasks and gather information online, and doing things the easiest way possible. The guide can be read sequentially by chapter, by browsing through large sections (for example, Part 2, "Financing Your Dream Home"), or by skipping around to certain areas that interest you.

How Do You Use This Book?

Sure you're already using this book, but it's not that silly a question. If this is the first *Complete Idiot's Guide* you've ever read, there are just a few things you should know.

First, the best way to learn is to follow along with the explanation for any procedure. If you need to select a particular menu, you'll see the name of that menu in **bold**, as in

Open the **File** menu and select **Print**.

The buttons and tabs in dialog boxes also are highlighted, such as

Click **OK** to save your changes when you're finished in the **General Options** tab.

Key combinations in this book appear with a plus sign between them. For example

Click **New** or just press Ctrl+N to create a new category.

This means you should hold down the **Ctrl** key and tap the letter **N**, and then release the keys in any order.

Finally, any text you type, such as Web addresses, appear in monospace type, like this:

Type www.mcp.com in the **Location** text box.

Extras

Along with presenting information on real estate Web sites and industry practices, this book offers insights and advice to navigate real estate's tricky waters. The following icons are used throughout the book:

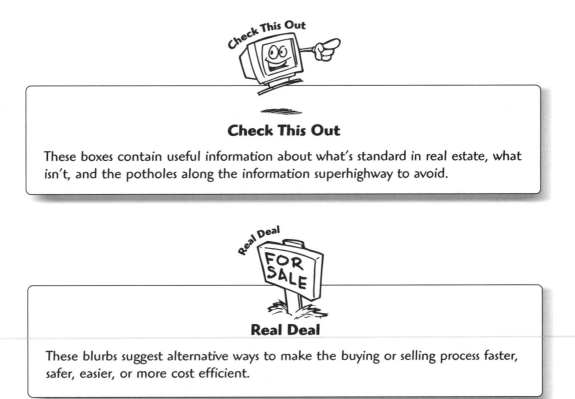

Check This Out

These boxes contain useful information about what's standard in real estate, what isn't, and the potholes along the information superhighway to avoid.

Real Deal

These blurbs suggest alternative ways to make the buying or selling process faster, safer, easier, or more cost efficient.

Real Estate Terms

Want to be an industry insider? These sidebars explain the odd lingo used by real estate professionals.

Part 1

First Things First: What to Do When You Are in the Market to Buy

Real estate professionals will tell you timing can make or break a transaction. Act too quickly and you might make a bad decision or pay too much for a property. Drag your feet, and you might lose your dream home. Most aspects of real estate do come down to timing. With that in mind, we will move briskly through Part 1 toward the meatier topics in real estate, yet still cover online basics so you can get up and running on the Internet.

Chapter 1

Preparing Yourself: This Is One of the Biggest Investments of Your Life

In This Chapter

➤ What resources are needed to get online

➤ A quiz to see if you're ready to buy a home

➤ The pros and cons of renting versus owning

➤ Understanding the mysterious real estate lingo

➤ A list of the many types of real estate

Before you can run you must first learn to walk. You will actually begin by crawling through an explanation of what the Internet is. The *Internet* can be summed up as a network of computers connected with one another for the purpose of sharing information and transferring files. Although there are many uses for the Internet—specifically email, the World Wide Web, chat rooms, and discussion groups—the key feature is information being shared by connected computers.

The real estate industry in particular is driven by information: how much homes in a particular area sell for, the current interest rate, the strength of school systems in a town, and so on. Like many good marriages, the union of real estate and the Internet was slow to develop. After it did, though, the two were a perfect fit and really took off. Real estate and the Internet go well together because the Internet puts information and control in the hands of the customer.

This chapter briefly describes what resources are needed to get online, and then dives into a meat-and-potatoes discussion about the various types of real estate and whether you're ready to own a home.

What You Need to Search Online: Online Search Engines

There are many ways to get on the Internet. Some of the easiest ways to gain access are

➤ Through online services like America Online (AOL), Netscape, CompuServe, The Microsoft Network (MSN), Prodigy, and Gateway.

➤ Through small, local Internet service providers; large, national service providers, such as PSINet, EarthLink, and Sprynet; or a school's computer network.

➤ Through your phone company or free community computer networks.

Search engines are used to search for topics on the Net. Key words and phrases are typed into the engine's search box, which simultaneously transmits the data to many individual engines and their databases of Web pages. Results from the search engines are produced in a matter of seconds. To find out if you can get a mortgage to buy a home, you would go to any number of search engines (Yahoo!, for instance) and type a set of key words, such as `mortgage pre-qualification`.

A limitation of search engines is the amount of matches, or responses, that turn up when commonly used words are searched for. The sheer number of responses can be overwhelming. The more unique and specific the key word you submit, the more effective the search will be. For example, `mortgage` and `pre-qualification` are better search words than just `loan`, because there are many types of loans other than loans to finance a house. Search engines are not perfect. They often misunderstand the logic behind your choice of a key word or phrase. The result is incomplete or inaccurate results.

Are Interest Rates Negotiable?

The interest rate you pay on your loan is negotiable. Buyers with near perfect or perfect credit get what's known as the lenders A rate. The weaker your credit history is, the less bargaining power you have with lenders.

There is a multitude of online search engines in existence, and the number seems to grow monthly. Here is a list of addresses of some of the bigger and better engines:

www.about.com	www.infoseek.com
www.altavista.com	www.lycos.com
www.excite.com	www.nothernlight.com
www.fastsearch.com	www.search.com
www.goto.com	www.webcrawler.com
www.hotbot.com	www.yahoo.com

More Search Tips

For more information about these and many other search sites, including power tips on getting the most for your queries, check out *The Complete Idiot's Guide to Online Search Secrets* by Michael Miller.

Remember, be concise and unique with your key word or phrase. There are more than 250,000 real estate–related Web sites on the Net, so it's easy to get lost in an avalanche of information. Following is a figure of Yahoo!'s Web site, just one of many search engines to use when looking up information. For an example of what a search engine looks like, see Figure 1.1.

Figure 1.1

Yahoo! is an easy-to-use search site.

Are You Ready to Buy a Home?

Nearly everyone dreams of owning their own home. The idea of finding the perfect piece of land, building the exact house you want, and putting roots down dates back to the settling of America. Romantic visions of a Robert Redford movie notwithstanding, owning a home is not for everyone. The advantages of owning do outweigh the advantages of renting, but there are some compelling reasons not to buy a home. First, let's explore the pros to owning.

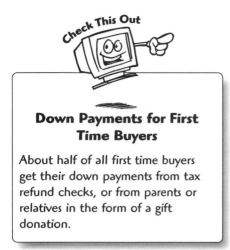

Down Payments for First Time Buyers

About half of all first time buyers get their down payments from tax refund checks, or from parents or relatives in the form of a gift donation.

Advantages to Owning a Home

The reasons to own real estate run the gamut from financial to psychological. A list of those reasons follows:

➤ Pride in ownership

➤ Tax breaks

➤ Investment/appreciation

➤ Builds savings or equity

➤ Strengthens credit history

➤ Control and privacy

➤ Fixed housing costs

There are numerous financial advantages to owning a home, but the single greatest reason might be pride in owning and caring for your personal dwelling. You can do whatever you want to with the place (within the boundaries of the U.S. Constitution or your neighborhood association, whichever is stricter) and have a great time doing it. (A disco ball and shag carpet in the master bedroom might hurt the home's value.) Another strong intangible reason is the control and autonomy owners enjoy. If you don't want to put up with loud, nosy, or obnoxious neighbors, buy a house with lots of trees or fence your problems away on all sides. Owning can empower you and give you more control over your emotional and financial destinies.

The financial advantages to owning a home are numerous and varied. To promote homeownership the government gives tax breaks—fairly large tax breaks—to home-owners. You can deduct most, if not all, of the interest you pay on the mortgage loan along with discount points incurred while financing the home and property taxes.

Appreciation is a fancy way of saying a home went up in value. By selecting the right home in an area of solidly appreciating houses, your monthly mortgage payment becomes an investment. Appreciation rates differ within cities around the country, even within subdivisions, or from block to block in some areas. (Homes in certain areas also can depreciate, or go down in value.) Normal ranges of appreciation are 3–5% per year, which is a nice return on your money because you have to live some-where. These numbers can fluctuate wildly depending on only a hundred or so factors in that particular marketplace.

Equity is the amount of the home you own. If your house is worth $100,000 and you owe the bank $90,000 on the mortgage, the equity, or amount you own, is $10,000. Equity is a savings account. You are forced each month to add to your savings account by paying the mortgage. The reward, along with having a roof over your head and enjoying the house, comes when you borrow from your savings account (take out an equity credit line, or second mortgage) to pay for junior's college tuition, the speed boat you've always wanted, or that room addition you've talked about for years. An even bigger reward occurs when you sell the home. The difference between what you owe on the loan (say $50,000), and what the home sold for (say $150,000) is given to the seller at closing in a proceeds check. $100,000 is a terrific down payment on your next house. There are a few other costs sellers must pay at closing, but your equity or savings account is largely determined by the amount you owe on the loan, known as the *payoff amount*, subtracted from the sales price of the home.

Less substantial advantages to owning are the strong credit history you can build by paying your mortgage on time each month (paying rent on time does this as well), and securing a fixed, unchanging mortgage payment every month. If you finance your home with a fixed mortgage rate for the life of a 30-year loan, your payment will never go up regardless of whether interest rates skyrocket, inflation escalates, or the stock market crashes. Landlords can raise rent payments at their discretion and usually do. An added bonus of owning is stability and comfort. Renters tend to move from place to place more often (besides owners of moving companies, who likes to move?) and don't have incentives to care for a property the way homeowners do. The result usually means owners live in higher quality dwellings.

Disadvantages to Owning a Home

Owning a home is always possible, and there are situations when it is not prudent. The disadvantages to owning are largely financial:

➤ Mortgage payments and taxes and insurance

➤ Maintenance and upkeep

Check This Out

How Are Mortgages Paid Off?

Title companies order the seller's payoff for the closing and overnight the check to the lender. The remaining balance on the loan is satisfied as of the day of closing.

Real Deal

Paying Off an FHA Loan

Unlike conventional loans, interest is charged through the last day of the month on FHA loans, regardless of which day of the month you close. So, sellers should always try to close at the end of the month if their current loan is an FHA mortgage. Closing early in the next month can cost you up to $1,000 in interest.

➤ Utility bills

➤ Risk of depreciation

➤ Lack of flexibility and freedom

Mortgage payments tend to be higher than rent payments. Lending institutions require property tax payments and homeowners hazard insurance to be added to the principal loan amount and interest charge. Failure to make your mortgage payments on time results in the lender seizing the property and selling it to recover their money. Owners must pay all the utility bills, whereas renters sometimes pay half or none. One of the biggest deterrents to buying a home is the responsibility involved. Maintenance and upkeep on the house can be a huge financial, physical, and emotional drain. Homeownership is a commitment, and many people are not ready, or able to make and honor the commitment.

Knowing when not to buy is just as important as knowing when to take the plunge. Red flags should go up when you know you're only going to live in a home for a short time, such as one to two years. If you're buying simply to make money (excluding investment rental properties), the plan can backfire and you can lose money, all the while living in a home you didn't like. If you don't feel knowledgeable or comfortable in a new city or area, renting is a great option while you familiarize yourself before buying. If you're worried about making the mortgage payments each month, paying a lower rent amount and saving extra money might be the smart decision. People with medical conditions should consider the maintenance work and upkeep homeownership requires. Renting basically means no responsibility, which is ideal for some people.

Home Warranty Plans

Home warranty plans are a type of insurance to protect owners from expensive home repairs. Most plans cost around $350 (with a $100 deductible) and cover all the major mechanical systems and appliances for one year. These are especially useful for older homes or homes in disrepair.

A Quiz to See if You're Ready to Own

Here are a series of questions to ask yourself to see if you're ready to own a home:

➤ Does it bother you each month when you write a rent check that you're throwing money away?

➤ Do you wish you had more control over the way your house or apartment looks?

➤ Are you tired of community living in an apartment and do you long for quieter, more private surroundings?

➤ Have you accumulated money in savings or checking accounts?

➤ Do you pay all your bills on time and have good credit?

➤ Have you rented the same place for a long time?

➤ Do you have difficulty taking care of possessions?

➤ Do you barely have money left over after you pay your bills?

➤ Will you be getting married or relocating to another place within a year or two?

➤ Are you self-employed or do you have large fluctuations in income from one month to the next?

Rent-to-Buy/Lease Options: The Best of Both Worlds

Lease options are a combination of renting and buying. People who are not yet ready to buy (because they don't have a down payment, their credit history needs to be improved, or they're not sure if they like the house enough to buy it) can enter into a contractual agreement with a homeowner to make payments for a duration of time. After that designated time, the person must decide to buy the home, where a portion of the payments will constitute a down payment, or move out, forfeiting the money paid. Rent-to-buy basically means putting a house on layaway until you decide if you want to buy it and if you can afford to buy it. Owners come out ahead whether the renter ends up buying or not, and renters get to try out the home with minimal risk before making a decision.

The key element to making rent-to-buy/lease options work is figuring out terms (payment amounts, interest charges, when the renter must decide, what portion of the payments will go toward the down payment) that please both the owner and the prospective buyer. Also, be sure you agree up front on what repairs you are responsible for and what the owner is responsible for during the period of the lease. You don't want to get stuck paying for a new roof and then not buy the home at the end of the contract period.

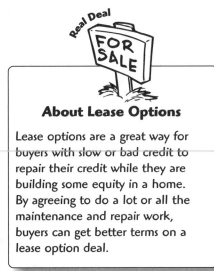

About Lease Options

Lease options are a great way for buyers with slow or bad credit to repair their credit while they are building some equity in a home. By agreeing to do a lot or all the maintenance and repair work, buyers can get better terms on a lease option deal.

Real Estate Lingo: An Online Glossary

adjustable-rate mortgage   A type of mortgage where the interest rate is tied to a particular economic index and is adjusted as the index rises and falls. Monthly payments go up or down depending on the current rates.

agent   A person authorized to work on another's behalf or assist another in the purchase or sale of a home.

13

To License or Not to License

Appraisers and real estate agents must be licensed by the state they conduct business in. Loan originators, home inspectors, and title company escrow closers are not required by law to be licensed.

appraisal   A determination of the value of an improved property or parcel of land by a licensed, certified, impartial individual.

balloon mortgage   A type of mortgage where the loan amount is amortized over the entire length of the loan (usually 30 years), but the loan comes due in a shorter time (typically 5 or 7 years). The balance of the loan is due in one final installment known as the balloon payment.

broker   An agent authorized to operate his or her own agency. A principal broker is the sole individual who runs an office.

Picture This: Photos Help

A home must be delivered to a new buyer at possession time in the same condition it was bought. Consider taking pictures during the viewing process and definitely during the inspection process. At the final walk through the day before closing, compare the pictures to the condition of the home. You also might be able to use the photos to negotiate a better price or home repairs if you find major defects.

When to Get Homeowner's Insurance

Homeowner's insurance and all additional insurance should be put in place the day of closing (even if you are a condo buyer who only gets contents insurance for furniture and clothes). If a fire burns down a home the day before closing, the seller's insurance pays for it. A fire the day after closing would be the responsibility of the buyer's insurance company.

closing   The process of finalizing all aspects of a real estate transaction. Title is passed from seller to buyer and all funds are dispersed at closing.

commission   The fee an agent earns during the sale of a home, typically a percentage of the gross sales price (2% to 3.5% depending on the local market).

conventional mortgage   A type of mortgage made by lending institutions where the buyer pays at least 5% of the purchase price as a down payment at closing.

counter offer   A counter response or new proposal that makes changes to terms in the original purchase agreement.

down payment   Money paid up front for the purchase of a home.

earnest money   Deposit made when an offer to purchase is written. Shows buyer's sincerity and ability to purchase the home.

FHA mortgage   A loan guaranteed by the federal government. Stands for Federal Housing Authority. A small down payment is made, but mortgage insurance is required.

fixed-rate mortgage   A type of mortgage where the interest rate is fixed for the life of the loan.

For Sale By Owner (FSBO)   A home being sold by the owner without the use of a real estate agent.

home inspection   A thorough examination of the condition of a home by a qualified, impartial individual.

interest rate   A percentage the lender charges for borrowing money.

Multiple Listing Service (MLS)   A computerized listing system of all the homes for sale by all real estate offices in a particular city.

mortgage   A legal document that pledges a property as security for a loan.

Realtor   An agent who belongs to a local or State Board of Realtors and the National Association of Realtors (NAR). These agents must follow the organizations' code of ethics.

subdivision   A large piece of land divided into numerous plots or parcels on which single family homes are built.

Negotiating FSBO Fees

For Sale By Owner sellers often pay commissions to Realtors working on behalf of buyers. If you are a buyer looking at By Owners and want to be represented by an agent, the way to get a seller to pay your agent's commission is to be completely loyal and unified with the agent. Tell the seller you won't buy a home without the agent, you can't pay the agent's commission, and you are a pre-approved buyer. Many By Owner sellers will give in. If you are selling By Owner, the way to avoid paying the agent's fee is to let the buyer see your home, get them attached to it, and then test the buyer's loyalty to the agent by refusing to pay the fee. Many buyers will drop their agents instead of losing the home they want.

title insurance   Insurance that protects the lender and buyer against liability or losses when the title is passed to a buyer. Title insurance companies host closings and preside over the proceedings.

VA loan   A type of loan available only to military veterans where no down payment is required. Known for its stringent appraisals.

Types of Real Estate

When you start your search for a home, you will have to decide if you want an existing home—one already built—or if you want to build a new home. There are pros and cons to both.

Existing Homes: The Traditional Dwelling

Existing homes are far and away the most popular choice of homebuyers. Seven or eight out of every ten buyers buy existing homes rather than build new-construction houses. This is because no one is making any more land to build on, and there are so many more existing homes to buy.

Established neighborhoods are one of the strongest advantages of existing homes. There's much less guess work in determining whether the home will appreciate in value if the area has done so for twenty to thirty years. Along with knowing what you're getting, existing homes usually have mature trees, sidewalks, and bigger lots. All the conveniences of modern living—grocery stores, banks, restaurants, video stores, and so on—are already in place and close by. There is no construction or building in these areas so they tend to be quieter and more private.

When Homes Become Outdated

Homes that are fifteen to thirty years old often need the most repairs. Many of the major mechanical systems, roof, furnace, central air conditioner, and plumbing are near or at the end of their useful life. Updating the décor in the kitchen and bathrooms also comes due around this time. A great time to buy an existing home is right after these repairs and updates have been done.

Existing homes typically have more personality and charm than new homes and the diversity in architecture is much greater than new-construction subdivisions where homes are slight variations of each other. Older homes often provide more space and amenities for the money. Adding a basement or Florida sun room to a new home might cost $20,000–25,000, whereas in an existing home the buyer might pay only half of that.

The negative factors of buying an existing home should be considered as well. You are buying someone else's dream. Does it satisfy your needs and wants when you can build your own dream? Existing homes often have tiny closets and bathrooms, small, detached garages, and impractical kitchens and laundry rooms. The maintenance of an older home is also a vital issue. The structure, roof, plumbing, wiring, furnace/air conditioning, and all the appliances might be near the end of their remaining useful lives. Older homes also can be plagued with problems like termites, water damage, radon, asbestos, and underground oil tanks. Few mechanical systems, if any, are under warranty in an older home, and the cost to keep them up can be expensive.

New-Construction Homes: Building Your Dream

Choice and newness are the biggest advantages of new homes. Builders offer a variety of floor plans, colors, styles, and levels of quality. You get what you want. Kitchens and closets are bigger. Garages are attached and great rooms have vaulted ceilings with more open, roomier airspace. New-home subdivisions have extra amenities such as a pool, tennis courts, playgrounds, and a clubhouse. Most new-construction sites are in the suburbs so the area is less highly traveled and crime might be lower. Everything in a new home is clean, in pristine condition, and under warranty. Maintenance should be little to nothing the first few years. If you like modern, contemporary home designs, new construction is the way to go.

Disadvantages to new homes are the lack of landscaping and trees; living out in the boondocks; lack of character, individuality, and warmth; and the small lots. There is less room to negotiate price with a builder or developer, and the association covenants and restrictions in the subdivision might limit improvements or modifications you want to make. Resale value in communities where building goes on for years can be a problem. Trying to sell your two-year-old, lived-in home when buyers can build brand new all around you is difficult.

Appreciation might not be established yet so the financial/investment part might be questionable. Building new doesn't usually give you value, especially if you're custom building. Buyers pay for all the wonderful little extras, and you pay top dollar. Building can isolate you from people, places, and things you are accustomed to because new building sites can be far out from the city.

Renter's Insurance for Condos

Unlike residential homeowners who are required by their mortgage companies to keep hazard insurance on their property, condo owners do not have to get homeowner's insurance when they close a transaction. The monthly association fee condo owners pay provides exterior structural coverage under a master insurance policy for the entire community. Condo owners can choose to carry contents insurance that covers furniture, appliances, televisions, stereos, clothes, and so on for only $100–200 per year.

Condominiums: A Lifestyle and Convenience Choice

Another type of housing that offers many of the benefits of ownership without the hassle of maintenance and upkeep is *condos*. With condos you own the actual living unit and all the air space from floor to ceiling and wall to wall. The roof, exterior housing, and grounds are jointly owned by everyone in the community. A monthly association fee is charged for maintaining the outside of the units and the common ground, which usually includes a pool, clubhouse, tennis courts, and the landscaping. Condos are especially attractive to retirees, professionals who travel a lot or who are not home much, or anyone who does not want to deal with yard work or home repairs. Condos appeal to people who want a certain ease of living, but might not be the best for large families or people with multiple pets because of the lack of privacy and autonomy.

Making Improvements to Condos

When condo owners want to make improvements to their units—such as adding a deck, installing a satellite dish, or putting in a hot tub—a proposal for the planned improvement must be submitted to the association's Architectural Control Committee (ACC) for its approval. This board is made up of owners in the community. The role of the ACC is to maintain consistency and uniformity so the overall values of the condos in the community increase.

Patio Homes/Zero Lot Lines

One of the most recent trends in new-construction building in the last twenty years is *patio homes*, also known as *zero lot lines*. This type of hybrid housing is a combination of existing home, condominiums, and new home. Most patio home communities are around ten years old or newer and offer many of the amenities of new homes, such as a pool, clubhouse, and warranties on the appliances. The owner is responsible for a tiny strip of land around the house, so upkeep is needed but minimal. The association maintains the common areas in the community for a small fee. The interior and exterior housing is owned, so many of the advantages to owning an existing home (pride, control, autonomy) are present without a lot of the hassles. Patio homes/zero lot lines are a nice mix and happy compromise of all three types of single family housing.

Duplexes and Multi-Family Homes

There are many pluses to owning a multi-family home, but there is a lot of risk involved. Investors are people who buy homes with the sole intention of making money. Rarely do they live in the home. *Duplexes*, or *doubles*, are two homes attached to each other that might or might not share common utility meters. They are specifically built to house multiple families in a cost-efficient manner. Both units, whether they are side by side, or downstairs and upstairs, usually have identical floor plans. The owner of a duplex might live in one side and rent the other unit to a tenant, or simply rent both sides out. Because owners pay one mortgage for the entire building, but receive two rent checks from two tenants, duplexes can be lucrative.

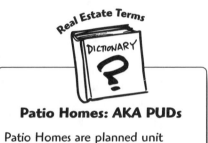

Patio Homes: AKA PUDs

Patio Homes are planned unit developments (PUDs). Developers plan out every facet of living in these communities. Many PUD homes are attached and share a common wall, but buyers own the house and small tracts of yard, unlike condo owners.

Multi-family homes are similar to duplexes in the investment aspect, but contain more units (anywhere from three to ten units) and are much more difficult to maintain and are a larger financial commitment. The monthly cash flow from renting investment properties can be extremely profitable, but the true appeal of these homes are the long-term equity that is built from tenants paying the mortgage for many years while the property appreciates in value. The down side is the amount of time, money, and effort investment properties require. There is huge financial

Cash Flow

The difference between the monthly mortgage a landlord pays a bank and the monthly rent a tenant pays the landlord for a rental property is the *cash flow*.

The Best Time for a Bargain

The best time of the year to get a bargain price for a home is during the holidays, typically Halloween to New Year's Day, and the dead of winter.

risk if units don't rent well or the property decreases in value. Multiple properties means multiple problems and headaches. Maintaining a three- or four-unit house is three or four times harder than caring for a single family home. The financial risk is also three to four times greater.

Vacation Homes or Second Residences

This type of housing is just what it sounds like: a second home to escape to or live in. Most vacation homes are bought for pleasure and enjoyment purposes, but they also can serve as a good investment. The upside is another home in a different locale (maybe on water, near the ocean, or in the mountains) that offers variety and amenities your first home lacks. The disadvantage is the cost and incurred traveling to it and the minimal time actually spent enjoying the second home. If you're lucky enough to have a vacation home, money might not be a primary factor in your decision making. Entertaining family, friends, and business associates is another benefit of second homes. An excellent source for information on vacation homes is www.4vacationhomes.com.

Seller's Market and Buyer's Market

A *seller's market* is when market factors favor home sellers so they have strong leverage when dealing with buyers. A *buyer's market* is when market conditions favor the buyer. The rule of thumb is a six-month supply of homes. Anything more designates a buyer's market. Anything less is a seller's market. Time of season, interest rates, the number of homes on the market, the economy, and trends within the real estate industry dictate whether a market is a buyer's market, a seller's market, or a level playing field.

The Least You Need to Know

➤ A computer, modem, and phone line—or access to this equipment at your workplace, school, or public facility—are needed to get online.

➤ Make sure you are ready to take on the responsibility of buying and owning a home before you take the plunge. The quiz earlier in this chapter will help you determine the answer.

➤ There are more advantages to owning a home than disadvantages, but you should consider the pros and cons of the issue to see if owning is right for you.

➤ People in the real estate industry speak a unique language filled with abbreviations, obscure definitions, and acronyms. Understanding real estate jargon is half the trick to understanding the home buying process.

➤ There are numerous types of real estate (residential home, new construction, condominium, and so on) and all offer different benefits and drawbacks to owners. Knowing the types of homes available and their strengths and weaknesses will help you decide which is right for you.

Chapter 2

Can You Afford Your Dream of Owning?

In This Chapter

➤ Calculating mortgage payments online

➤ Analyzing various Web sites' payment estimators

➤ Up-front costs to buy a home

➤ A breakdown of closing costs

➤ Home inspections and environmental inspections

➤ Figuring buyers' total expenses

Of all the important aspects of buying a home, money is the most important. If you don't have cash or can't obtain a loan to finance your dream, the rest of the process is meaningless. This chapter will show you how to calculate your mortgage online and list some payment estimator Web sites. The costs of buying a home and when the money is due will be explained, as will the different inspections that take place.

How to Calculate Your Mortgage Payment Online

Start by entering the Web address of the site you want to visit in a search engine's search box. Start with a key word or phrase like mortgage calculator or home affordability if you don't have an address. The biggest and best site might be www.quickenmortgage.com, shown in Figure 2.1. A full range of services is offered on Quicken's home page. To calculate mortgage payments, select **home affordability**.

(This can be tricky because the names of services can be vague or misleading. Common sense and trial and error are your guides.) You will be asked to input information on your gross (pretax) income, minimum monthly debt, cash available for down payment, the term of the mortgage (usually 30 years), the interest rate (a national average is provided), and self-imposed maximum monthly payment limit. Helpful icons assist you in determining what to include and what not to include, such as salary, commissions, bonuses, and child support.

Figure 2.1

Quicken's mortgage site at www.quickenmortgage. com provides online access to powerful financial calculating tools.

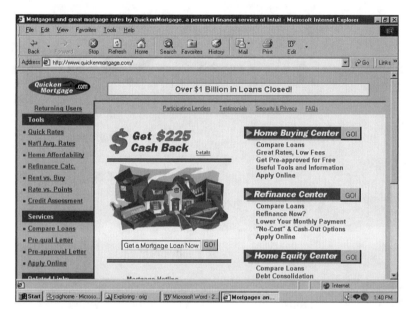

After the date is calculated, the results are presented in the form of a low estimate and a high estimate. The information given is home sales price, loan amount, interest rate, total monthly payment (this includes *principal* loan payment, *interest* on the loan, property taxes, and homeowners insurance), down payment amount and closing costs, down payment percentage (10% of sales price, for example), and the limiting factor that poses the biggest problem (low income, little cash available for down payment, and so on).

The limiting factor response is particularly helpful because it isolates what you need to improve to get a more expensive house or keep the monthly payment down. Quicken is an excellent site because it offers a huge menu of services and is fast and easy to use.

Some other popular sites to calculate mortgage payments are www.eloan.com, www.iown.com (formerly www.homeshark.com), www.lendingtree.com, www.mortgage.com, www.cyberhomes.com, and www.homeadvisor.msn.com. Online payment estimators are an excellent way to figure out the price range you should be looking in. The interest rate is the one factor that can fluctuate greatly from the online payment estimators to an actual mortgage company's or bank's estimate. Rates change daily, sometimes drastically, and payment estimators use a national average that could be vastly different from the rate you'll receive from your personal lender.

Up-Front Costs of Buying a House

Now that you have a strong idea of the price range you want to search in, let's discuss the costs you will have to pay and when you will have to pay them.

Down Payment   Nearly every type of mortgage loan requires a down payment. (VA loans for military personnel are the big exception. Some lenders offer special programs to qualified buyers on a local basis. See Chapter 4, "Help! What Type of Loan Is Best for Me?") The down payment is the borrower's (buyer's) initial investment in a property. The larger the down payment, the less risk the borrower is in the lender's eyes. The down payment is collected at the closing, normally about one month after the purchase agreement is accepted.

Pre-Qualification Versus Pre-Approval

Getting pre-qualified is a ten-minute verbal interview in which a loan originator asks questions concerning income and debt ratios, job history, and money saved for a down payment, and runs a credit check. With a pre-approval, the buyer's information is actually verified by the lender. The buyer supplies bank statements, pay stubs, income tax forms, and so on, three to six months prior to starting the house hunting process. Buyer's financing information should always be included in the purchase agreement offer to show the financing will be approved. Pre-approvals show more strength, but when buyers want to act quickly on a terrific home in a fast-selling area, pre-approvals might take too long. Pre-qualifications still show the buyer will get the loan.

At the time of making an offer to buy a house, the buyer submits an earnest check with the offer to demonstrate sincerity and good faith, and to show the ability or wherewithal to buy the home. Earnest money is part of the down payment, and must be deposited within 48 hours of acceptance by the listing agent's office or the seller in an FSBO transaction. In most markets, the typical earnest money deposit is 1% to 2% of the sales price, but in some markets it is as high as 10% or more.

Down payment money can come from alternative sources if you don't have cash in the bank. A relative or close friend can give the borrower the down payment in the form of a *gift* when FHA or conventional (20%+ down payment) financing is used. Lenders won't allow the down payment to be borrowed, but gift donations are not expected to be paid back. (Whether they are or not is between the borrower and the relative.) Many lenders will also loan money against a borrower's collateral, such as a car, to raise the down payment money. The downside to a "collateral loan" is that the down payment counts against the borrower's income-to-debt ratios, which limits the amount of money the buyer qualifies for.

Check This Out

How to Pay at Closing

Buyers should bring down payment and closing cost monies to closing in the form of a cashier's check or certified check. Title or escrow companies do not accept cash or personal checks over approximately $500. The checks can be made out to the title company or attorneys' office that closes the transaction or put in the buyers' name and they can endorse the check over to the title company at closing.

One third of all buyers use gifts for down payments when purchasing their first homes, according to the National Association of Realtors. Builders sometimes decrease or waive the down payment in exchange for sweat equity, buyers doing work themselves. FHA loans require a down payment of approximately 3.5% to 4% of the contract sales price. Insured conventional loans require 5% or more of the sales price. To qualify for a true conventional loan and avoid paying PMI (private mortgage insurance), 20% or more of the sales price must be paid at closing.

Application fees paid at the time of loan application are the appraisal fee and credit report. Lenders require appraisals to determine the value of the home you are purchasing. Appraisals for a new mortgage deal cost between $350–500 depending upon the lender and the city. (Re-finance appraisals cost around $150–250.) The credit report will be in the range of $60–150.

What Does Under Appraising Mean?

Being cut by an appraiser or *under appraising* means a home did not appraise for the sales price in the purchase agreement. The appraiser cannot adequately justify the contract sales price with comparable sales of similar homes in the same geographic area. For example, if a seller and buyer settle on a price of $120,000 with a loan amount of $116,000, but the home appraises for $114,000, the lender will not loan $116,000 for a home deemed to be worth only $114,000.

You can check your own credit online by visiting any or all of the three major credit service sites. For $8 you can get a credit report at www.equifax.com, www.experian.com, or www.transunion.com. Quicken mortgage will do a merged or tri-report of all three credit services for $24. This is the most comprehensive credit search available; mortgage companies and banks use it, and it can potentially help you get the best interest rate possible when negotiating your rate with lenders.

Breakdown of Closing Costs

Many buyers want to break down and cry when they hear what their closing cost will be. Worse yet, some buyers don't find out what those costs will be until right before the closing. A good lender will give an itemization of all closing costs, a *good faith estimate*, during the pre-qualification or pre-approval process prior to you starting house hunting. Those numbers should be accurate weeks or months later when you close the transaction. Closing costs can vary from lender to lender, so make sure you ask for a list when shopping around. (Interest rates might be negotiable depending on the buyer's credit history and knowledge of the market; closing costs are somewhat negotiable.)

Some common lender fees are the loan origination fee (usually 1% of the loan amount), the document preparation fee, the tax service fee,

Hud-1 Settlement Statement: The Closing Bible

The *Hud-1 Settlement Statement* is a two-page document that breaks down all the costs charged to the buyer and seller and the credits given them. Title or escrow companies prepare the settlement statement one to two days prior to closing and collect and disperse all monies at the closing table.

and the underwriting fee. These three fees typically range in price from $300–500 (sellers must pay for these when the buyer is using FHA or VA financing). Like the loan origination fee, they are charged to the buyer the day of closing. When a buyer makes a down payment of less than 20% of the sales price, mortgage insurance is required. Mortgage insurance on a $100,000 house would be approximately $2,000–2,500. Smaller fees include flood insurance certification (at $25), recording the deed and title (at $40–50), and surveys (at $100–500).

Another closing cost for buyers is money set aside to start escrow accounts, also known as *impound accounts*. Money is collected from the buyer at closing to set up escrow accounts. These accounts were devised by banks to ensure buyers would pay their property taxes and keep insurance on their homes. Homeowners only have to write one check a month to their mortgage company and the lender pays the insurance and property taxes out of money accumulated in the impound accounts. Think of escrow accounts as a pocket to hold money for you so you don't forget to pay insurance or taxes. Using a complicated formula that is regulated by the government, lenders collect three to six months of payments for your property taxes and put them in the pocket.

As months go by and you make mortgage payments, a portion of each payment is put in the escrow pocket. The pocket grows until the escrow balance is large enough to pay the taxes when they are due (normally twice a year). Lenders will waive impound accounts typically with down payments of 20% or more. This should be arranged at the time of loan application. Getting escrow accounts waived after closing the transaction is extremely difficult. Escrow accounts are convenient for homeowners, but make no mistake about why banks use them. They want to protect their investment.

Home Inspections

One of the most important and least understood aspects of purchasing a home is the home inspection. The purpose of an inspection is to determine the condition of the property, not the value. Professionals with completely diverse backgrounds do inspections and appraisals for vastly different reasons. Home inspections are important because, like the financing process, the contract to purchase is contingent upon the home inspection being done and buyer and seller agreeing on what items, if any, will be repaired. The inspection is typically done within one to two weeks of the purchase offer being accepted. The buyer picks the company to do the inspection and pays for it. Home inspection prices range from $100 to $500.

A general inspection should cover all the major mechanical components of a home, such as the furnace, water heater, air conditioning, plumbing, electrical wiring, roof, and structure. In addition, some lenders require a wood-destroying infestation report, better known as a termite report. The buyer may opt for a termite inspection or other environment-related inspections, such as radon, lead-based paint, and asbestos tests.

Home inspectors should be qualified, certified (members of the American Society of Home Inspectors, ASHI, or the National Association of Home Inspectors, NAHI) professionals who work full-time in the field. Besides being thorough and impartial, they should interpret their findings so buyers know the difference between items that are major defects, items that are broken or defective but aren't major defects, and items that are simply maintenance issues and reflect normal wear and tear of a home. Major defects are items that affect the habitability of the home or violate a safety code. Some cities require inspectors to be certified and others do not. When in doubt, consult a Realtor to ensure you hire a qualified and reputable inspector. A complete list of home inspectors can be found at www.ashi.com or www.nahi.com (National Association of Home Inspectors).

Buying As-Is to Get a Better Price

If you want to get a better price on a home, consider writing in a clause that allows you to have a home inspection, yet buy the home in As-Is condition. The clause could read: *Buyer has five days from acceptance of purchase agreement to have all inspections done. At the end of the five-day inspection period, buyer must either buy the home in As-Is condition or sign a mutual release thereby dissolving the contract. If contract is dissolved, the buyer's earnest money will be promptly returned to buyer. Seller may continue showing the home and take back-up offers during this five-day period.* This clause protects the buyer while giving you leverage to negotiate a better price for the As-Is sale, but still allows the seller to market the home while the inspections take place. It's a win-win situation for both parties.

One of the more challenging parts of a real estate transaction is complying with local, state, and federal environmental guidelines. Every few years a new issue seems to crop up, yet the old ones don't go away. Some of the most common inspection items are radon (at $75–150 for the test); termites or wood-destroying insect reports (at $50–100); well, septic, and water test (varies according to local markets); asbestos (depends on local specialist); and underground oil storage tanks ($100–3,000). The buyer typically pays for these inspections before closing or at closing.

Getting Home Repairs Done by the Seller

If you are having trouble getting a seller to make repairs on a home inspection report, check with your loan originator to see whether your lender will require the repairs. If your lender calls for the repairs because of FHA or VA financing, the seller will have to make the repairs if they want to sell the home to you.

Existing homes are not perfect homes and buyers should remember that at the time of inspection. More than anything, the home inspection is an insurance policy for the buyers. Buyers can choose to have any inspection done, but getting a seller to make repairs is another story. Like appraisals and credit reports, the home inspection is usually paid for outside of closing.

A general guideline in real estate is closing costs often equal approximately 1.5% of the contract sales price, so costs to close a $100,000 home would be around $1,500. This rule is not perfect, but it does give a ball-park estimate of total closing costs. One way to defray closing costs is to ask the seller to pay some or all of them. To entice a seller to do this, a buyer would have to raise the sales price the equivalent amount. This saves the buyer money out of pocket at the closing table, but raises the monthly mortgage amount around $10–50 a month depending on the interest rate and the amount of closing costs the seller pays for the buyer.

The Least You Need to Know

➤ Monthly mortgage payments and down payment amounts can be calculated online to determine what price home you can afford.

➤ Many sites have excellent online payment estimators that figure monthly payments. Some of the best sites are www.quickenmortgage.com, www.e-loan.com, www.lendingtree.com, and www.mortgage.com.

➤ The up-front costs of buying a home are the down payment, the earnest money deposit, application fees (credit report and appraisal), pre-approval fee, if applicable, and the home inspection fee.

➤ Standard buyer closing costs are the loan origination fee, document preparation fee, tax service fee, underwriting fee, flood certification fee, recorders fee, survey, and pre-paid funds to set up escrow accounts.

➤ Home inspections are thorough and impartial examinations of a home's mechanical systems and structure by a qualified professional.

➤ Buyers' total closing expenses are the closing costs (roughly 1.5%–2% of the contract sales price) and the down payment minus the earnest deposit.

Chapter 3

EENY MEANY MINNY MO'!!!

Picking a Home-Buying Web Site

In This Chapter

➤ Picking the right site for you

➤ Shopping at the megasites

➤ For Sale By Owner sites

➤ New-construction sites

➤ Pros and cons of various sites

Even starting your online real estate adventure can be a daunting task. In the fluid environment of the Internet, with such a bewildering array of choices, it's hard to say with certainty that you've found the best available anything. Indeed, things change so quickly on the Net that some of the Web addresses given in this book could be different or obsolete by the time you're reading this. New sites seemingly pop up every other week. The answer to the question: "Which is the best site to use when buying a home online?" is *there is no one best site*. Different sites offer different services and information. You should pick the site or sites you feel most comfortable with and find most effective for what you are doing.

Right Site for You

I'm a big believer in doing things the simple or easy way if possible. One approach to use while house hunting online is to pick one Web site and stick to just that site. This exclusivity will make the process a great deal easier and faster, especially for those who are first-time homebuyers, or novices on the Internet. If you fall into both of those categories, I urge you to find one site you are comfortable with and stay with it from the start of the process to the end.

More advanced Net surfers might want to move from site to site to capitalize on the staggering amount of information that can be found online. This process takes longer and might be more difficult. The reward is greater information that enables you to make a more informed decision. Even if you are jumping around a lot, some sites do specialize in key areas like researching neighborhoods and getting financing information.

One-Stop Shopping at the Megasites

There are two megasites that offer a step-by-step, guided tour of the entire process, from checking your credit to researching neighborhoods to finding a lender. homeadvisor.msn.com and www.iown.com epitomize the one stop shopping philosophy that has worked so well for retail giants like Wal-Mart and Meijer.

Check This Out

Most Visited Home-Buying Site

REALTOR.COM is partly owned by the National Association of Realtors and is the most visited home-buying site on the Internet. Currently the site boasts over 1.3 million listed homes nationwide.

Because you didn't buy this *Idiot's Guide* to get bogged down in complex processes, let's start with the easiest way to buy a home online. The two megasites, HomeAdvisor (homeadvisor.msn.com) and iOwn, (www.iown.com), formerly homeshark.com, offer all kinds of services imaginable. Each site has strengths and weaknesses.

What you're looking for will determine which site you use. HomeAdvisor is simpler, faster, and more convenient. I recommend it to first-time buyers and people not well versed in surfing the Internet. The Net is a wonderful tool to gather information, but it can be difficult to move around in. If you type homes for sale on the AltaVista search engine, for example, you'll get 13 million links.

Pros and Cons of Various Megasites

HomeAdvisor's greatest strength is its simplicity (see Figure 3.1). Easy-to-follow instructions prompt you to select buttons that chronologically walk you through the home-buying process. The screens are laid out well and visually appealing. Directions at the bottom of each screen tell you where to go next. The site also enables you to click real estate jargon terms to retrieve definitions or figure out where to go for additional information. HomeAdvisor even offers a free personal computer if you secure your financing through them. Those of you uncomfortable with home buying or surfing the Net will soon feel like an old pro on this site.

The problem with HomeAdvisor, if there is one, is the limited amount of data and resources the site offers. This causes two glaring weaknesses. The first is the number of listings available, approximately 400,000 homes. With so few houses to pick from, odds are you might not find any homes in the town or area you're searching. The reduced number of listings also could mean fewer legitimate options to choose from. The second problem is the lack of regional or local lenders in HomeAdvisor's database. Right now the section on financing only provides information and access to national lenders. These problems can be fixed, and should be in time. When that happens HomeAdvisor would be the strongest home buying site on the Net. Nevertheless, HomeAdvisor is the simplest and most user friendly of the megasites. You can see HomeAdvisor's site in Figure 3.1. Think of it as online home buying for idiots 101.

A Listing

A *listing* is a home put on the market for sale by a real estate company and agent. The word *listing* comes from the Multiple Listing System (MLS), which is a database, or listing, of all homes in a specific city or town for sale. Realtors pay dues to gain access to this database.

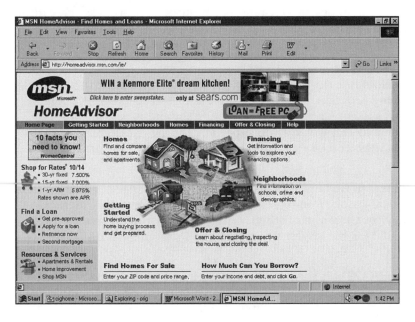

Figure 3.1

One of the most user-friendly online realty sites is homeadvisor.msn.com.

iOwn is the opposite of HomeAdvisor. Homeshark (an Internet mortgage broker) and Homescout (a homes listings Web site) merged to create iOwn. iOwn's strength is the amount of data it provides. Because it links to other sites, particularly www.amshomefinder.com, iOwn's resources are vastly superior to HomeAdvisor. If loads of information is what you crave, and you feel comfortable navigating a less user-friendly site, www.iown.com is the place to go.

iOwn is so comprehensive the site takes you through a comparison of renting versus owning all the way up to closing a transaction. Advice is given and resources provided for nearly every real estate–related topic. A major plus is the links to other Web sites, which enables users to gain access to over one million listings.

iOwn is not simple or user friendly. It doesn't guide you page by page the way HomeAdvisor does. The screens are not set up with convenience or speed in mind. Often you have to go back and forth between screens or use the Forward and Backward keys on your Web browser excessively. While it is not the easiest site to move around on, iOwn does provide the most information on community demographics, schools, and financing data, and is ideal for savvier buyers and Net surfers.

Another large realty Web site is CyberHomes. This site is mostly geared toward home listings, but does provide financial tools and mortgage calculators. It also supplies school system information for free. You can input criteria you want to search for and your email will notify you when new matches (new homes) come on the market. The mapping functions on CyberHomes are outstanding. You can hunt for a house within a geographic radius of your choice. The age-old buyer's request of not being more than a thirty-minute commute from work has never been measured so accurately before this pinpoint function.

The downside to CyberHomes is the frequency in which the program crashes, particularly during the mapping function. Another negative is how difficult the calculators are to find and use. This site isn't as strong as HomeAdvisor and iOwn, but the mapping function alone makes it worthwhile, especially for the experienced surfer who is visiting multiple sites. You can view the home page of CyberHomes in Figure 3.2.

The last megasite is REALTOR.COM. This site is predominantly a place to find homes and Realtors. The National Association of Realtors (NAR) partly owns this site, and 450 multiple listing services share their listings. More than 1.3 million homes can be found here. REALTOR.COM is the largest single Web site for home listings on the Internet.

The downside to REALTOR.COM is the lack of strength in financial tools and mortgage information. Also, the site has discontinued its mapping function, community environmental reports, and some other functions.

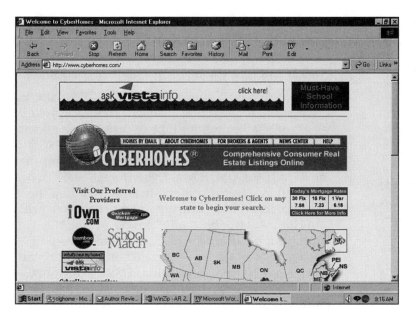

Figure 3.2

*You can shop for
homes online at*
www.cyberhomes.com.

Online Real Estate Advertising Is Big Business

Forrester Research out of Cambridge, Massachusetts, reports that real estate–related businesses are expected to devote nearly 20% of their advertising budgets to online promotion in the next two years. In the year 2000, Internet advertising among realty–based firms will reportedly reach an estimated $59 million, up from $5 million in 1997.

They Handle Everything from Step A to Step Z

These megasites offer suggestions, insights, and resources on almost every facet of the home-buying process. The first step in this process is making the decision to either continue renting or to buy a home. iOwn tackles that question on its site. The next step is finding out if you are credit worthy and can afford to buy a home. Researching areas and neighborhoods and gathering demographic data follows. HomeAdvisor, REALTOR.COM, CyberHomes, and iOwn offer these services, although iOwn is

No-Pressure Sales

The Internet gives buyers unlimited control over when to browse for homes and how to do it. An added bonus is the lack of sales pressure from Realtors. Buyers don't have to talk to agents until they've narrowed their search down to a short list of five to ten homes they want to view.

strongest in this category. Next is choosing a lender. Both iOwn and HomeAdvisor provide these services with iOwn's database being much larger (QuickenMortgage and E-LOAN also are good sites).

The next step is finding a Realtor. REALTOR.COM is the best site for selecting an agent. Following your selection of a Realtor, it's time to search for a home. Most agents will search for homes through their local MLS systems, but the best Internet sites for this are REALTOR.COM, iOwn, CyberHomes, and HomeAdvisor in that order. After you've found the right home, an offer is written to purchase it. iOwn and HomeAdvisor both offer tips on writing the contract and closing the deal. The final step—post closing odds and ends—is covered on both sites, but iOwn tends to have more information. Remember, HomeAdvisor is much easier to use, but iOwn has more information and access to a larger number of home listings.

Muddling Through Different Sites

The more sophisticated Internet traveler desiring as much information as possible might want to use different sites in his search. The following is a list of some of the more popular home-buying sites on the Internet. They all can be used to search for homes, do research on neighborhoods, and uncover demographic information.

    www.amshomefinder.com

    www.bagi.com

    www.century21.com

    www.cyberhomes.com

    msn.homeadvisor.com

    www.homeseekers.com

    www.iown.com

    www.realtor.com

    www.relocate-america.com

Figure 3.3 shows the Web site for HomeSeekers.com.

Figure 3.3

*HomeSeekers.com is
another popular online
realty site.*

For Sale By Owner Sites

For Sale By Owner means exactly what it sounds like. A homeowner decides to sell his or her home without using the services of a Realtor or any other type of real estate professional. The Internet has made it easier and more effective for By Owners to market their homes. There are two major sites, www.owners.com and www.fsbo.com, where By Owners can advertise their homes and buyers can shop for By Owner properties.

Owners.com is the largest assembled list of For Sale By Owner homes on the Internet. The benefit of this site for buyers is the sheer number of properties to view. Another advantage is that it links directly to E-LOAN's mortgage assistance program. For buyers big is definitely better and this is the site for lots of By Owner homes. A negative is the lack of photos of homes on this site. Most By Owner sellers advertising on this site don't spend the extra money to have pictures of their properties appear online. Another potential problem for less desirable homes is the comparison factor. With so many other By Owner properties being marketed the lower-quality homes get passed over.

New-Construction Home Sites

There are a few megasites for new-construction homes. Some of the most popular are www.newhomesearch.com, www.newhomenetwork.com, and www.homebuilder.com, shown in Figure 3.4. Of the three, NewHomeSearch offers the largest list of builders and homes under construction. Buyers are able to search in specific price ranges and by builders' names. This site enables you to view floor plans and check amenities. The major negative of the site is the layout and graphics, which are hard on the eyes. Confusing headings and symbols make it even tougher to decipher. The information on this site is substantial, but the way it is presented leaves a lot to be desired.

Figure 3.4

At HomeBuilder.com, you can shop online for a new—not pre-owned—home.

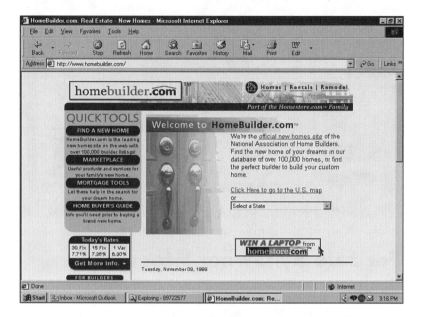

Local Board of Realtor Sites

Most cities and large towns across the country have boards of Realtors that govern how real estate is practiced in that community. These boards have been front runners in pushing real estate online. All of these boards have their own addresses. For example, MIBOR's (Metropolitan Indianapolis Board of Realtors) is www.mibor.net.

The link to all these boards is the National Association of Realtors (NAR). NAR's official Web site is www.realtor.com. This is the best site on the Net for information about local boards, Realtors and real estate offices. These local board sites offer much of the same information as the megasites, but the home listings are only properties in that particular market. A small disadvantage is the inferior resources and information on these sites compared to the major, all-purpose sites.

Check This Out

How Boards of Realtors Govern

Realtors who are members of local boards follow a code of ethics that governs how they practice business. Disputes are settled by mediation or arbitration. Realtors must follow the disciplinary actions set down by the boards.

Big Sites Versus Little Sites

I'm not sure if better or worse matters when it comes to grading the bigger sites and the smaller ones. There definitely are sites that are stronger in some categories than others. The larger sites tend to have greater resources, access to more information, and the capability to link up with other sites. CyberHomes's mapping function is an example of a terrific feature on a large site, as is iOwn's seemingly unlimited information.

The larger sites are generally harder to navigate (with the exception of HomeAdvisor) and can be more difficult finding precisely what you want. The smaller sites specialize in giving you just what you want without all the bells and whistles. There also is a bit less advertising on the smaller sites.

Hopping from One Site to Another

Only the experienced surfer or those comfortable zipping around the Net should jump from site to site. There is a limitless treasure on the numerous real estate–related sites, but you can be overwhelmed if you don't know what you're doing. Most people are using the Net as an introductory research tool before hooking up with a Realtor and mortgage company. One or two sites offer all the information you would need, and then your agent can take over from there.

Hopping around sites would be extremely useful for the adept Internet surfer who plans on buying or selling a home By Owner. This person will not benefit from a Realtor's input or the MLS listing service, so the extra information uncovered online would be an immense plus. If you are using key words or phrases to search for real estate–related topics, remember to be specific and unique, be persistent, and try a lot of different combinations. Search engines don't necessarily use the same logic us idiots do, so keep at it.

The following is a compilation of frequently used search words or phrases that are particularly effective:

> ➤ real estate for sale
> ➤ home
> ➤ homes for sale
> ➤ house
> ➤ houses
> ➤ property
> ➤ realty
> ➤ realtors
> ➤ relocation
> ➤ moving
> ➤ relocating

- buy
- sell
- rent
- flat
- residential
- rural
- farm
- homestead
- residence
- owner
- fsbo
- for sale by owner
- condo
- condominium
- townhouse
- vacant lot
- broker
- sold
- owners
- buying
- selling
- buyer
- seller
- mls
- foreclosure
- community
- information
- mortgages
- listing
- listings
- land
- commercial

The Cafeteria Plan: Taking a Little from Each Site

The same way you would pick and choose your lunch at a cafeteria, the Net enables you to pick and choose what services you want to use from many different Web sites. A hodgepodge of various sites can be employed to get the best information possible. A buyer could start out by using both QuickenMortgage and E-LOAN to check credit before going to iOwn, REALTOR.COM, HomeAdvisor, and CyberHomes to research neighborhoods and find demographic information. REALTOR.COM is the site to visit in selecting a real estate agent.

There are an unbelievable number of lenders online (some were mentioned in Chapter 2, "Can You Afford Your Dream of Owning?") and iOwn and HomeAdvisor can lead you to even more. Searching for a home can be done on REALTOR.COM and a host of other sites previously discussed in this chapter. iOwn offers the best resources and detailed information, whereas HomeAdvisor is the simplest and easiest to use. Homegain.com provides market analyses of what homes in a given neighborhood are selling for and what they are worth.

Comparative Market Analysis (CMA)

A *Comparative Market Analysis* (CMA) is the tool Realtors use to set the list price on homes. Appraisers also use CMAs to determine value when appraising a home. CMAs compare recent sales in the immediate vicinity of a subject house. Sales occurring within the last year are the most comparable because they show the most recent trends in that market place.

The point of a cafeteria plan is to provide the consumer with lots of choices. The buyer then gets to select what he or she thinks is best for them. Whether the decision is meatloaf or chicken in your cafeteria, or iOwn versus the local board's site in your hometown, the options are there for your consideration. The Internet is the world's largest cafeteria plan. You can get almost anything you want.

The Least You Need to Know

➤ There are home-buying Web sites for Internet and real estate beginners and seasoned veterans, so pick a site according to your skill, confidence, and comfort level.

➤ The megasites offer every type of service imaginable and are particularly strong in researching neighborhoods, gathering financing data, and showing the largest number of home listings available.

➤ Two major For Sale By Owner sites offer sellers the benefit of saving money while advertising the home online.

➤ New-construction sites provide online floor plans, designs, and detailed information about building a new home.

➤ Every site has advantages and disadvantages, so it's important to evaluate your needs and skills to find the best site for you.

Part 2
Financing Your Dream Home

Before you move ahead and actually start zipping around the Internet in search of your dream home (crawling might be more accurate), you must first get your financing in order. What bank or mortgage company should you use? Exactly how much home will they pre-qualify or pre-approve you for? Do you want to spend that much or more? What should you be looking for in a lender? These questions and more will be addressed in Part 2.

Chapter 4

Help! What Type of Loan Is Best for Me?

In This Chapter

➤ VA and FHA loans made simple

➤ The basics of conventional loans

➤ Fixed-rate and adjustable-rate mortgages

➤ Special financing and creative financing

There is a lot of misinformation about financing a home. Everyone and their brother seems to have advice on what type of loan to get, whether or not you should go with a fixed rate or adjustable rate, 15-year notes as opposed to 30-year ones, and so on. The one thing you should listen to is the recommendations from family, friends, or co-workers concerning a loan originator they received outstanding service from. After that, what you decide to do in the way of financing your home is between you and your lender (tell them I said so).

FHA Loans

FHA (Federal Housing Authority) loans are government-insured loans that require a down payment of approximately 3.5–5% of the sales price. Popular with first-time buyers who do not have money for a larger down payment, the maximum amount for FHA loans is regularly raised to combat inflation (the FHA max is at $125,000 but it varies from state to state). You do not have to be a first-time buyer to use FHA financing. One of the drawbacks to this type of financing is mortgage insurance that must be paid. The larger the down payment you make, the smaller the risk you are to a lender.

Terminating Termites

FHA guidelines stipulate a clear wood–destroying insect (termite) report must be provided at or before closing for an FHA financed deal to go through. If termites are found, the seller in the transaction must pay for the bugs to be sprayed and treated. The buyer cannot pay for the treatment.

FHA loans are extremely popular with first-time buyers or people buying in price ranges up to approximately $150,000. The two major benefits of FHA financing are the small down payment and the capability to receive down payment funds in the form of a gift. Most FHA buyers are younger, have purchased fewer homes, and typically stay in a home less than five years. A smaller down payment makes sense for these people, even more so if the money comes from another source. Throw in the added bonus that FHA loans allow for higher income-to-debt ratios than conventional loans, and it's easy to see why FHA mortgages are the favorite type of financing for more than just the 20- and 30-something set.

Along with the small down payment, another advantage of FHA loans is the $300–700 in financing fees the seller must pay for the buyer and a relatively intense appraisal that protects the buyer from the roof and major mechanicals being in poor condition. FHA loans are assumable, which means a buyer can take over the loan from you. This potentially makes your home easier to sell. There are no penalties for paying off an FHA loan early, but the loan must be paid to the end of the month instead of the date of payoff when selling, so make sure you close at the end of the month.

The required dual mortgage insurance payments are the disadvantage of FHA loans. Buyers must pay an up-front, one-time MIP fee (mortgage insurance premium) to ensure they won't default on the loan. Each month, buyers pay additional private mortgage insurance that is factored in to the mortgage payment. FHA buyers are considered larger risks than their conventional counterparts are, so the interest rate is normally .25–.50% higher than those making a down payment of more than 20%.

VA Loans

Another government-backed loan is the VA loan. This mortgage is reserved for military veterans and is guaranteed by the Veteran's Administration. VA loans are appealing because they are virtually the only loan that does not require a down payment. In addition, there are some $600–1,000 in closing costs that a seller must pay for a VA buyer. When sellers agree to pay all or most closing costs for VA buyers, this type of financing requires literally no money to be brought to closing. A downside to VA financing is the high loan amount. A funding fee is charged to buyers and some of the closing costs get rolled into the loan amount so the amount to repay the bank is often higher than the sales price of the home. If a buyer stays in a home for a long time this isn't a problem, but if the buyer sells after a few years he can get burnt and have to bring money to the closing. VA buyers must apply for an eligibility certificate if they don't have it. This takes up to two months to secure, so a VA buyer should allow ample time to navigate the mounds of paperwork and bureaucracy.

What Are Income-to-Debt Ratios?

Income-to-debt ratio is the percentage of your monthly income compared to the amount of monthly debt you pay out. The lower your income-to-debt ratio is, the less risk you are to a lender. For instance, buyer 1 whose outgoing debt is 20% of her total income will qualify for a more expensive home than buyer 2 who makes the same amount of money but whose outlay in monthly debt is 40% of his income.

If you've ever heard a friend or relative tell a VA appraisal horror story, they must have been the sellers in the transaction. VA appraisals are the toughest in the business. The purpose is to protect the buyer from expensive repairs to the structure, roof, and major components of the home. The guidelines a home must pass are extremely stringent. The maximum limit for a VA 100%-financed loan is $203,000. With down payment assistance from the buyer, the maximum loan amount is $240,000. VA's address is www.va.gov.

Insured Conventional/Conventional Loans

Buyers who have more money to put down obtain an insured conventional loan (5–19%) or a conventional loan (20% or more). Insured conventional buyers pay mortgage insurance, while conventional buyers do not. Putting more money down makes you less of a risk to a mortgage company so you should get a better interest rate (other factors such as credit, job history, and income/debt ratios also come into play). Conventional borrowers are expected to pay all their own closing costs, and because you are viewed as a well-heeled borrower, the appraiser looks entirely at the value of the home, not the condition as appraisers do in VA and FHA appraisals.

All About FHA and VA Loans

Not all mortgage companies and banks offer FHA and VA loans in their portfolio of loan programs. Lenders have to be accredited to do FHA and VA loans. Frequent audits are done to make sure lenders are complying with federal guidelines governing these loans.

Fannie Mae, Freddie Mac, and Ginnie Mae

Some of the oddest names in real estate belong to the agencies our government has set up to buy mortgages (this is not a team of rapping grandparents). Fannie Mae (Federal National Mortgage Association), Freddie Mac (Federal Home Loan Mortgage Corporation), and Ginnie Mae (Government National Mortgage Association) buy loans from lenders. The criteria most lenders use to approve or turn down loans actually come from these agencies. If your loan is sold, don't fret; the only difference you'll see is a new address to send your coupon and payment to. These government agencies work hand-in-hand with lenders to buy and sell loans, but rarely will you even notice. Their addresses are www.fanniemae.com, www.freddiemac.com, and www.ginniemae.com.

Fixed-Rate Loans

Fixed-rate loans are as traditional as baseball and apple pie. Nearly all loans were fixed-rate mortgages until the early 1970s when inflation and stagnation sent interest rates soaring to 20% (and you complain about your 7.85% rate). Lenders came up with a new type of interest rate, the adjustable-rate mortgage, where borrowers could share in the feast or suffer in the famine. The advantages of fixed-rate loans are the security of knowing your mortgage payment will be the same in the year 2000 and the year 2025. If you know you're going to live in a house for a long time, fixed rates make a ton of sense. If rates are particularly low, fixed rates are almost a no-brainer. Lock in a super low rate and pay the same amount for twenty plus years. Retirees and people with fixed incomes or jobs where their income might decrease over time find the stability of fixed mortgages appealing.

When interest rates are high, fixed rates might not be the best route to go. You might not even qualify for a fixed-rate loan, and why would you want to lock into that high rate for 30 years, anyway? You can actually lose money over the first few years of a fixed-rate loan compared to the savings of an adjustable-rate loan. When interest rates are high, adjustable rates should be considered. After a few years of enjoying the lower rate and saving money, you can refinance your loan into a fixed-rate mortgage and lock in that lower rate for the life of the new loan.

Adjustable-Rate Mortgages

Adjustable-rate mortgages (ARMs) are just what they sound like: The rate adjusts up or down depending on the index it is tied to. As the index rate adjusts up, so do your payments (rarely do they go down). Rate caps limit the amount the rate can go up or down during the adjustment period. Payment caps limit how much your payment can rise during the adjustment period. Typically, your rate will increase by the largest amount the terms of the loan enables for. The adjustment interval dictates how often your rate will go up. For example, a one-year ARM adjusts every year.

The advantages of adjustable rate loans are enticing and potentially risky. You might have an easier time getting a loan by going with an adjustable rate, or you might qualify for a more expensive home. If you are confident your income will rise, or more money will be freed up (kids graduate college, your student loans are paid off), adjustable rates might not be a gamble. The best time to employ an adjustable rate is when interest rates are high and you know you'll live in a house for a very short time. By selling or refinancing the loan in one to three years, the rate never gets a chance to climb too high. Used the right way, adjustable-rate mortgages can be calculated risks.

When to Get an Adjustable-Rate Mortgage

If you are fairly certain or know for sure you are going to live in a home for only a few years, seriously consider getting an adjustable rate unless fixed rates are incredibly low. You will save a ton of money in those first two to three years with the lower, adjustable rate, and then sell the house before the rate goes up high enough to hurt you.

The cons of adjustable-rate loans are fairly evident. If you get stuck with one in a poor economy, your payments will go up year after year. The stress of not knowing if you can make your mortgage payment is hardly attractive. You might end up refinancing your loan all the time (it's become a simple process in recent years), or have to sell a home you love because your rate has raised your payment to the point you can't pay it. One thing to remember about adjustable rates: the rate might not go up each year, but it will go up. Count on it.

The most popular loan is a 30-year fixed-rate mortgage. Payments are amortized over 360 months. You also can get a 10-year loan, a 15-year loan, or a 20-year loan. The 15- year mortgage is becoming more popular because you pay so much less interest on the loan, and own the home in half the time (the monthly payment is at 25% more than a 30-year).

Table 4.1 illustrates the differences between a 15-year loan and a 30-year loan for a mortgage amount of $115,000 at 8% interest. The 15-year loan saves over $100,000 in interest and you own the home in half the time.

Table 4.1   15-Year Versus 30-Year Mortgage Table

	15-Year	30-Year
Interest Rate	8%	8%
Monthly Payment	$1,099	$844
Principal	$115,000	$115,000
Interest	$82,820	$188,779
Total Paid	$197,820	$303,779

Short-term loans are great, but you have to be sure you can afford the payments. Another option is to get a 30-year loan and make extra payments each month toward the principal only. If you do this, make sure you write a separate, second check and put "principal only" in the memo section, or the lender might apply the money to interest or your escrow balances. By paying $50 extra every month, you will turn your 30-year loan into a 20-year loan and save nearly $50,000 in interest.

Discount points are a lender's tool (or trick) to lower the interest rate of a loan. One point is equal to 1% of the loan amount. If rates are high, buying down the interest rate might be a wise decision, especially if you know you're going to live in the home a long time and you're dead set against adjustable-rate loans. A lender can offer you an interest rate of 8% with no points. Or you might opt for a 7.5% rate and pay 2 points. Points lower your interest rate over the long haul of the loan, but add to your bill the day of closing. All lenders offer different loan packages and points deals. Be sure you consider points as an effective way to lower your mortgage payment, but be careful to ask questions and review the financing material because lenders can make a great deal of money on points, sometimes at the borrower's expense. Points are tax deductible when you buy a home (an itemized expense); when you refinance, they must be spread out and deducted over the life of the loan.

Lending Referrals from Realtors

Realtors are a superb source of referrals for finding a mortgage company or bank. Ask your agent for two or three names of loan originators. Be wary of an agent that refuses to give you more than one name. Realtors should have favorite lenders, but they also should be able to recommend reputable backups. An agent that gives only one lender's name might be receiving a kick-back from that lender.

Portfolio and Jumbo Loans

If you have trouble getting financing because of Fannie Mae and traditional lenders' guidelines, *portfolio loans* are another option. Many loans are packaged, grouped with other loans, and sold in a bundle, so they have to meet certain guidelines. Portfolio loans are not sold on the secondary market, so they don't have to adhere to Fannie Mae or the other government agencies' guidelines.

Jumbo loans are loans that exceed the maximum borrowing limits of Fannie Mae, Freddie Mac, and Ginnie Mae. Only certain lenders deal in loans this large because of the risk involved, and the interest rate is usually .25–.50% higher than conventional rates. The current maximum loan amount for Fannie Mae is $240,000.

What's a Balloon?

Loans that hold the initial payments lower for a specified period of time by financing over a long term are called *balloon mortgages*. The loan never reaches the full term. The entire balance is paid off in a large lump sum at the end of the specified period. Usually balloon mortgages are refinanced into another type of loan, the remaining balance is refinanced, or the home is sold (thereby executing the balloon payment). Most of the initial payments go toward interest, so equity is not built up quickly, but the payment is kept low.

Balloons are attractive because they offer a lower initial interest rate than fixed-rate mortgages, but they can blow up in your face if you can't refinance them or sell the house. This type of financing is risky. The longer the term (seven to ten years), the safer the loan.

Swing loans are used when a buyer has not yet sold his current residence, but absolutely has to write an offer on his dream home before someone else buys it. If this buyer does not have the funds to buy the dream home without selling his current home, he can get a swing loan, or gap loan, to make the down payment on the new home and bridge the two properties. After his current home sells, he would pay off the swing loan, thereby having only one mortgage payment.

Swing loans are risky because until the buyer sells the current residence, he potentially makes payment on three loans: the current home loan, the swing loan, and the usually larger payment on the new dream home loan. This type of financing is not very common (there are many less-risky ways of selling your current home and buying your next one) and should be used when most other options fail.

Handling Problems with Your Lender

If the interest rate your lender has quoted you seems high or if you have questions about the closing costs and fees being charged, ask your Realtor before calling your lender. The agent might be able to explain things to your satisfaction or intercede on your behalf, especially if the agent referred you to the lender.

Assumptions

Assumable loans, or *assumptions*, occur when a buyer assumes the responsibilities and terms of the seller's loan. This is attractive to buyers because they do not have to pay for a new loan to be originated, or wait a long time for loan approval. If the interest rate is low, they are locked into that desirable rate. Some buyers with poor credit cannot get financing the traditional way, so assumptions are their only way to purchase a home.

Most new loans are qualified assumptions, which means the current lender must approve the new buyer before they can assume the loan. If a seller sold a home for $100,000 to a buyer who wanted to assume the loan, the buyer would have to pay the difference between the loan amount ($90,000) and the sale price. There would be few, if any, financing closing costs, but the buyer would still have to come up with $10,000 for the down payment. Not too many loans are assumable these days (most are FHA), but it doesn't hurt to ask your lender if yours will be.

Non-Conforming and Special Loans

Loans that meet the requirements of Fannie Mae and the other loan-buying agencies are known as *conforming loans*. Those that exceed Fannie Mae's maximum amount are *non-conforming loans* or jumbo loans. These loans are riskier in nature and might require a higher interest rate. Many lenders will not do non-conforming loans, and the guidelines for approval might be strict. Non-conforming loans are also known as *shelf loans* because the lender can not sell them on the secondary market, so they are shelved or held.

Real Estate Terms

Locking In an Interest Rate

Lock in or *locking* a rate means a loan originator will guarantee an interest rate for a certain period of time, usually 60 to 90 days. Most lenders charge a fee to lock in a rate after the 60- or 90-day period is up.

Some lenders offer first-time buyers or lower-income borrowers special deals to entice them to take the plunge into homeownership. Typically a break is given in the amount of down payment the buyer has to come up with, or in a reduction of the interest rate. With one popular program, the Nehemiah loan, the buyer pays a small down payment (1% of the sales price) or no down payment at all. The seller has to pay a fee (4% of the sales price) and some of the buyer's closing costs, as well as provide a clear roof inspection, clear termite report, and a one-year home warranty plan. Nehemiah gives 3% of the fee to the buyer as a gift for the down payment.

If you're wondering why a seller would do this, a lot of them won't. The way to persuade a seller to participate in the Nehemiah program is to make a full price offer, or pay top market price. If the Nehemiah program is your only way of buying a home, this makes a lot of sense. This program is not just for first-time buyers. Anyone having trouble acquiring a down payment can use this program. Nehemiah's address is www.nehemiahprogram.org.

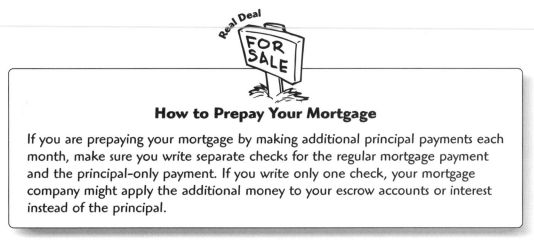

Real Deal

How to Prepay Your Mortgage

If you are prepaying your mortgage by making additional principal payments each month, make sure you write separate checks for the regular mortgage payment and the principal-only payment. If you write only one check, your mortgage company might apply the additional money to your escrow accounts or interest instead of the principal.

Local housing authorities across the country offer first-time or low-income programs for buyers having problems getting money for a down payment. These programs vary from state to state. Usually the programs reduce the interest rate or offer down payment assistance. For detailed information about these programs, contact a local lender or look in the yellow pages under Non-profit Housing Programs. You also can contact HUD (Department of Housing and Urban Development) at www.hud.gov.

There are some loan programs offered nationwide that allow for 100% financing for homes bought in designated rural areas. Houses within city limits do not qualify for these programs, only those in outlying areas. The purpose of these loans is to promote homeownership in rural areas and provide assistance to people living in lower-income counties. In many communities, churches and nonprofit organizations work with banks and mortgage companies to provide down payment assistance programs similar to the rural program. All the standard guidelines of a traditional FHA or insured conventional loan apply, and there might be some additional income parameters and job history requirements the borrower must qualify for.

Buying Down a Lower Interest Rate

Discount points or *points* are a lender's tool to lower the interest rate. Buyers can buy down the rate by paying for a discount point (usually 1% of the loan amount). This is a good idea if you know you're going to live in a home for a long time, the current interest rate is high, and you don't want an adjustable-rate mortgage.

A final program to discuss is historical restoration or urban revitalization loans. Often times the interest rate is reduced for the borrower if they restore a home to the historical society's standards. In addition, grants are given to homeowners to refurbish properties in historical districts. If the work meets the requirements of the historical society and the lender, the grant money does not have to be paid back. These loans foster homeownership and revitalization of urban areas and preservation of historical districts. Two sites that deal with chambers of commerce and historical city issues are www.digitalchambers.com (shown in Figure 4.1) and www.clickcity.com.

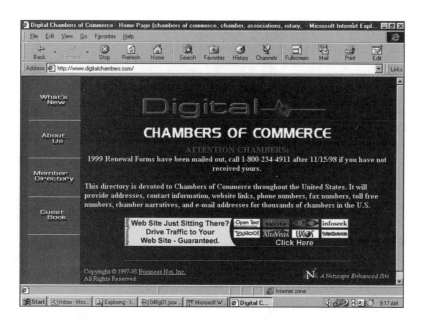

Figure 4.1

Digital Chambers deals with Chamber of Commerce and historical city issues.

For those with less than perfect credit, there are ways to improve your credit history. Think of it as a financial check up or an economic diet plan. No one's in perfect credit shape; we could all be a little bit healthier (even Bill Gates's team of accountants probably forget to pay the light bill once in awhile). The first thing to do is get a copy of your credit report online (refer to Chapter 2, "Can You Afford Your Dream of Owning?"). After you have your credit report, contact a local lender or one you found on the Net. They can interpret anything in the report you don't understand. They should be more than happy to do this because they want your business. Lenders are most interested with your credit history over the past twelve months. Yes, they look at everything on the report going back five, seven, or ten years, but the last year tells them the most about projecting credit behavior in the upcoming months and years.

Lenders can provide you counseling based on what they find on your report. Certain items should be paid off first, others might be explained with a letter of clarification (lenders will help you write these letters), and some credit problems listed might not even be yours. If traditional financing is not possible, the lender can steer you to the many down payment–assisted, special programs previously mentioned. The service you get from a loan originator during this process of cleaning up your credit will tell you a lot about the service you'll get when it comes time to formally apply for a loan.

Financing Hoops for the Self-Employed

Self-employed individuals are analyzed closer by lenders because of the potential for volatility and fluctuations in income. Self-employed workers should keep thorough and accurate records of all income generated and debt expenditures. The longer you've been in your current occupation and field, the better chances you'll have of getting a loan.

One unique group of borrowers is self-employed individuals (a group near and dear to my heart because I'm one of them). Instead of being rewarded for their industriousness, entrepreneurial spirit, and contribution to the economy, self-employed people are penalized at tax time and when they purchase a home. All the standard hoops must be jumped through to secure a loan, but there are a few tighter, stricter requirements for those who are self-employed. Lenders require longer time on the job (three years as opposed to two for non–self-employed), and evaluate the last two years' tax returns and take the average of that income.

Self-employed loans are scrutinized more closely by loan originators and underwriters to make sure there will be stability in income. Reserves in checking and savings accounts also are reviewed carefully. You are more of a risk if you are self-employed (in lenders' eyes; I'd give you a medal), so they are extra cautious about lending you money.

The Least You Need to Know

➤ VA and FHA mortgages are government-backed loans designed to make home buying more attainable for military veterans and young or first-time borrowers buying in lower price ranges.

➤ Insured conventional loans (down payment of 5–19% of the sales price) and conventional loans (down payment of 20%+ of the sales price) are types of financing employed by financially solid borrowers.

➤ Fixed-rate mortgages are set at a specified interest rate for the life of a loan, while adjustable-rate mortgages fluctuate (typically up) from year to year based on economic indexes.

➤ Some lenders offer creative or special financing to buyers who are bigger risks because of spotty credit histories or extremely large loan amounts.

Chapter 5

The Mortgage Process: Getting Your Ducks in a Row

In This Chapter

➤ When and where to check creditworthiness

➤ Credit company Web addresses

➤ Slow credit versus bad credit

➤ Repairing bad credit

➤ Searching for the right lender

Sometime during high school between freshman gym class and senior prom, an economics teacher or guidance counselor should have pulled every student aside and explained what credit history is and how important it will be. They spend entire semesters in high school teaching algebra, calculus, and trigonometry, and 95% of the population will never need those skills—but everyone needs to understand the importance of good credit.

The Advent of Your Credit History

One of the first things that happens in college is credit card companies throw card after card at naïve, 18-year-old freshmen. Anyone can get credit, but not everyone can maintain good credit. This chapter deals with the role your credit history plays in buying a house. If you are one of those people who learned about credit the hard way (like me), take heart: There are things that can be done to improve your credit rating. This chapter will give you what we all should have learned in high school. Take care of your credit rating; it's the only one you'll get and it has to last a lifetime.

I learned about credit my freshman year of college. I got two credit cards with no annual payments and low interest rates (19.9% seemed low at the time) because I was a college student and they believed in me (yeah, right). What they were really saying is we want to make it easy for you to get a credit card because you've never had credit, don't know how it works, will spend outrageous amounts of money, and then pay back the minimum amount each month. They should have told me that because that's exactly what I did. Brake repairs on my car that cost $275 ended up costing about $1,200 because I paid $10–20 a month for nearly two years. By the time I was a senior, I had cut up all my credit cards and vowed to never use credit again (and haven't except to buy homes and cars).

Trying to Establish Better Credit?

Here's a tip that can actually get credit cards working for you in reestablishing good credit. Get three to five credit cards that you won't use, cut them up, and throw them away. Credit checks include all revolving charge accounts. The cut-up cards will never have a late payment in the period you've had them.

I was lucky. My credit history was not damaged or ruined by that experience, but I did learn a valuable lesson. Credit follows you for a long, long time. The good news is good credit follows you as long and far as bad credit. After you develop a strong pattern of credit, it becomes quite easy to keep it up. Conversely, bad credit becomes a noose around your neck that is very hard to break free from.

Overcoming Bankruptcies and Foreclosures

If you've filed for bankruptcy or lost a home to foreclosure, it is still possible to get a loan to buy a home. The farther back in your past the bankruptcy or foreclosure took place, the better your chances are. Contact a lender to see what you have to do to be credit-worthy again.

When to Check Your Creditworthiness

Two key words to discuss when talking about credit are *pattern* and *habit*. Credit is a habit that we act out, good or bad, almost unconsciously. After you get in a habit of paying bills on time, or not paying on time, the habit is very hard to break. Lenders look for patterns in borrowers' credit history. Fair or unfair, they will judge you based on credit patterns and loan you money, or deny you money, based on the patterns they see.

Even if your credit history is less than perfect, there are steps you can take to clean it up and improve your overall credit history. Like most things, reviewing credit comes down to "What have you done for me lately?" The last twelve months are the most crucial time of your credit history. Lenders feel that what you did during the past year gives the strongest indicator of what you will do in the immediate and long-term future. If your credit was superb until six months ago, lenders will want to know why and you will be penalized for it. On the other hand, if your credit has been up and down for a couple of years, but for the last fourteen months it has been spotless, lenders will be more likely to loan you money.

The best time to check your creditworthiness is three to six months before you start the pre-qualification or pre-approval process. If you're worried your credit might be average to poor, start earlier so you have time to work on repairing the bad credit. The more time and distance there is between slow or bad credit and the present, the better off you will be. Even if you are confident your credit history is strong, give yourself a month or two to make it as sterling as possible (occasionally things show up on reports that are not yours, have been paid but aren't appearing that way, or you forgot about them or never knew they existed). If you have to clear up a mistake or erroneous information, you'll be glad you started checking your creditworthiness ahead of time. It can take many weeks to straighten out inaccurate data on a credit report. Don't lose your dream home because you didn't begin the process soon enough.

The way to check your credit before talking to a lender is by visiting the Web sites of the three major credit services. Equifax (www.equifax.com), Experian (www.experian.com), and Transunion (www.transunion.com) offer online credit reports for $8 that are accurate, thorough, and confidential. QuickenMortgage (www.quickenmortgage.com) and E-LOAN (www.eloan.com) (see Figure 5.1) also provide credit reports. The age of technology certainly has helped this aspect of home buying. There simply is not a quicker, easier, less expensive way to find out what your credit history looks like.

Figure 5.1

Using an online credit service offers a quicker, easier, and less expensive way to find out what your credit history looks like.

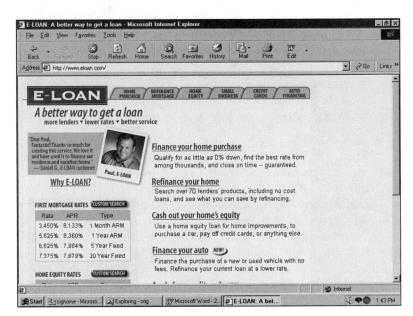

There is a big misconception that slow credit is okay; bad credit, not paying a bill at all, is what you want to avoid. To many lenders, slow credit (late payments) is almost as bad. Consider the following two scenarios: Buyer #1 has good credit over the last five years, but has not paid three bills during that time span. Buyer #2 has paid over half of his bills late during that same time span, but has paid all of them. Who do you think is the bigger risk to the mortgage company? There is not one definitive answer, but many lenders would frown upon the person consistently late, even though he had no unpaid bills. Once again, lenders look at patterns of behavior.

Often long, consistent patterns of slow or late credit looks worse to lenders than a short history of poor credit. Don't be misled to believe paying late is okay as long as you end up paying. Slow credit can scare lenders off just as quickly as bad credit will. Having too much credit, being leveraged to the hilt, can throw your income-to-debt ratios out of whack and can turn lenders off as well. Be careful with excessive credit along with slow credit. Unless you are paying cash, you're a risk to a lender. The key is to appear to be as small a risk as possible.

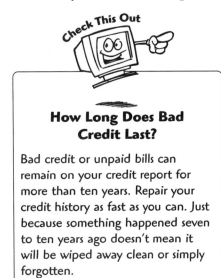

Check This Out

How Long Does Bad Credit Last?

Bad credit or unpaid bills can remain on your credit report for more than ten years. Repair your credit history as fast as you can. Just because something happened seven to ten years ago doesn't mean it will be wiped away clean or simply forgotten.

Repairing Poor or Inaccurate Credit

Very few people have absolutely perfect credit. Fortunately, perfect credit or near perfect credit isn't needed to buy a home. If late or non-payments appear on your credit report, contact the creditor and satisfy the debt. Make sure to request written confirmation to show the debt has been paid, and have the creditor notify the credit services so they can update their records. If you have already selected a lender, they can advise you on what outstanding debt should be paid off first. If you cannot resolve the problem, document your explanation as thoroughly and accurately as possible. This explanation will be included in the credit agency's report.

If a mistake shows up on your report, the reporting agency should correct it. This is extremely hard to get them to do, sometimes harder than clearing a valid outstanding debt. The best way to correct a mistake is to call first and obtain an individual's name, preferably a manager or supervisor. Write that person a complaint letter and continually call and write until they correct the mistake. Don't worry about being a nuisance. You will have to be persistent to get the inaccurate information removed. Remember, they were wrong in the first place. Slow credit should be addressed just as non-payments are. Write letters of explanation as to the reasons you paid the bills late. (Pride should not enter into this. Use every explanation possible, including the dog ate the phone bill.)

Dealing with Lenders About Your Credit History

Be completely honest and forthright when telling your lender about your credit history and your income and debt ratios. He's going to find out the truth soon enough when he verifies everything. The loan originator's job is to help you get a loan, not get you turned down. A loan originator only gets paid when he closes a loan, so he has every reason to want you to be approved for a mortgage, not rejected.

Take extra time to document why mortgage payments or rent payments were late, particularly in the last twelve months. Lenders will look closely at these late payments because that is the very thing they will be loaning you money for. Clear up as much or all of bad or slow credit as you can before you talk to a lender. Your loan being approved and the interest rate you get might depend on it.

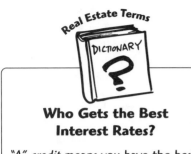

Who Gets the Best Interest Rates?

"A" credit means you have the best credit possible, a perfect or near perfect credit history. People with "A" credit get the best interest rates from lenders because they are less of a risk.

Having an average to bad credit report does not mean you cannot buy a home. It might mean you will have to search a bit harder to find a lender who will loan you money. The interest rate you get will probably be higher if your credit is below average to poor. Often times it is better to go with the higher rate. If you make your payments on time and establish good credit for a year or two, you can refinance to a lower rate. Your credit history has been rebuilt while you were enjoying the many perks of ownership (that is, tax breaks, equity savings, and control and pride).

Overcoming Slow or Bad Credit

Lenders often have borrowers write letters of explanation detailing why payments in past years were late or never paid. Originators and their processors coach borrowers on how to address past problems and explain what was done to correct the situation (fewer credit cards, lower interest rates, and credit lines on the existing cards). These letters can balance out or cancel some poor credit in a borrower's past.

Verifying Credit: Items Your Lender Will Request

When you talk to a lender, you will have to provide them with information so they can check your credit. All lenders are supposed to ask for your correct legal name and any other names you have amassed credit under. They also will need your Social Security number and your last two years' address(es) of residence. Even if you are worried about your credit, provide accurate information. Lenders will find it soon enough and this type of deception does not help when you are asking to borrow large sums of money. Lenders will usually do a second credit check right before the loan is approved, so do not run up huge debts or bad credit in the interim months between applying for the loan and closing the deal.

Searching for the Right Lender

There are many places to find a moneylender. Locating a good lender is sometimes a different story. Money is lent a lot more freely today than it was ten years ago. Turn on the television or look in the newspaper and you'll find numerous lenders offering their services. The number of lenders on the Internet has exploded in the last two years. There are tens of thousands of online lenders hawking their financial services. QuickenMortgage and E-LOAN are two of the bigger and more popular online lenders. Most major home-buying sites offer mortgage information and services on their home pages (refer to Chapter 3, "Picking a Home-Buying Web Site").

Key words to search for online lending sites are `mortgages`, `mortgage loans`, `conventional loans`, and `home mortgages`. Depending on the economy and interest rates, you might periodically get cold calls from banks around the country pitching a loan consolidation program or refinance deal. There is a monumental difference between a lender and a good lender. Any lender can quote you a rate, move paper around a desk, and close the transaction 30–45 days later. That kind of service will give a hollow, "I'm just a statistic" feeling.

Check This Out

Estimating Closing Costs and Fees

A good loan originator will provide you with a good-faith estimate that is extremely accurate, if not a tiny bit high. When you get your closing, figures a few days before closing or the day of closing, those figures should match what your lender gave you weeks or months before.

The best way to find a lender is through referrals from family members, friends, or trusted co-workers who have used the individual and had a good to great experience. Another terrific source is your real estate agent. If you know this agent well, or she came highly recommended by a trusted friend or family member, she should be able to refer you to a few reputable, credible lenders. Agents are a wonderful source because they work in the business and know who is good and who isn't. Plus, they have a lot at stake. If they were to give you a bad referral they might lose your business and be out potentially thousands of dollars in commissions.

I want to briefly explain the difference between a lender and a loan originator, and talk about the various types of lenders. *Lender* is a generic, all-encompassing term that describes a bank, mortgage company, or credit union. Lenders are companies, or financial institutions that loan money. *Loan originators* are the individuals at banks or mortgage companies that initiate, or originate loans for customers. (For the sake of simplicity, and in light of real-world practice, loan originator and lender are often used interchangeably in this title.)

Loan originators (LOs) offer advice on different mortgage programs, provide good-faith estimates on projected closing costs, quote interest rates and then lock them in, and generate the massive paper trails that document and verify all aspects of the loan process. Working with a good loan originator is probably more important than working with a big, strong bank or mortgage company. An inexperienced, incompetent, or dishonest loan originator can mess up a deal beyond repair even if he or she works at the biggest and best financial institution in town.

Conversely, a seasoned, knowledgeable, honest, hard working originator can work for himself or the smallest lender in town and do a wonderful job on your loan. Ideally, you will find a balance between the two: an excellent originator who has the support and resources of a strong institution behind him or her. With the vast number of lenders competing aggressively for your business, you should get exactly what you want from a lending institution and its employees. Remember, you're the customer and lenders will make a large amount of money on your loan, so you might as well have the best experience possible.

The Role of Loan Processors Is Vital

The person who actually compiles all the paperwork, verifies all the information in your file, and does the leg work for your loan originator is the *processor*. Get to know your processor during the loan process, but don't bug him because he is extremely busy. A nice note or pleasant email or voicemail to the processor goes a long way in making the loan process go smoothly.

I'm a huge believer in service. Real estate is driven by two factors: money and service. There will always be people who make decisions based solely on value and how much money they can save (there's absolutely nothing wrong with this—I've been this way a great deal of my life). There also will always be people who are willing to pay for quality and service (I've become more this way as I've aged). A healthy combination of both will serve you well when selecting and working with a loan originator. Everyone wants the best interest rate they can get. Too many people sacrifice service, however, and end up not getting their loan approved, paying extra in fees or down payments, or having a nightmare experience buying a home. Many people aren't in their homes long enough to justify shopping just for the best rate. Service is a key part of the loan process. Make sure when you're picking a lender that you look at the service you'll get, not just the interest rate and fees you'll be charged.

Qualities of Good Lenders

Good loan originators are competent and knowledgeable about the market they work in. They understand the market in general and the programs they offer and can explain them in a straightforward, non-condescending way. Listening skills are crucial to an originator's job. Good lenders also are competitive, result-oriented, and detailed. Lenders that approve loans locally usually have quick turnaround times, but lenders that send loans out of state for approval can still be fast, efficient, and easy to work with. Loan originators that have superb processors and underwriters behind them are wonderful to work with. When a lender's support staff is strong, the originator will be that much stronger because of it.

Finally, maybe the best quality a loan originator can have is honesty and trustworthiness. If the originator is genuinely interested in your well being and acts in your best interest, you will have a good experience. Any problem that arises during the loan process can be overcome if the originator sincerely wants what's best for you. A lender with this attitude will give great service and will be highly successful and well compensated for superior service.

Your loan originator might talk to you about getting pre-qualified or pre-approved before you start looking for a home. Every buyer should do one or the other (I personally won't show buyers homes until they do). Your Realtor will write in the contract to purchase or submit a pre-qualification or pre-approval letter with the offer. This shows your strength as a buyer and lets the seller know that you will be approved for the loan. Pre-qualifications can be done over the telephone or computer. They take about fifteen minutes and consist of the lender doing a credit check and asking about your income and debt, your job history, and available money in savings or checking accounts. They cost nothing.

As long as you are honest during this interview and nothing drastically changes from the time of the pre-qualification to the closing, you should get a loan with no problems. Pre-approvals take one day to a week, cost around $100, and the information you provide is verified a lot more thoroughly. Pre-approvals look stronger to a seller, but a good lender can pre-qualify you and, if your information is accurate, the pre-qualification means essentially the same thing. The important thing to remember is have one or the other done so you're not wasting your time, or anyone else's. Plus, having done this up front does make you a stronger buyer in the seller's eyes. (Would anyone go to McDonald's and order a Big Mac value meal without first checking to see if they had money to pay for it?) This is the same idea with buying a home except on a much larger scale.

Showing the Seller You're a Strong Buyer

At the time an offer is presented to a seller or the seller's Realtor, your agent should submit a written note verifying you have been pre-qualified or pre-approved. The lender's name, phone number, and address also should be included or written into the further conditions part of the contract. This will save everyone time and trouble and show the seller you are a serious, strong, worthy buyer.

The Least You Need to Know

➤ Creditworthiness can be checked online at the major credit report companies and should be done three to six months before you start to shop for a home.

➤ Experian, Equifax and Transunion offer individual credit reports or merged reports.

➤ A long, habitual pattern of slow credit (paying late) can be nearly as bad (sometimes even worse) as failing to pay at all.

➤ Bad credit can be repaired with diligent work, persistence, and increased discipline and commitment over a period of time.

➤ Look for a loan originator who is honest, hard working, understands the market, listens well, is detail oriented, and will give excellent service with competitive rates and fees.

Part 3

Research: Your Happiness Depends on It!

After you have selected a lender and are pre-qualified or pre-approved for a loan, the next step is to figure out where you want to live. The way this is done (if you haven't already lived in a specific area, or have relatives and friends begging you to move close to them) is through online research. If you are not familiar with the town, city, or state you are moving to (job transfer, relocation against your will, and so on), you will have to become as familiar as possible so you can make the best informed decision possible. The old way of doing things was to trust your real estate agent's judgement, or cross your fingers, say countless prayers, and throw pennies in every water fountain you could find. The new way is to jump online and surf the Net.

HEY. HOWZ IT GOIN!...

Chapter 6

Research Areas: Don't Get Stuck Living Next to the Addams Family

---

In This Chapter

➤ Locating city maps online

➤ Why location IS most important

➤ Factors that influence price

➤ Doing research online

➤ Online comparative market analyses

I was twelve years old the first time I heard the adage "The three most important things in real estate are location, location, location." I only remember this because I heard it on a television show I was not supposed to be watching (*Cheers*). As I grew older and eventually entered the real estate industry, what stuck with me was the adage being on the most popular sitcom of the 1980s. This age-old real estate maxim had become part of popular culture when Norm and Dr. Frasier Crane discussed it around the bar. The more time I spend selling real estate, owning rental property, and writing about real estate, this maxim becomes all the more true. Location really is the end all, be all, deciding factor on what a home is worth.

Finding City Maps Online

One of the coolest sites on the Net is MapQuest, shown in Figure 6.1. You can find this site by typing www.mapquest.com or the key word mapquest in the search box. This site offers overview maps of cities and towns all over the country and the world (international referral networks are a huge source of business for large real estate offices like Century 21 and RE/MAX). Along with providing maps of cities all over the U.S., MapQuest gives the most detailed, door-to-door directions imaginable (no more stopping at gas stations to get directions).

Figure 6.1

Use MapQuest to find city maps online.

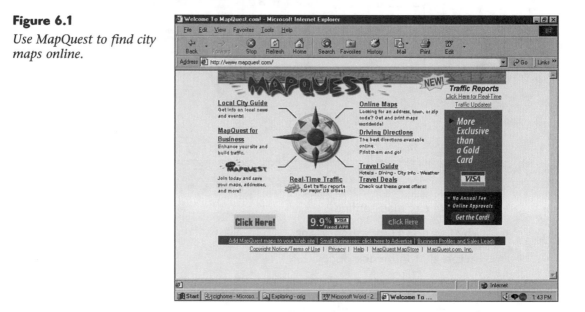

Shortcuts to Finding Maps and Directions

MapQuest offers a cheat sheet with pre-set addresses in a variety of categories, such as museums, sports facilities, universities, and monuments, so you don't have to look up addresses when searching for directions from one place to another.

Here's how it works. Type the address or as much of an address as you have in the box marked **From**. (I'll use 100 South Capitol Avenue, the address of the RCA Dome in downtown Indianapolis.) Then type the address of your destination in the box marked **To** (for this example, I'll use the most famous address in America: 1600 Pennsylvania Avenue, Washington D.C.). Click which option you want to use (**Door-to-Door** is more accurate and thorough then **City-to-City**), and select route and avoid preference options. You can pick the shortest route or the fastest route, and avoid limited-access highways, toll roads, and ferry lanes if possible. After you input the information, click **Calculate Directions** and your door-to-door guide will appear (directionally challenged marriages are being saved).

Neighborhood Locators

One of the biggest problems with the Internet is its lack of organization. The information superhighway has no speed limits, no consistent direction for passengers to follow, and no rules to govern how it is traveled. This can make research difficult. Persistence and trial-and-error searching will come in handy, but there are some tricks that can help you locate neighborhoods and areas online.

Before I go any further into Web sites and resources to research neighborhoods, I want to talk about why location is so important in determining the value of a home (value refers to worth during this discussion). Real estate is a disorganized, fragmented, homogeneous industry. Crossing over one street or intersection can mean a difference of $100,000. The same exact home can be worth $120,000 in one location and $300,000 in another area of town. The only difference is the value of the homes around it. That is why location is so important. Location is one of the two biggest factors buyers consider when selecting a home (price range is the other). Home values are dictated by the value of homes in the same subdivision or immediate vicinity. You could have a five-bed, four-bath home in an economically depressed area of town and the most the home might sell for is $90,000. Conversely, another home might be a two-bed, one-bath bungalow in one of the hottest selling areas of a city and be worth $150,000–200,000.

Realtors and appraisers use other sold homes in the same area to calculate real estate value. In the end, what a seller is willing to sell for and what a buyer is willing to pay determines what a home's true value is. Many factors make an area attractive: school systems, shopping and entertainment districts, safety, proximity to business districts, interstate systems, and scenic beauty (water, mountains, and so on). Supply-and-demand principles are hard at work in real estate. When more and more people want to buy into an area, the values of homes are driven up. This causes resale and appreciation rates to go up, making the area even more appealing.

After an area gets a strong reputation, it will usually stay that way unless negative factors halt the growth. Good or bad, homes are slaves to the values of homes around them. A great home in a bad area will only sell in the top range of *that* neighborhood or subdivision. Likewise, a terrible home in an excellent area will be pulled up by the high values of the surrounding homes. It will sell at the bottom range of that subdivision, but when the entire range is high, the seller will still benefit from being in such a good location.

Other factors that influence price are the size of the house and the lot it sits on. Larger homes with more square footage, bedrooms, baths, and lot size are worth more than smaller homes.

Key Areas to Update

The kitchen and bathrooms are the two most important areas to update for resale and appreciation reasons. Many people believe women make the final selection when picking houses, and the kitchen and baths are often the most important areas of the house for women.

Condition of the property is also an important factor in figuring value. A large home in a strong area can be pulled down significantly if the home needs $50,000 in repairs, updates, and renovations.

Amenities or extras also can play a role in figuring value. Elaborate decks, patios, sunrooms, impressive garages, swimming pools, basements, and fireplaces can all add value and raise the selling price. Tasteful, neutral décor makes a home more desirable, thus increasing value. As you can tell, many factors *affect* the value of a home; only one thing *determines* the value. Location, location, location says it all.

Online Research

One effective way to search for information is by going to a search engine (refer to Chapter 1, "Preparing Yourself: This Is One of the Biggest Investments of Your Life"). Type the city you are researching, and then the key word demographics (for example, Dallas demographics). A host of non-related subjects will probably appear, but by scrolling through the list of matches you will find data on communities in Dallas. Along with the major house-hunting sites discussed in Chapter 3, "Picking a Home-Buying Web Site," Relocate-America.com is another good source for information on neighborhoods. Relocating is an excellent key word to search under, as are relocation, moving, communities, and real estate for sale. iOwn, shown in Figure 6.2, is probably the megasite with the most comprehensive information on neighborhoods. If you are able to buy a home anywhere in the U.S., a fantastic guide to the best communities in America is money.com's Best Places to Live.

Figure 6.2

Get the most comprehensive information on neighborhoods at iOwn's Web site.

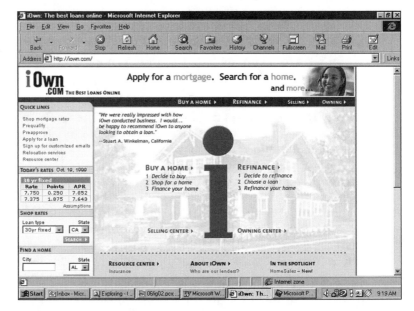

A wonderful source of research information is local Board of Realtors Web sites. Whether you are doing research on communities in other parts of the city or state you live in or across the country, these sites offer some of the most comprehensive information on areas and neighborhoods. A state-by-state listing of local Board of Realtors addresses can be found at www.realtor.com, the official Web site of the National Association of Realtors.

Another source is local chambers of commerce. A boat-load of information, city statistics, and demographic data can be found by contacting these organizations at www.digitalchambers.com and www.clickcity.com. They will be more than happy to send you relocation packets about their cities. Be aware that chambers are in the business of promoting their cities, so the information will be painted with a rose-colored brush.

An extremely useful tool when researching areas is a *mapping function*. Many of the large home-buying sites offer this feature. (REALTOR.COM discontinued this feature.) You can target certain areas in relation to your office or day-care center. For instance, CyberHomes provides a radius search that enables you to input the address of your office or church. You can instruct the program to search in a ten-mile radius of that address for all homes with your required criteria (three beds or more, two baths or more, two-car attached garage or more, up to $150,000).

If you have a basic idea of what town or city you want to live in, but aren't sure what part of that town best meets your needs, try iown.com or homeadvisor.msn.com. These sites offer information on crime, schools, and demographics. iOwn provides better school and demographics data, but you do have to register your name, which means junk mail and advertisements. The trade-off is information on median income, utility costs, home sizes, homeowners' ages, educational levels, commute times, nearby shopping and entertainment, and health care facilities.

Check This Out

Researching for Current and Up-to-Date Information

Real estate is constantly changing and evolving because of economic, political, seasonal, and social factors, so make sure the information you're getting about neighborhoods, areas, school systems, taxes, and so on is as current and up to date as possible.

iOwn's school information is so detailed you can find data comparing various school systems, special education programs, computer-to-student ratios, athletic and educational-resource facilities, the percentage of students who attend college, scholarship and award winners, and standardized test averages.

HomeAdvisor's strength is crime data. The site provides information from the FBI. You can select information on a county-by-county basis. The frequency of seven types of crimes are outlined, including murder, grand theft auto, assault, and robbery. All the real estate sites discussed in Chapter 3 can be used to do research, as well as www.bagi.com.

Online Comparative Market Analyses

One of the most frequently asked questions I hear in real estate is "How do Realtors know what a home is worth and how do they come up with list prices or asking prices for homes?" (I wonder that myself when I see some of the crazy list prices on homes.) As mentioned earlier in the section concerning location, the single biggest factor that determines what a home is worth is the area it is in and the homes around it. Realtors use this information to compile a *comparative market analysis* (CMA). A CMA is what it appears to be: a comparative look at similar homes in a similar area. Sometimes the analysis is simple because the subject home (the home either being put on the market for sale or to be bought) is in a large subdivision with many homes that are identical in bedrooms, baths, garage, square-footage size, and so on.

Homes like this are easy to comp out because all Realtors have to do is average the sales prices of the identical floor plans and compare the condition of the subject property to the other homes. If the subject property's condition is above average, the price will be at the upper end of the range in that subdivision. The opposite holds true if the condition is below average.

Homes in rural areas and those not in planned communities are much harder to comp. Realtors must be competent and knowledgeable about the area the home is in. They also must understand what amenities add value and decrease value, and be able to accurately determine what the dollar amounts of those increases or decreases are. For instance, if there are not many four-bed homes in an area, three-bed homes have to be used for comparisons. A Realtor must know how much to deduct for the lack of that fourth bedroom. Various features like fireplaces, decks, extra half baths, and so on all increase or decrease value in different ways. Appraisers use this same method of comparison when appraising home values.

A savvy, intelligent real estate agent can accurately come up with the true range in value for a home, thereby ensuring the seller a fast sale for the most amount of money possible. On the other hand, Realtors working for buyers have access to this same information (the Multiple Listing Services computer database) and also should perform a CMA to see how accurately priced a home is compared to the other homes in that area or subdivision. This helps a buyer understand how much a home is worth, and possibly benefits them in negotiating a better sales price.

The key to a good CMA is to accurately assess value when comparing different items from one house to another. For instance, two homes might have similar layouts and bedrooms and baths, but one might have a basement and fireplace, yet be in below-average condition. The second home might be in perfect condition, sit on a large, beautiful wooded lot, but back up to a busy street. Both of these homes are essentially the same: three-bed, two-bath ranches with similar square footage on the same street.

Understanding What Comparable Sales Are

Comping out a home means doing a comparative market analysis (CMA) to see what the home's value is in comparison to other similar homes in that subdivision or area. Buyers should have their agents comp homes before writing an offer to purchase to see how accurately a home is priced and to determine what the offer price should be.

The trick in doing this CMA is attaching value to the different amenities. The only way to do this effectively is to study the homes that have sold in the last two years, preferably the last twelve months (this reflects the most current trends) and figure out a pattern. This is difficult because trends can change without a moment's notice, and are usually easier to spot after they've stopped, not before or during.

Appreciation rates can be calculated by tracking the sale prices of homes in a specific area over a period of a few years (the longer the better). As you track the patterns in sales, you can determine if homes are appreciating at the citywide rate, which is 3–4% for many metropolitan cities, or faster or slower. The other way to figure appreciation is to contact a Realtor well versed with trends in that market place. He should be able to tell you if you are having trouble determining appreciation rates.

CMAs are vital to an online homebuyer because you must learn the range of price in different areas to know if you will consider looking for a home in that part of town. You can see a typical CMA form in Figure 6.3.

Figure 6.3

The CMA form.

75

Using Sold Homes for Comparing Value

Only sold homes should be used in a CMA because there is no guarantee active or pending homes will definitely sell or to know what they sold for until after they close.

Sites that buyers can use to do comparative market prices are www.dataquick.com, www.experian.com, and www.homegain.com. DataQuick, HomeGain.com, and Experian charge $10 per comparable home so pick them wisely (HomeGain.com offers one free comparable sale). REALTOR.COM and iOwn are good sites to view to see what current homes are listed for. Active listings (homes currently on the market but not sold yet) provide a frame of reference, but really don't determine value. A home with a list price of $249,900 might end up selling for $202,000, or possibly not at all. To use $249,900 as a comparable price would be grossly inaccurate.

It is important to note that Realtors have the greatest source of information at their fingertips because of the centralized multiple listings service (Realtors pay thousands of dollars in dues per year for access to the MLS). If you have any questions or concerns about the value of homes in an unfamiliar area, contact a real estate professional. She will do a CMA for free whether you are looking to buy or sell.

The Least You Need to Know

➤ Maps of most American cities and directions to any address or location can be found online at www.mapquest.com.

➤ Real estate prices are determined by comparing similar homes in the same geographic area, which makes location the single greatest factor in determining a home's value.

➤ Other factors that influence what a home is worth include the following: the size of the home and lot, the condition of the home, the décor and amenities of the home, and market conditions (such as time of year, interest rates, and other market factors pertinent to specific areas).

➤ Online research can be done by going directly to a Web site, browsing search engines, visiting real estate megasites, or searching local cities' Board of Realtors and chamber of commerce sites.

➤ DataQuick, Experian, and HomeGain.com offer online comparative market analyses that compare and contrast similar homes in the same location to determine the range in value for that neighborhood.

Chapter 7

Property Taxes and What That Means for You

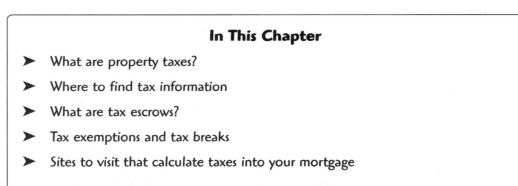

In This Chapter

➤ What are property taxes?

➤ Where to find tax information

➤ What are tax escrows?

➤ Tax exemptions and tax breaks

➤ Sites to visit that calculate taxes into your mortgage

As a kid I remember hearing my parents complain about rising property taxes. As I got older Mom and Dad griped about what their property taxes were being spent on, or weren't being spent on (certainly not roads, our family car fit snugly into many Indianapolis chuckholes). When I got into real estate as a career, many people asked me how property taxes were assessed. This chapter deals with one of the more confusing and irritating parts of real estate: property taxes.

Tax Laws Online

Property taxes are taxes levied by local city governments against homeowners. The revenue generated by this tax funds new schools, police and fire stations, parks, libraries, and the infrastructure of roads, highways, bridges, and so on in a particular township or county. Some owners feel property taxes are a penalty for owning. The theory behind the tax is homeowners have put down roots and will live in an area longer and enjoy the benefits of the city's improvements, so they should share in the cost of the improvements. Property taxes are most counties' largest revenue generator.

Why Escrow Accounts?

Escrow accounts were devised by lenders to make sure homeowners paid their property taxes. Without escrows people might not pay property taxes and schools, libraries, parks, and roads would deteriorate.

The vast majority of states in America pro-rate taxes through the date of closing, which is the most equitable way of negotiating the future payment of taxes. There are a handful of states that pay in arrears (paying backwards for time already lived in the home), which makes very little sense.

There are some issues concerning property taxes that are not debatable. The tax is deductible on your income taxes. Newer homes and more expensive homes have higher taxes. Treasurer's offices often miscalculate or overcharge property taxes because their information is incorrect. For example, if the treasurer's office shows your home having a two car garage instead of one, or if their records indicate you have a basement when you don't, *you're paying too much in taxes and are entitled to a refund for all the years you have overpaid.* You can appeal your tax bill through the Assessor's office and seek a refund. Contact your real estate agent or local Assessor to find out how to appeal your taxes in writing.

The place to find online tax laws is city and state governments. Go to the search engine of your choice (Chapter 1, "Preparing Yourself: This Is One of the Biggest Investments of Your Life," discusses search engines in detail). Type the words `city government`, and then the name of the city you are researching. For example, if you're considering a move to Charlotte, North Carolina, you would type `city government Charlotte`. Information on when taxes are due, how they're assessed, and tax laws for various counties in Charlotte can be found this way (see Figure 7.1). This same method can be used by typing the words `state government` and the name of a state. Tax laws can differ within a state, though, so searching by city government is the most accurate, efficient method to use. A final way to research taxes online is through local chambers of commerce. The best two sites for this are `www.digitalchambers.com` and `www.clickcity.com`.

Another source of property tax information is mega house-buying sites such as iOwn, HomeAdvisor, REALTOR.COM, and CyberHomes. These sites are supplemental sources to find tax rates.

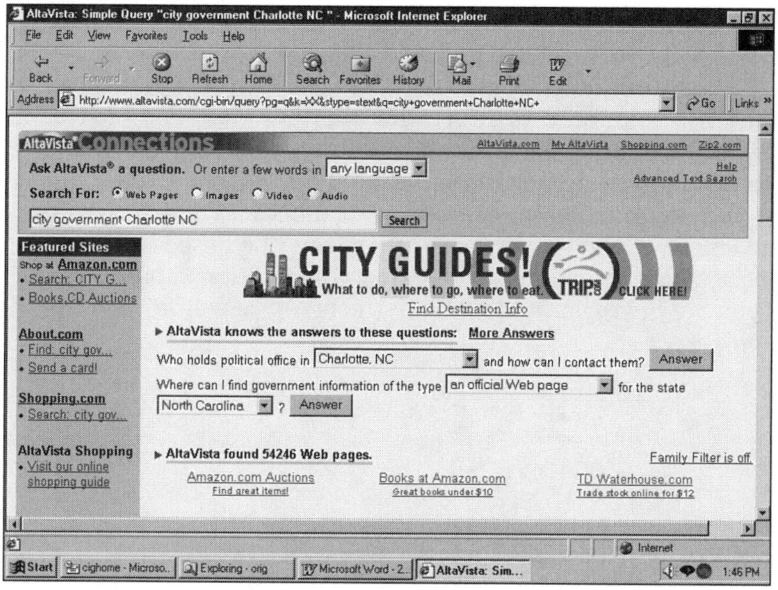

Figure 7.1
This site shows how to search for property tax information.

Tax Escrow Accounts

Banks and mortgage companies will escrow your property tax payment into your mortgage to make sure you pay the tax. Each month a portion of your mortgage payment will go into an escrow account your lender has set up. Lenders don't do this because they want you to write only one check per month (that is a nice benefit of escrow accounts for taxes and insurance). They do it to protect themselves and their investment from homeowners not paying their taxes. City governments everywhere would have liens on endless homes and tens of thousands of homes would be forced into foreclosure.

If taxes are due twice a year, your lender will pay the tax twice a year with the money collected from your monthly payments. The federal government regulates banks and mortgage companies to make sure they do not keep too much of your money in escrow accounts. Lenders are required to audit their escrow accounts, usually once a year, to make sure they have not overcharged homeowners. If there is an excess in your escrow account, it will be returned to you so you can invest the money or use it in a manner you see fit.

A good lender will explain the purpose of escrow accounts and how they work during the pre-approval interview or at the time of loan application. The good-faith estimate the loan originator provides you will have all your closing costs and estimates for setting up your escrow accounts. A few months of escrow payments are collected from buyers at closing to establish a positive amount in the accounts. As you make monthly payments, the escrow balance will rise so enough money is in the account when the first property tax payment is due.

Remember: Your monthly mortgage payment is made up of *PITI*. *Principal* payment on the loan, *interest* payment on the loan, *taxes* paid to the county, and *insurance* paid to maintain homeowner's hazard insurance against risk of loss. Because taxes are part of your monthly payment, it is important to know what they are. They can have a significant effect on how much you pay each month. Inquiries concerning whether or not taxes are going to be raised in the near future should be directed to the Assessor's office in the county you are looking to buy in. Just because taxes have been a certain amount for the last few years doesn't mean they won't be raised in the next year or two. This is especially true in counties where new-construction subdivisions are being built. Even if you are buying an older home, the brand new homes in the area can drive up your property taxes.

Are Tax Rates on MLS Sheets Accurate?

Never assume the tax rate listed on a multiple listing sheet will be the tax rate you will pay for five to ten years in the future. Ask your Realtor about the chances of taxes going up in that county, especially if there are a lot of new-construction subdivisions going up. The local Assessor's office also can provide information on tax changes.

How Are Taxes Assessed?

There is no single method in which taxes are assessed. In many states tax assessments leave people scratching their heads in confusion or anger because their next-door neighbor pays nearly half of what they do. Tax rates vary from county to county within a state, and can be markedly different in various regions of the country. An old rule of thumb suggests taxes are 1–2% of a home's purchase price (generally around 1.5%). For instance, a $100,000 home would be assessed a tax of approximately $1,000 to $1,500 per year if the owners did not have any exemptions filed to lower the taxes. In recent years there have been changes in tax laws. A more cynical, but pragmatic view is taxes are assessed according to the value of a home and how much money a particular county needs to raise for future projects. Taxes used to be re-assessed every seven to ten years. Lately, there appears to be a trend to re-assess taxes every two to five years, particularly in areas where new-construction housing is prevalent.

Politicians routinely pass legislation for tax re-assessments every two or three years in counties where new schools and infrastructure facilities (that is, roads, bridges, libraries) are being renovated or built. This is done to raise money. They like to call them re-assessments instead of tax hikes when in essence that is exactly what they are. (Hard to believe politicians do this, isn't it?)

In my hometown there is a five-year study under way to review and change the way taxes are currently assessed. Nobody seems to know how they're assessed in Indianapolis, so no one will really know if the new way is better, or even that there is a new way. The best source of information on how taxes are assessed is your local Assessor's office or through your city-county council. These offices have a vested interest in looking good, so understand you will get a rosy picture of property taxes from these agencies.

Tax Exemptions and Tax Breaks

Because our government wants us to feel warm and fuzzy while they are taxing us outrageous amounts of money (America became a country because of a tax revolt, remember?), tax exemptions were created to give money back to homeowners. The two most common and beneficial exemptions are the homestead and mortgage exemptions. The *homestead exemption* is a credit given to homeowners for living in a dwelling as their primary residence. This tax break encourages and rewards home-ownership. The idea (right or wrong) is that a community will be stronger, safer, and more attractive if there are a high number of people who own homes and live in the home.

Real estate investors who own rental properties and individuals who own vacation homes or multiple houses can only receive a homestead exemption for the one home they live in, their primary residence. Homestead exemptions vary from state to state. Each state Assessor's office can provide information on what that respective state's exemption is worth. If the assessed value of a home is $100,000, a $2,000 homestead deduction will make the assessed value $98,000. You would only pay taxes on the $98,000 assessed value.

A second exemption is given for carrying a mortgage on the property. The *mortgage exemption* rewards homeowners for contributing to the economy and provides relief from the burden of mortgage payments. A $100,000 loan repaid over thirty years ends up costing well over $200,000 because of interest (that's a lot of contributing and quite a burden). As long as a homeowner is paying a mortgage, this exemption can be received. The mortgage exemption

Check This Out

How Are Taxes Handled at Closing?

Your lender will estimate on your good-faith estimate the taxes you will be credited for at closing. The credit will appear on the Hud-1 Settlement Statement as a credit to the buyer and a debit to the seller.

is typically worth less than the homestead exemption, and also varies from state to state. The deduction on your assessed value might be only $3,000 to $5,000 per year, but as my parents said: every little bit helps.

Some title companies will file these exemptions for you when you close on your home. Others will give you the documents already filled out and instruct you when to file the paper work. *Tax exemptions must always be re-filed when a home is bought or re-financed.* If you don't file the exemptions, one year later your taxes will go up. If you have questions about filing exemptions, ask your Realtor or contact the title company where you closed your transaction. Most states charge a miniscule fee, around $1 to $5, to file these exemptions and they save hundreds of dollars per year in property taxes. So make sure they are filed!

Filing Your Exemptions

When paying the fee to file your homestead and mortgage exemptions, always send a check even though the fee is $1. If you send cash, a clerk in the Assessor's office might enjoy a Snickers bar and Coke with your money and your exemptions will never get filed. Also, hold onto the receipt you get in the mail from the Assessor's office as proof the exemptions were filed. If you don't receive a receipt within three months of sending in the paper work and check, contact the Assessor's office.

A final tax break is given to homeowners with physical infirmities. Individuals with sight, hearing, or other disabilities might qualify for an additional exemption. Local Assessor offices have information on this exemption. This tax break also varies from state to state.

Calculating Taxes into Your Mortgage Payment

Many sites allow you to calculate property taxes into your mortgage to see what your monthly payment would be. Remember: Your monthly payment is made up of principal payments, interest charges, taxes, and insurance (PITI). The best sites to figure monthly payments are www.quickenmortgage.com, www.mortgage.com, www.eloan.com, and www.iown.com. mortgage.com, shown in Figure 7.2, is particularly easy to use.

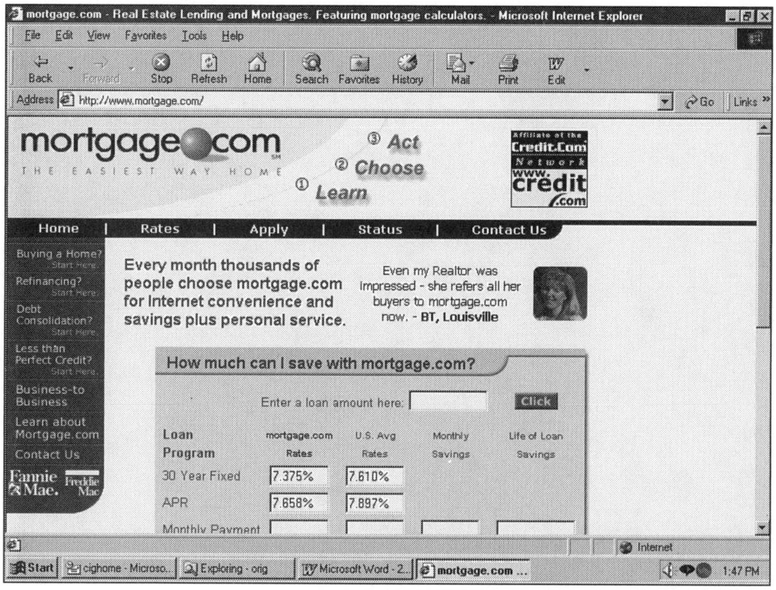

Figure 7.2

The following figure shows the home page of mortgage.com, which offers a monthly mortgage calculator.

The Least You Need to Know

➤ Property taxes are taxes levied by local governments to generate revenue to maintain and improve schools, roads, parks, libraries, and government facilities in a specific area.

➤ Tax information can be found online by going to a search engine and typing `city government` and the city name you are searching for. Local Assessor's offices also have tax information.

➤ Tax escrows are accounts set up by lending institutions the day of closing to make sure homeowners pay their property taxes on time. A portion of each monthly mortgage payment goes to an escrow account to pay the property taxes.

➤ Tax exemptions are discounts or breaks given to homeowners to reduce the amount of property taxes paid. Homestead exemptions are received for living in a home as your primary residence and mortgage exemptions are given for carrying a mortgage on the property.

DIRTY STEVE'S
FINDER O'HOUSES

Chapter 8

HOWZ IT GOIN'...

Choosing a Real Estate Agent

In This Chapter

➤ The different types of real estate professionals

➤ Agency relationships and commissions

➤ What to look for in an agent

➤ Finding an agent online

➤ Hiring and firing an agent

The term *agent* brings many different thoughts to mind. Some people think of a Hollywood agent or sports agent who secures multi-million-dollar deals for his clients. Others might think of an insurance agent who comes to your home and talks about life insurance for hours in a monotone voice. There are FBI agents and agents of the state who work for state government agencies. The term invokes negative or distrustful feelings in a lot of people.

Agent actually describes any person acting in a fiduciary responsibility for someone else. In plain English, one person is getting paid to act in someone else's best interest. This sounds simple enough, but the day-to-day complexities of real estate and the large amounts of money at stake make this picture more gray than black and white. In this chapter we will examine the role agents play in the real estate process and discuss how to find a good one.

Types of Real Estate Professionals

The terms agent, salesperson, Realtor, and broker are thrown out loosely in the real estate industry. Many people do not know the difference between the designations and what they signify. One person can be all these designations because they have passed the course work and state licensing requirements. On the other hand, an individual might just be a salesperson or agent and not have acquired other certifications. I will use the terms agent, Realtor, and salesperson interchangeably throughout this chapter and the rest of the book.

Agents possess a salesperson's license, which is the minimum designation required to sell real estate. Salespersons and agents are the same thing. *Brokers* are real estate agents, or salespersons, who have attained a higher designation through advanced class work. These individuals can own or manage a real estate office because of their broker status. Brokers hold both a salesperson's and broker's license, whereas agents hold only a salesperson's license to sell. Laws vary depending on the state you live in, but brokers typically have to hold a salesperson's license for one or two years before they can sit to take the broker's class and state licensing exam. Principal brokers are individuals who own the controlling share of a real estate agency. They are the primary owner of an office, and are often called broker/owners.

Many real estate professionals have their broker licenses and do not own or manage an office. They have taken the broker's classes to improve their skills or to market themselves as more of an expert. There is nothing wrong with being an agent or salesperson, but brokers have reached a higher level of professional accreditation.

There is nothing wrong with maintaining a salesperson's license. Many agents choose not to pursue their broker's license because they have no interest in owning or managing an office. Others don't want to commit the time to take the classes. A broker's license can make an agent a better real estate professional, but the license isn't a guarantee that the individual will work harder or be more ethical. We'll talk more about what makes an agent good later in this chapter.

Realtors are salespersons who are affiliated with their local Board of Realtors and the National Association of Realtors. These agents pay yearly dues to be members of these state and national organizations. They also agree to adhere to the code of ethics the local and national organizations set forth. If disputes arise concerning the agents' conduct during a real estate transaction, Realtors must abide by the decision of the Board that oversees them. Realtors have to hold a salesperson's license, but they also can have their broker's license.

Check This Out

What's a Broker's License For?

The classes and state exam to become a broker are more detailed, thorough, and intensive than a salesperson's course work and exam. The material covered focuses on owning and managing a real estate office, and the administrative duties of running an agency.

There are many advantages to affiliating with a local Board of Realtors. Agents cooperate with each other (split commissions) and share information in the Multiple Listing Service. Although they have a responsibility to serve their client's best interests, a professional courtesy exists between real estate agents that promotes the industry in general. Agents that are members of local boards tend to practice real estate in a more professional manner because there is a governing body watching over their conduct. Boards also require minimum amounts of continuing education that sharpen agents' skills and keep them apprised of new legal, environmental, and ethical laws. There is really no downside for customers to work with a salesperson or broker who is a member of the local Board of Realtors, only an upside.

Real Estate Commissions and Representation

Real estate commissions vary from 5% to 7% of the gross purchase price depending on local custom. The entire commission is usually paid by the seller. Buyers pay the costs to originate the mortgage loan and most other closing costs. If a home is listed at 6%, the seller will pay a 3% commission to the listing office, and a 3% commission to the buyer's agent's office. Commissions are negotiable; they cannot be fixed or set. However, big, reputable real estate offices and agents normally do not lower their commissions because they're in demand and don't have to.

Typically the commission is split evenly, but there are many instances where one of the agents has altered his or her commission structure. Some buyers do pay their agents a fee or commission to find a home for them, but this is rare (except for real estate investors who are constantly looking to buy property).

The thing to remember about real estate commissions is they are all-or-nothing opportunities. Real estate sales is a 100% commission-based business. If you produce, you get paid. If you don't produce... Well, you get the picture. Agents only get paid when they sell a home and close the transaction. They might work for six months trying to sell a $50,000 home, but if the home doesn't sell and close, they get paid nothing. Conversely, a Realtor might show a $350,000 home one time and get paid an $11,000 commission for less than ten hours work.

Agents receive their checks the day of closing just as sellers do. Because agents are independent contractors, the commission checks are made out to the real estate office the agent works out of. The office then takes a percentage out of the check for administrative costs and writes a check to the agent.

There are three types of agency relationships in real estate sales. The first type of single agency is *buyer agency*. In this form of agency the agent works solely for the buyer and has no responsibility to the seller even though the seller pays the buyer's agent's commission. The second type of single agency is *seller's agency*. The agent works only for the seller and is paid by the seller.

Agents to Steer Clear From

The last thing in the world you want in a real estate professional is an agent who is short on money or desperately needs a sale. Agents work on a 100% commission basis. If an agent needs a sale to close to make commission money, you might not get the best counsel. Instead, you might get advice that gets the deal done so the agent can get paid. Work with agents that don't need a fast paycheck to pay their bills and you'll get unbiased representation.

The third type is *limited* or *dual agency*. This form of agency arises when one broker office represents both the buyer and seller in a transaction. Many people believe dual agency occurs when the same agent represents both the buyer and seller in a transaction. This is an example of dual or limited agency, but there is another more common situation where it occurs.

If buyer #1 is looking to buy a home in a specific area and is using Realtor A from ABC Realty Company, that Realtor is working for the buyer in a buyer's agency capacity. If seller #2 puts their home on the market in this same area with Realtor B from ABC Realty Company, this Realtor is working for the seller in a seller's agency capacity. The moment Realtor A tells buyer #1 about seller #2's house and provides information about it, the agency relationships for both buyer and seller have changed concerning that particular home. Because Realtor A and Realtor B work in the same office and have the same broker (ABC Realty), both Realtors are now working in a dual or limited agency capacity. If a Realtor were selling a home for seller #2 and brought buyer #1 to the home to view it, this also would be dual agency. Anytime two agents under the same broker are involved in a transaction, the agency relationship becomes dual or limited.

This type of situation can be both advantageous and detrimental to buyers and sellers. It is potentially hazardous if the agents act unethically to raise or lower the sale price to get a deal done or line their pockets. The possibility of impropriety is much greater when one agent is handling both sides of a transaction or two agents in the same office are involved in a deal. A conflict of interest could arise that harms one or both parties (usually the buyer).

What to Look Out For in Dual Agents

The way people are typically harmed in a dual or limited agency situation is being talked into buying a home they shouldn't buy. Many people think a dual agent will try to raise the sales price to make more commission money. If an agent gets the buyer to pay $1,000 more for a home and the commission rate is 3%, the agent only makes an extra $30. But if an agent is tired of showing homes or fears a home might never sell, they might give the client bad advice to buy the home, ensuring they receive a commission.

A dual or limited agency situation can sometimes be a good situation for buyers and sellers if the agent or agents involved are honest and ethical. Information flows quicker and more smoothly if there is only one agent or if the agents know each other and work in the same building. There is more at stake to the agent involved and the company, so the Realtors should be more motivated to work harder and make the deal go as well as possible. If normal problems arise, say in the inspection process, the agents and office have more to lose so they might do more or possibly give up some commission money to make the deal go through.

The key to a dual, limited agency transaction is the agent's intentions. As long as the agent or agents involved have the clients' needs in mind at all times, not their own, the deal should close without incident. Even though agents work for their respective clients and serve their best interests, there should be a sense of cordial professionalism and community among agents. They share the same information with each other from the Multiple Listing Service and agree to cooperate with each other for the purpose of selling real estate.

Agents must rely on other agents to show listings, bring offers from buyers, and close deals. The vast majority of agents are hard-working, trustworthy professionals who enjoy their jobs. Like any industry, a few bad apples can make the whole barrel look rotten. With so many good agents in the business, it's up to buyers and sellers to find the good ones. There's really no reason every client can't be represented by a good real estate professional.

Split and 100% Agents

Split agents have a contract with their broker/office that determines how much of the commission they bring in they will keep. Typically split agents have to give up 40–50% of the commission for administrative costs. *100% agents* keep 92–95% of the commissions they bring in but have to pay a monthly rent to the broker/office.

Why Agents Add Value to a Transaction

How many times have you heard a friend or family member say "I'm going to sell real estate and make a lot of money"? There's a perception that real estate agents work very little and make tons of money. Real estate can be lucrative, but few agents make good money without being really good at what they do. In addition, there's no such thing as working a little and making a lot in real estate or any field. Somewhere along the way long hours were put in and sacrifices were made. With Realtors that usually means nights and weekends.

Agents wear many hats in the course of a transaction. There is no single job description that covers all the things they do. Good Realtors do whatever has to be done to serve their clients and close a deal. Because their pay is a percentage of the sales price of a closed home, agents don't know if they will even be paid (some homes don't sell and buyers can change their minds after house hunting for three months and not buy). Agents don't know at the start of a transaction how many hours they will work or how much money they will spend assisting a client.

On some deals agents might make $8–10 per hour. Other deals they can make as much as $500 an hour, depending on the size of the commission and the amount of time invested in the transaction. Remember, agents don't have control over this and they spend on average five to seven hours of preparation time for every one hour you actually see them.

If your house caught fire, the natural thing to do would be to call the fire department. Most people don't home school for a reason: They're smart enough to teach their own kids, but they're not trained to do it. If you had a $20,000 tax problem, would you handle it yourself or call an accountant? Why not call a Realtor on a $120,000 home issue?

What Do Agents Do?

The iceberg philosophy applies to real estate agents. Ninety-five percent of an iceberg is not seen in plain sight, but we know it's there and it's huge. The vast majority of the work agents do is unseen, but it's being done and there's a lot of it.

When working for a buyer to find a home, an agent adds value in many ways. The initial work an agent does happens long before the agent starts working for the buyer. A Realtor must understand the local market place and local customs. This takes years of studying the market and continually staying abreast of market factors that change and evolve. An agent's initial job when contacted by a buyer is to get the buyer pre-qualified or pre-approved through a quality, reputable lender if the buyer isn't already (it's amazing how many aren't). If the buyer does have financing in place, the agent must verify the lender is credible and strong.

An agent must educate a buyer on the areas and neighborhoods the buyer wants to search in. The numerous factors that determine value—location, condition, amenities, appreciation rates, and current economic factors such as interest rates, inflation, the job market, and the stability of the stock market—all influence value, as does the time of the year and the nuances of a particular subdivision or area. These factors are constantly changing, as are amenities in an area such as new schools, churches, retail malls, and roads.

An agent's next job is to actually take a buyer out and tour homes. While buyers look at décor, layout, and functionality issues, agents focus on the structural soundness, safety, resale ability, and appreciation potential of homes.

When a buyer has selected the home of his choice, the agent prepares him to write an offer by doing a comparative market analysis of the subdivision or area to determine what range the offer price should be in. The agent walks the buyer through each step of the purchase agreement, explaining the ins and outs of the contract. Deals often go through because of a well-written contract that is clean and contains few contingencies. Conversely, a poorly written contract with a high offer price can be rejected or countered.

After the offer has been written, the agent must present it to the listing agent who represents the seller. The agent then assists the buyer in negotiating the price and terms of the contract (closing and possession dates, tax payments, and so on). A good agent is worth his weight in gold if he negotiates effectively for his client. Thousands of dollars can be saved or lost in the negotiating process alone.

After the offer has been accepted (congratulations!), the agent helps the buyer select a reputable home inspection company, set up the inspection, and attend it. When the inspection report comes in, the agent advises the buyer on what items should be repaired by the seller, gather information on the cost of repairs, and informs the buyer on environmental and ecological laws that have to be complied with. When the inspection amendment is written and presented, an agent negotiates for the buyer what repairs will be done and who will do the work.

What Are Contingencies?

Contingencies are subject to clauses inserted into a purchase agreement stipulating that an activity must be done in order for the transaction to close. After the contingency is satisfied, it is removed and the contract is no longer subject to that activity being done. The two most common contingencies are a buyer's mortgage loan being approved, and a home inspection being done and buyer and seller agreeing on what repairs will be completed. When all contingencies are removed, the transaction closes.

All About Inspections

Inspections are done as insurance policies so buyers know what they are buying and are protected from making a mistake if problems were hidden from them or not disclosed. Inspections are not a tool for buyers to get any or all repairs done or to make a home perfect. Even new-construction homes are not perfect. Homes sometimes seem to be sold twice because the inspection negotiations can be so difficult and strained. Sellers usually don't want to fix many things in an inspection and buyers often want as much as possible repaired in the inspection process. Compromise and common sense usually prevail and deals go forward and close.

The next step is the title search and coordinating the closing. The agent prepares the buyer for the closing and instructs him on what will be needed. The agent also assists the buyer in securing homeowners insurance if he doesn't have an insurance carrier. Closing day is finally here, and the agent attends the closing and handles any last-second issues that arise (there always seems to be one or two). The final thing the agent does is assist in the moving process. From selecting a moving company to canceling memberships, getting kids enrolled in schools, or whatever other information is needed, the agent's job is to take care of all the big things and the little things.

Realtors working for homeowners for the purpose of selling a home perform many of the same functions as agents working for buyers. The difference comes when the listing agent puts the home on the market. The listing agent must be competent about the local market and understand local customs and practices. The agent educates the seller to what the market is doing and what she can expect.

The agent tours the seller's home and offers suggestions on how the home can be improved to sell faster and for more money. Ideas might range from repairing or replacing things to simply painting, caulking, or wallpapering. The agent prepares a Comparative Market Analysis (CMA) to determine the range in value in that particular area and helps the seller pick a list price.

A large part of the listing presentation is spent explaining the current market conditions and outlining the marketing plan the agent will utilize. The rest of the listing presentation consists of documents being signed and all paperwork being taken care of. After the home is listed, the agent must market the home. Any number of the following items are done by the list agent as well as a host of other activities: advertising the home, networking with agents, conducting open houses, distributing flyers, placing phone calls and emails, working within referral networks, and getting feedback on showings.

What's a Listing Presentation?

The *listing presentation* is the interview sellers give agents to decide who will put their home on the market and hopefully sell it. During the listing presentation the agent makes suggestions on ways to spruce up the home, measures the home's dimensions, reviews the values of nearby homes, educates the seller on current market conditions, explains the marketing plan she will use to sell the home, and collects signatures on all relevant documents.

When an offer is received, the agent presents the offer to the seller and qualifies the buyer to make sure he will be approved for the mortgage. From this point on much of the work the list agent does is similar to the buyer's agent's activities.

Over-Improving a Home

Unless major repairs are truly needed or there is a glaring problem, such as 25–year-old orange carpet, agents typically do not advise sellers to put a lot of money into a home to sell it. Home values in an area only go so high, so over-improving is dangerous. Much of the money will never be recouped when the home sells and you don't get a chance to enjoy the improvements you made.

What to Look For in an Agent

There are some common qualities all good agents possess:

➤ **Good agents put your needs first**   Agents that are mindful of what is in your best interest, not theirs, rarely make mistakes or give bad advice because you're the boss and they understand that.

➤ **Good agents educate you and explain all your options**   Agents should be knowledgeable about the marketplace and provide you with all possible information before every decision you make. Good agents should never be pushy or demanding with you and should not take advantage of you in any way.

➤ **Good agents are full-time professionals**   The home buying and selling processes are unbelievably complicated, time consuming, and extremely important because your personal safety, happiness, and financial well-being are at stake. This significant an endeavor requires a professional who is qualified and readily accessible at all times.

➤ **Good agents bring in other professionals for second opinions or to do work the agents aren't qualified to do**   Agents should recommend inspectors, contractors, insurance people, or attorneys (I shudder to say those last ones) to provide thorough and accurate information when the agents are not able to advise their clients.

➤ **Good agents continually work to learn and improve their skills**   Agents should constantly strive to broaden and sharpen their skills to provide better service for their clients. Continuing education, additional classes and designations, and work in the field improve the ability of agents, resulting in better service for buyers and sellers.

➤ **Good agents should work with quality vendors with strong reputations**   The lenders, title companies, home inspectors, and other vendors agents refer you to should be reputable. If an agent refers you to a vendor, chances are that agent is as good or bad as the vendor she referred you to.

There are many other qualities good agents possess. They should never make decisions for you. Instead, they should explain in detail all your options (even those that might kill the deal). Agents should be fairly generous with their time. This includes the extremely successful agents. After all, you're paying for the agent's expertise, not her assistant's.

Good agents must be honest and communicate well. You need to hear the truth about why your home isn't selling or why your three offers to purchase were all rejected. Your agent can be your friend after the transaction is over. During the transaction brutal honesty is needed to ensure the best results.

Finding a Good Agent

There are almost as many places to find a strong agent as there are strong agents. You might have known a trusted real estate professional twenty years and never used them or you might bump into a good agent at the hardware store and see something in that person that you really like. There are some excellent places to find good agents. The point isn't so much where or how you find them, just that you do.

Before I discuss the best source for finding a good agent, here is a list of some places you can find an agent:

➤ Referral from your lender
➤ Title company referrals
➤ Home inspector referrals
➤ Church newsletter ads
➤ Local Board of Realtors
➤ Newspaper production ads
➤ Real estate magazines
➤ Yard signs in neighborhood

The best place to find an agent is a referral from the people closest to you. Family members, friends, and co- workers who have had terrific experiences with an agent are a wonderful source. The people you trust most, a parent, sibling, best friend, or boss at work, are the people you should ask for a referral. If they have always been there for you and given good advice, they will not let you down on something so important as buying or selling a home.

Full-time Versus Part-time

So what do you do if you are referred to an agent who is a policeman by day and a Realtor by night? This is a tough situation because the agent has pleased someone you know enough to be recommended. A lot of factors influence this decision. How soon do you need to buy or sell? Is the area you're looking to buy into or sell out of a hot, active market or a slow, inactive market? What job does the agent do during the day and how accessible will they be when you need them?

Pitfalls of Part-time Agents

Many part-time agents do not have MLS access because they don't want to pay the high fees to associate with their local Board of Realtors. This costs you time and access as a buyer. Part-time agents usually don't have the support system behind them that full-time agents do because large offices don't like to hire part-timers. If you're not seriously looking to buy or sell, a part-time agent would probably work fine. If you are serious about buying or selling, full-time agents are the way to go.

A policeman moonlighting as a Realtor is probably not a good fit. There's no way the agent will stop chasing down a burglar to go show you homes. That's an extreme example, but the point is home buying or home selling is too important to entrust to someone who is not completely qualified, not completely well-versed in the business, not accessible to you when you really need them, and not able to devote 100% of their time, effort, and focus on you and your needs.

There are too many good agents in the business that work full-time to take a chance on an agent who does it on the side or for extra money. This includes family members and friends that are part-timers. You aren't looking for an average house to buy or half-heartedly trying to sell your home. For most people, a home is their largest and most important investment. Would you let a part-time surgeon operate on your heart or brain? Then why use an agent whose focus and attention are divided between two or more occupations?

If you have a close friend or family member who is a part-time agent, there is a way to ask for their help yet still use a full-time agent. Explain to the friend why you want to use a full-time agent, but ask them for the name of a good Realtor. Your friend will receive a referral fee from the Realtor (usually between 20–40% of the commission earned) and you will get a full-time agent giving you the best service possible. If you want to include the close friend, you can show them documents or ask questions as you proceed. But chances are they will be happy to receive a check for basically doing nothing, and you won't have to include them unless you want to.

Picking an Agent Online

The best site to find an agent online is the National Association of Realtors (NAR's) site. REALTOR.COM is the official site of the NAR and provides access to more Realtors (and home listings) than any other Internet site.

You can see REALTOR.COM's home page in Figure 8.1.

Figure 8.1

RAELTOR.COM helps you find Realtors as well as home listings.

Most, if not all, national real estate franchises are online and easily accessible. Century 21, RE/MAX, Coldwell Banker, Carpenter Better Homes and Gardens, and ERA can be found online by entering www., their name, and .com. For instance, to gather information on Century 21 offices and agents in Orlando, type in www.century21.com. Data on all facets of securing a broker/office and agent can be found by contacting these Web sites. For a look at the Century 21 national Web site, see Figure 8.2.

Figure 8.2

Century 21's Web site offers an abundance of agency information.

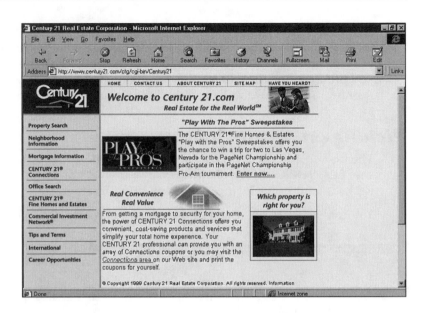

Interviewing an Agent

Determining if you are a good match with an agent you find online is really not that different from picking one over the phone or in person. The same questions are asked: How long have you been in the business? How many homes have you sold so far this year, all of last year, and the year before? How many homes have you sold in this area or subdivision? How many buyers and sellers do you sell to each year? How many buyer clients do you have right now? How many listings do you have?

What is difficult about the Internet is the anonymity it provides. People are faceless, almost emotionless if they want to be. This is exactly what you don't want from your agent. You have to build some kind of rapport with the agent to determine whether this person can be trustworthy, hard working, will serve your needs to the best of her ability and get the job done. Unless you do everything online and have a high level of trust with an agent or are an excellent judge of people, I recommend meeting your agent in person to make sure you will work well together.

The Internet is a wonderful tool to gather information and expedite numerous duties and activities in your day-to-day life, but the human aspect of buying and selling real estate is vital to the process. Most people need to get that warm feeling in their stomach to make a decision so large and significant as which agent they will use to buy or sell their most valuable asset.

The interview process can take place any number of ways. You can meet over lunch or dinner, in the agent's office, or in your home if you are selling your home. If you are listing your home for sale, you should conduct the interview in your house. This is known as a listing presentation (described in detail earlier this chapter). If you are interviewing agents to help you find a home, any place will do. The interview should not be a police interrogation, rather an exchange of information and personalities to see how well you will interact.

Many people recommend interviewing three to five agents when you are going to sell your home. I've always thought this number a bit high. If you find yourself feeling extremely comfortable and have high levels of confidence and trust in the first or second agent into your home, follow your instincts. Chances are the next two or three agents will be wasting everyone's time. If you are in a hurry to get your home on the market, this is particularly true. But if you have an extra few hours in a week to listen to agents present their spiel, invite as many agents as you think appropriate.

Ask agents during the interview for references from past clients (you can even do this prior to the interview so they have the information available) and consider posing questions to see how they respond. What you're looking for is a positive feeling that this is the right person to work for you. That feeling can come because of many different reasons. What's important is that you make the best decision for you.

Firing an Agent

Hopefully, you will never be in a situation where you have to fire an agent. If you are, there are a few things you can do. When you list your home with an agent, you also list with that agent's broker/office. In the listing contract there are stipulations on how the contract can be terminated by both parties. Review this carefully when signing the list contract. Most contracts contain an "out" clause. Typically this clause will get you out of a listing contract if you give written notice and wait a certain amount of days. Often the clause enables the broker/office or agent a chance to remedy whatever problem is troubling you. The period is usually ten days to one month.

A quicker way to get out of a listing contract is to simply ask to be released. If you do not cooperate with your agent or refuse to show the home to prospective buyers, the home will not sell. The agent and broker/owner will understand this and should let you out of the contract.

If you are working with a buyer's agent and have not signed an exclusive buyer's broker agreement, firing the agent is easy. You simply tell the agent you no longer want to work with them. If you have signed a buyer's broker contract, you must give written notice you want to terminate the contract and possibly wait for the time period to expire. The other way is to refuse to look at any homes with that agent and ask to be released from the contract. If the contract binds you to a buyer's agent for three to six months and you can't look for homes with other agents because the first agent is entitled to a commission, you should consider contacting a real estate attorney.

The Least You Need to Know

➤ The different types of real estate professionals are salespersons, brokers, and Realtors. Agent is a collective term that describes all three.

➤ Sellers pay real estate commissions that are usually split by buyer's agents and listing agents, but the buyer's agent works exclusively for the buyer in his best interest and the listing agent works exclusively for the seller in her best interest.

➤ Agents add value to a transaction through their expertise, counsel, legwork, negotiating skills, and many other functions that typically are done behind the scenes.

➤ Traits to look for in an agent are honesty, unselfishness, hard working, competent, experienced, and easy to work with.

➤ Referrals from trusted people, such as family members, friends, and co-workers, or lenders, title companies, and insurance agents, are excellent sources to find a good agent.

➤ The best places to find an agent online are REALTOR.COM and any of the large real estate offices, such as Century 21, RE/MAX, Coldwell Banker, Carpenter Better Homes and Gardens, and ERA.

➤ Hiring and firing agents is spelled out in the contract you sign when listing a home or searching for a home. If you really want out of a contract, it's hard for the agent or broker/office to keep you in it.

Making the Decision Not to Use an Agent

In This Chapter

➤ Selling By Owner might be the thing to do

➤ There's money to be saved

➤ Are Realtors really necessary?

➤ What buyer's agents offer

➤ Quiz to see if you should sell By Owner

Sweat equity in a new-construction building occurs when the builder allows the buyer to do some of the work to lower the cost of the house. We live in a nation of do-it-yourselfers and penny pinchers. A dollar saved is a dollar earned. For Sale By Owners epitomize this mindset. These are people who want to sell their homes themselves and save money doing so. This chapter will explore the issue of selling By Owner and why it can be a very good thing for homeowners or possibly a dangerous endeavor.

Selling a Home Yourself CAN Be the Right Move

Many of my Realtor friends will get mad at me for writing this chapter or not even read it. I believe For Sale By Owners can be a wise decision for some homeowners. There is primarily one reason to sell By Owner: to save money. The potential exists to save a lot of money. A $200,000 home in a market where the standard commission is

6% would result in $12,000 in commissions being paid by the seller (both the listing agent's commission and the buyer's agent's fee is paid by the seller). Who wouldn't want to save $12,000 if they could?

You might be wondering why we even have Realtors. Let's go back to that same $200,000 home. The sellers might receive a proceeds check for $60,000 after paying off the mortgage, the commissions, and all other fees. Most people would take $60,000 any day of the week over the $0 they would receive if the home does not sell. The issue isn't so much *should* you sell By Owner, but *can* you. If selling a home yourself was easy, everyone would do it and I would be writing a much shorter book.

Often people sell By Owner because they have no choice. They might have only lived in a home for two years and have built up no equity or have a second mortgage to pay off. Regardless of why money is tight, some sellers cannot afford to pay the real estate commissions that go with listing a home through the multiple listing service. Their choices are stay in the current home they're living in or sell By Owner. The decision to sell their home themselves is essentially made for them. Ironically, many of these homeowners do not want to sell their homes themselves, but have to.

There are other homeowners not in such desperate financial straits who are qualified to sell a home. These people include attorneys, bankers, accountants, and persons who work in the real estate industry. Because of their knowledge and access to information and resources, homeowners in these fields can usually successfully sell their homes themselves, thereby saving thousands of dollars.

A final category of By Owner sellers is those who are not necessarily qualified to sell their homes themselves, but do so because of the money they can save. These are the people I will discuss the most because, if you are reading this chapter, you probably fall into this group.

Check This Out

Fees By Owner Sellers Must Pay

Items sellers are responsible for paying at closing are their mortgage payoff, real estate taxes, FHA or VA fees if applicable, title insurance, and the release of their mortgage. Sellers pick the title insurance company of their choice.

Selling By Owner Means Saving Money

Far and away the biggest reason to sell By Owner is to save money. Some would go so far as to say saving money is the only reason. The financial advantages to selling your home yourself can be huge. Consider a $300,000 home in an area of town where homes are moving quickly (an average of 30 days or less). If the commission structure in this city were 7% of the gross sales price, the seller would save $21,000. That's a lot more money to put down on a new house, or money to buy a new boat or pay college tuition.

The down side is the time, effort, and advertising and attorney bills incurred during the process. Still, for $21,000 that's not too bad of a down side. Consider this scenario with the same $300,000 home. If a pre-approved buyer comes through your open house with a Realtor and wants the agent to write an offer on your house that includes you paying the agent a 3.5% commission, you still save $10,500. The up side is now there's an agent involved who will end up doing work for you in her effort to close the deal for her buyer. Homeowners still have to pay all the other normal seller fees (refer to Chapter 2, "Can You Afford Your Dream of Owning?" for a breakdown of closing costs), but real estate commissions are the second largest seller fee behind the payoff of the first or second mortgages.

We can't discuss the benefits of selling By Owner without discussing the negatives. A ton of money can be saved or made (depending on how you view it) selling your home yourself. As stated before, every seller would do it if they could. Why they don't is the question to ask.

If a home is in an area where homes don't sell quickly or have trouble selling at all, By Owners might not be possible. If the real estate market is slow (during winter and the holidays) and there are few buyers looking, selling your home yourself might not be feasible. If you have to sell extremely quickly because of a job transfer or divorce, selling your home yourself might not be effective.

The work involved in selling By Owner might rule it out for some homeowners. If you have never sold a home before, don't feel knowledgeable enough, and don't have access to information or people in the business who can assist you, selling your home yourself might not be the right decision. If the time spent marketing your home, answering phone calls, and showing your house to buyers (some who are serious and others who are nosy neighbors) bothers you, this isn't the way to go. If you are worried you might accidentally or inadvertently do something wrong and open yourself up to a lawsuit, you probably shouldn't consider selling By Owner. If your home is somewhat lower in value (under $50,000) or high in value (over $500,000), selling your home yourself probably won't work because not many buyers search for FSBOs in those price ranges.

I say all these things for two reasons. There are way too many people trying to sell homes themselves who shouldn't be, for any number of reasons: They're not qualified, they're in an area where it's incredibly difficult, the time of year makes it virtually impossible, whatever. There are many people who can and should be selling themselves. The problem is both seller and buyer can be harmed if By Owners aren't careful.

I often get phone calls from people who have been trying for three or four months to sell their home themselves and now have to list their home and sell it in 30 days. To accomplish this, they have to put an aggressive price on the home and they end up getting less money than if they had listed it from the outset. Buyers are sometimes leery of For Sale By Owners, especially if they do not allow the buyer to be represented by a buyer's agent. On the positive side, buyers should get a little bit better price because the seller isn't paying 6–7% in commissions. Some of those savings might be passed on to a buyer to entice them to buy.

The second reason I mention all the negatives to selling By Owner (no, it's not because I'm a Realtor) is to assist you in determining if you can do it yourself. If you've read this far and still feel comfortable and want to sell your home yourself, my guess is you can and should. There is a lot of money to be saved. You can ask 5–10% below market value because you are not paying commissions, sell your home quicker, and still net the same amount you would if your home was listed.

Figure 9.1 shows the largest Web site on the Internet to market For Sale By Owner homes.

Figure 9.1

The largest Web site for homes being sold by owner is FSBO.COM.

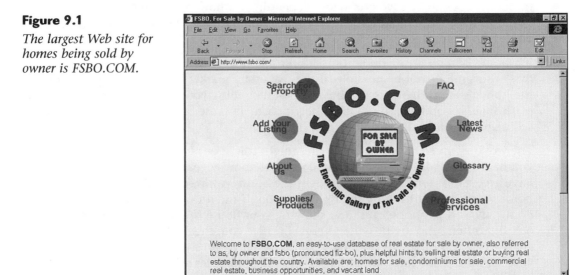

If you know people in or around the business, you might be able to get free help or advice. There are reference sources like this one designed to help people do exactly what you're attempting to do (Chapter 20, "Selling Your Home Yourself," is devoted exclusively to selling By Owner). Another option is the semi-By Owner. This transaction saves you half or most of the commissions but cuts down on your time and work involvement.

The first type of semi-By Owner sale is when a seller pays an agent a reduced percentage of the sales price or a flat fee to manage the transaction. This is especially useful when you know a good Realtor personally and money is tight. By paying the agent a flat fee or possibly half to three quarters of his standard commission the agent is compensated for his time, work, and expertise, but you still save money, save time and effort, and get professional assistance.

The other type of semi-By Owner is when a buyer is represented by a buyer's agent. If the buyer is pre-approved for a mortgage and will not buy your home unless her agent is allowed to work for her, pay the agent's commission or a reduced amount. You've saved thousands of dollars by not listing your home and now have a professional agent working for both parties to close the deal. I like to save as much money as possible, but the goal is to sell the home first, and get the most money possible second.

Qualifying Potential Buyers for Your FSBO

If you are selling By Owner, make sure a buyer has been pre-qualified or pre-approved before letting him view the home a second time. Get the information in writing and call the lender to verify he will be approved for a loan in the amount you are asking for your home. Ask the lender how long the buyer has been at his job, if a credit check has been done, if the buyer's income and debt ratios are in line, and if there is two months' reserve or more in the checking and savings accounts. Do not accept an offer and stop showing your home until you are confident the buyer will get the loan.

Can Agents Be Trusted: Realtor Horror Stories

Another possible reason not to list your home with a real estate company is your lack of confidence or trust in Realtors. A light-hearted saying among real estate professionals is buyers are liars. This refers to buyers who say they are looking for a certain type of home, yet when their agent finds a home that seemingly meets all the criteria, the buyer doesn't like it. Another example is the buyer that starts the pre-qualification process by stating he makes $80,000 a year income and has good to very good credit. When the information is verified, the buyer is found to make $60,000 and have average to good credit. Many agents are skeptical of clients because of past negative experiences.

This is not only true with agents and their clients. The public's perception of real estate agents is less than wonderful. Realtors rank near the bottom of most public opinion polls of most trusted or respected professionals. Typically only car salesmen and attorneys fare as poorly as real estate agents. There are a few reasons Joe Q. Public holds Realtors in such low regard.

Sooner or later most people have to buy or sell a home, so the exposure to real estate agents is high. Certainly, everyone knows someone who has bought or sold a home, so the exposure is extremely high. Most people's largest and most valuable investment is their home. There's a lot at stake if something goes wrong. If you can't sell the old washing machine in your basement, it really doesn't matter much. If you can't sell your $140,000 home to move into your dream home, your Realtor must be a moron.

Because homeownership is such an integral (and interesting) part of most people's lives, the subject is talked about a great deal. What ends up happening when something goes awry during a transaction is the old disgruntled customer adage. This theory says a happy customer will tell three to five people about the wonderful experience he had. An unhappy customer will tell seven to ten people about his negative experience. An angry or offended customer will vent to everyone he knows.

Realtor Code of Ethics

Agents that join their local Board of Realtors follow a code of ethics set forth by the National Association of Realtors and the local Board. The foundation of this code is the agent's responsibility to work in the client's best interests at all times. Agents must serve the client's needs above all other considerations.

This is what happens in real estate. Agents that give great service and do terrific work get lots of referrals. They are extremely successful because of their excellent work, yet some people see this and think Realtors make tons of money and don't do that much. Transactions where things go bad or the agents make mistakes result in unhappy clients who tell people about their bad experiences.

Deals where agents flat out lie to clients or steal from clients are the worst. These clients have every right to rant and rave—and should. Agents practicing real estate in this manner should be reprimanded or have their licenses suspended or revoked. Unfortunately, the fallout from these transactions is the view that not just a particular agent is crooked, but most agents can't be trusted. Like most industries, there are many more good professionals in real estate than bad, but the bad ones make all the noise.

The best way to ensure your agent can be trusted is to receive a referral from someone you trust. Get references from the agent and contact these past clients to see what kind of experience they had with the agent. Find out if they have used the agent more than once. The truest test of an agent's skill, professionalism, and honesty is repeat customers.

Determining Whether an Agent Can Be Trusted

When interviewing an agent to work for you, ask for a list of references of past clients. See how many used the agent more than once in the past. If an agent does not have clients who have used him more than once, be wary about this, especially if the agent is a big producer. Contact the clients and ask if the agent practices integrity and honesty.

If you think you've been on the receiving end of some rotten treatment from a real estate agent, here's a list of some infamous ways agents dupe clients:

➤ **The classic bait and switch with contracts**   Agents have clients sign the wrong contract, forge a signature, or alter numbers on a contract. One example is lowering the list price on a home so the home sells much faster, saving the agent extra time, work, and money. Another example is changing or lying about a sales price on a purchase agreement. The client shows up the day of closing and finds out they bought or sold the home for $5,000 more than they thought.

➤ **Agents buy homes from their sellers after devaluing them**   A clever, yet dishonest trick some agents use to buy properties for themselves far below market value. The agent will list the home at a low price and either not put it in the MLS system or prevent buyers from looking at it or writing an offer. At or near the end of the list period, the agent will buy the home at an even lower price, arguing the home clearly isn't worth the asking price because it didn't sell in six months.

➤ **Faking inspection reports or paying for friendly inspections**   To get deals done, dishonest agents can fake, manufacture, or fabricate an inspection report. An example is a termite inspection that comes back clear when there are termites or a roof inspection where the contractor states the roof has five remaining years of useful life left when in reality it needs to be replaced. Contractors and handyman are sometimes paid to say what agents want them to.

➤ **Padding interest rates for a kick back from lenders**   Some agents will quote high rates to buyers and give erroneous information, and then send the buyer to their favorite lender. The lender charges an excessive interest rate and gives money back to the agent for setting the buyer up to be taken.

➤ **Giving bad or inaccurate advice to make a commission**   This is a more subtle, yet dangerous ploy unethical agents use to sell homes faster or for more money. When working up a comparative market analysis to determine a home's value, an agent can manipulate the numbers to sway a seller into listing their home at a price far below its true value. Conversely, an agent doing a CMA for a buyer can massage the figures to influence a buyer to pay a lot more for a home than the buyer should. Another ploy is to simply talk clients into something that isn't in their best interests. Senior citizens and less-experienced clients are especially vulnerable to this maneuver.

Now that I have turned you off to all real estate agents, let me assure you these examples are done by only a rare few of the bottom feeders in the business. The vast majority of agents, brokers, and Realtors are ethical, hard-working, straight-shooting people who got into the business because they like working with people, love architecture and homes, and want to make a good living. Remember, there are plenty of strong agents out there. It's up to you to find one.

Why Buyers Should Use a Buyer's Agent

In this discussion of making the decision not to use an agent, I want to talk about buyer's agents. Most people selling their home By Owner do it because they want to save money. Many would like to have a professional working for them, but for any number of reasons they can't afford to pay the 5–7% in commissions. If they could get representation and have someone work for them and not have to spend any money, how many FSBOs do you think there would be? Correct. Almost none or none.

This is what buyers get when an agent serves as a buyer's agent: a professional working for you in your best interest with no ties to the seller, and you don't have to pay one dollar in commissions. I am asked all the time by first-time buyers who pays the real estate commissions. I will say it here and in a sidebar because this is a very important point. *Buyers do not pay any real estate commissions. Sellers pay them.* Buyers receive representation from agents who work only for them but do not have to pay the commission. Buyers pay the cost to originate the mortgage loan, the closing costs on the loan, and all inspection and appraisal fees. Sellers pay the real estate commissions.

Having someone do legwork, educate and advise you, negotiate for you, and represent you as a buyer is invaluable. Getting all this for free is priceless. Buyers should take advantage of all the services agents provide them. A buyer represented by a Realtor will have a much better chance to get the best home in an area at a better price than an unagented buyer looking on her own.

Who Pays the Real Estate Commissions?

Sellers pay all real estate commissions. Buyers pay the costs to originate the mortgage loan, close the loan, and all fees associated with inspections. Even though buyer's agents work for the buyer and serve the buyer's best interests, the seller pays both the listing agent's commission and the buyer's agent's commission. Buyers should always use the services of a buyer's agent.

If a buyer does not use an agent to find a home and simply drives around town calling agents from signs in yards, the process will take much longer and be much more difficult. If a buyer surfs the Net and emails agents, that buyer will have five different agents show them five homes. When the buyer decides to write an offer on one of those homes, he will have to get help from the listing agent to write the offer. Many buyers would not feel comfortable having the seller's agent write the offer for them. Many buyers also would not feel comfortable negotiating with the seller when the seller's agent is the go-between (this is known as a dual or limited agency situation, see Chapter 8, "Choosing a Real Estate Agent," for more details).

At all times during this type of transaction, the buyer might be wondering, "Am I being treated fairly, or am I being taken advantage of?" Having an agent of your own will alleviate these concerns. Having an agent of your own will make the transaction go faster and smoother.

One might argue that a dual agent would have greater incentive to work hard to get the deal done because she will receive the whole 6% or 7% commission. This is true, but the agent also will have more reason to act dishonestly or unethically to give one party an advantage over the other to get the deal done. Who will get the short end of the stick—the seller who the agent has known longer (sometimes years) and is paying the commission, or the buyer who has looked at just that one home with the agent and is not paying the agent anything?

People are human. They can't help play favorites a bit or lean in one direction over the other. Even the best intentioned sometimes have moments of weaknesses. As a buyer, you don't want to be in a situation where a Realtor is faced with a decision on which way his loyalty should go because 99% of the time it will go to the seller. There's really no need to be in this situation because there are fantastic buyer's agents out there who all work for free.

Only investors looking to buy rental property or debilitated real estate should consider working without a buyer's agent. These individuals have enough experience to write an offer and negotiate on their own. They also can benefit from the dual-agency situation because the listing agent might be thrilled to get both sides of the commission and not have to do much work on the buyer's side. A savvy investor can sometimes negotiate a better price because he knows the agent can reduce her commission a bit to make the deal work for the seller and still come out ahead dollar-wise because the agent gets both ends of the commission.

What Is a Fiduciary Responsibility?

A *fiduciary responsibility* exists any time an individual or company represents someone else. Agents work in a fiduciary capacity when they represent a buyer's or seller's interests. Done the right way, a fiduciary relationship is advantageous for both the real estate agent and the client. Taken advantage of or abused, the relationship can be extremely harmful for the buyer or seller.

Buyers Agency Versus Sub-Agency

This argument is a no-brainer. Sub-agency is the old, outdated form of representation in real estate. In this type of agency relationship, an agent would take Mr. and Mrs. Jones all around town hunting for the perfect home. The Joneses would confide in the agent what they wanted and how much they would pay for it. When the Joneses found their dream home and wrote an offer to buy it, they disclosed all sorts of confidential information to the agent, thinking the agent was working for them.

Unbeknownst to the Joneses, the agent was a sub-agent of the owner of the dream home because the seller was paying the agent's commission. The agent would proceed to take the offer to the seller's Realtor and pass along all the Joneses' confidential information that was spoken in confidence. Sellers had a huge advantage over buyers. You can see where buyers felt violated and taken advantage of with this type of agency relationship.

To rectify this situation, laws were passed by state legislatures everywhere to protect buyers' interests in the home-buying process. The buyers agency was created to level the playing field. Buyer's agents are still paid a commission by sellers, but buyer's agents have no fiduciary responsibility to serve the seller. The homeowner has their own agent working for them, and buyers have an agent as well. The relationship between listing agent and buyer's agent should be cordial and professional, not adversarial.

The buyers agency is the system currently in place. As far as I know, across the country sub-agency has gone the way of the dinosaurs. There is no longer a need for sub-agency. Because buyers don't pay commissions and still receive representation, all buyers want agents working in a buyers agency capacity. (Does the term 8-track tape ring a bell?)

Basic Criteria for Selling By Owner

For those of you considering selling your home yourself, there are a few essentials to ponder. The following is a checklist for any one wanting to go the FSBO route:

➤ What are your reasons for selling By Owner?

➤ Do you live in an area and price range where homes sell quickly (30 days or less) and a lot of homes sell By Owner?

➤ Do you have the ability and knowledge to sell yourself?

➤ Do you have the time and temperament to prepare the home to show, market it, receive inquiries, schedule showings, negotiate an offer, and close the deal?

➤ Do you have access to applicable state and federal guidelines for financing, inspections, and environmental health hazards?

➤ Will a slow FSBO sale limit you or prevent you from buying the right home you want to move into?

➤ Does the risk of liability or possible litigation worry you if something goes wrong in your transaction?

Quiz to See if You Can Sell By Owner

1. Will you barely make any money by selling your home or fight to just break even?

2. Have you lived in your home less than three years, taken out a second mortgage, or used VA financing to buy your current home?

3. Do FSBOs routinely go on the market in your area and sell within three months?

4. Do you work in an occupation where you are knowledgeable about real estate or do you have family members or close personal friends who do?

5. Do you have to sell your home quickly or do you have a few months to see how it goes before you get serious?

6. Have you had a horrible experience in the past with real estate agents and refuse to use one?

7. Are you crunched for time in everything you do or is there extra time in your schedule to market and sell your home?

8. Have you found another home already, will you look for your next home after you sell, or will you write a first-right contingency offer dependant upon your current home selling?

9. Are you aware of all city, state, and federal environmental laws affecting the sale of your home?

10. Is money the only reason you are selling By Owner and will you pass some of the savings in commissions on to a buyer?

The Least You Need to Know

➤ For people who are not in a huge hurry to sell or live in a hot area where homes sell quickly, selling By Owner makes sense. If homeowners have a lot of real estate experience, FSBOs should be an option.

➤ The single strongest reason to sell By Owner is the large amount of money you can save by not paying the full real estate commissions or just paying a portion of them.

➤ For the most part Realtors are ethical and hard working, but like every profession there are some incompetent, dishonest agents that tarnish the industry's reputation. There is an abundance of good agents, so steer clear of ones that give bad signals or raise red flags within you.

➤ As a buyer, you should always use a buyer's agent when shopping for a home because you will receive full representation and sellers pay the buyers agent's commission. If you don't use a buyers agent, the seller's agent becomes your agent and writes the offer for you, which is detrimental.

➤ Listing agents work exclusively for the seller and act in their best interest, and buyer's agents work exclusively for the buyer and solely serve the buyer's needs.

➤ Selling FSBO can save you a significant amount of money, but you should be sure you are able to do it and your home is in an area and price range that is feasible.

Part 4
Finding Your Dream Home

You've been patient, done your homework, and gathered as much information from the Internet as possible. Now that you've researched areas, studied property tax laws, and picked a Realtor, it's time to put all the data to use and begin hunting for the perfect home. This section of The Complete Idiot's Guide to Online Buying and Selling a Home *focuses on finding just the right place, whether it be an existing home or condo, or a new-construction house.*

Chapter 10

Existing Homes

In This Chapter

➤ Searching listings on Web sites

➤ Picking a lender

➤ Researching sales histories of target homes and their utility averages and bylaws

➤ Comparing target homes to "Needs" and "Wants" checklist

➤ Picking a home inspection company and getting insurance

You've learned how to get online and move around from site to site. You understand how to search for different real estate subjects. You're up to speed on what various Web sites offer and know which ones you want to use. Timing is the name of the game in real estate (as well as life), so let's start shopping for a home.

Searching Listings

Our motto is do things the simplest way possible. For that reason we will search for homes on HomeAdvisor, the easiest home-buying site to navigate. Start by typing the address www.homeadvisor.com in your search engine's search box and click **Go**. After HomeAdvisor's home page appears, click the menu selection **Homes**. Another list of menu items will appear. Click **Home Finder**.

To install the Home Finder software, click **Yes** in the dialog box (the screen prompts you). When you see a house appear on the screen, click **I See the House**. Downloading takes a minute or two. (You only have to download the software the initial time.) The Home Finder menu page will now be on the screen, as shown in Figure 10.1.

Figure 10.1

The Home Finder home page gives you a menu of options to help with your house search.

You can search by specific address if you've already located a handful of addresses in your previous research or by state, region, and neighborhood. Multiple neighborhoods can be searched simultaneously.

Easy-to-follow prompt buttons enable you to input data on price ranges (say $100,000–150,000) and amenities such as central air-conditioning, forced-air heat, a garage and fireplace, and at least three bedrooms and two baths. The number of matching listings is shown. You can scroll down and click each match individually to pull it up.

Complete listing information for each home appears (some listings have exterior photos of the homes). A menu bar enables you to choose to have listings emailed to you, your agent, or your co-buyer, or you can stamp a listing as one of your favorites so it can be quickly accessed.

Some basic neighborhood demographic information is provided, or you can go to the main menu for more detailed demographic data. You also can add map points to customize your search. The map points show where each particular home you've found is located in relation to the town or city parameters you inputted. There is an additional function to find local shops, businesses, and services so you know how far they are from the home you're interested in.

116

HomeAdvisor's Strengths and Weaknesses

HomeAdvisor is the simplest, most convenient home-buying site on the Net. The menus and screen prompts are easy to find and understand. The page layouts make sense and are visually easy to follow. HomeAdvisor's problems are the small number of available home listings and a lack of demographic information.

A mortgage worksheet is offered after the mapping function. You can enter the asking price of a home you've found, an interest rate, and the down payment you want to make. From this information the calculator will crunch the numbers and figure what the monthly payment would be if you bought the home at the full asking price. You can easily search for mortgage information by clicking **loan finder**. This will take you to a new menu of financing-related functions.

One of the newest and coolest features of the Internet is virtual tours of homes (touring the inside of a home on your computer). HomeAdvisor is linked with www.ipix.com, a leading virtual tour Web site. By clicking the **ipix** prompt, you can tour homes in the comfort of your own home. The other leading virtual tour site is www.bamboo.com. With these virtual tours, you are able to see literally every room of a house and extra features such as a deck overlooking a pool, a gazebo, or a picturesque lake view.

Virtual tours are replacing Sunday open houses as the means for viewing large numbers of homes without your agent present. Virtual tours are a great tool because they are so much more efficient time wise. Buyers don't have to drive around neighborhoods looking at the outside of homes nor be shown homes that have twenty-year-old shag carpet or the smallest kitchen ever built. Realtors don't have to show ten homes to clients and have only one or two be remotely close to what the buyer wants. Even sellers benefit. They don't have to round up their kids and pets and be out of the house for an hour only to have a buyer hate their home. Virtual tours help narrow a potentially large list of pretenders (agents make all homes look good on those MLS description sheets) down to a smaller, realistic list of true contenders.

You can see the home page of IPIX.com in Figure 10.2. To see an example of a virtual tour from bamboo.com, see Figure 10.3.

Figure 10.2

At the IPIX.com home page, you can take a virtual tour of some homes...

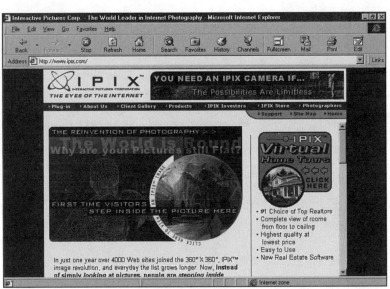

Figure 10.3

...and you can do the same at bamboo.com.

Virtual tours can be taken on other Web sites such as REALTOR.COM, iOwn, and Century21.com, or by visiting individual agents' home pages (you'll only be able to see their respective listings). Try to narrow your list to a short list of the ten or so best homes. Too large a list can be cumbersome and confusing. Each subsequent home you like should drop one off the list so you are working with a manageable number of homes.

Selecting a Lending Institution

There seems to be an unlimited number of lenders on the Net these days. Type in a lender's Web address (www. plus *lender name* plus .com), or go to one of the major home-buying sites (HomeAdvisor, iOwn, REALTOR.COM, CyberHomes, HomeSeekers.com, and Century21.com) and click **financing**. A few of the major online lending sites are QuickenMortgage, E-LOAN, LendingTree.com, and mortgage.com.

There's no shortage of sites to visit, but how do you know which lender is right for you? Most people shop for a lender by shopping strictly for the lowest interest rate and fees. There is absolutely nothing wrong with this (actually I encourage it if you're picking a lender online). There isn't too much guess work in shopping rates. You simply visit as many sites as you want and get quotes on what your rate will be and how much closing costs will be. If you've been referred to a bank or mortgage company by a trusted relative, friend, or co-worker, visit its site first and check a few other lenders to see if the recommended lender is competitive. If so, my advice would be to go with it. You cannot put a price tag on good service.

Speaking of service, the Internet presents some new and challenging problems in the way of security and safety. By now you might have heard of all the credit card theft that has occurred online. The nameless, faceless features of the Net have enabled white collar, financial crime to explode in the last few years. Loan originators and mortgage brokers can be shady enough when you go to their offices and meet them. Imagine what it's like when you're doing a loan transaction across the country and never actually meet them or any of their staff. The potential for illegal activity or simply unethical activity goes through the roof when you secure a loan online.

If you were going to drive down to the corner of your neighborhood street and get a loan from the friendly banker you've known twenty years, service should still be a factor. If you're going to get a loan from a lender 2,000 miles away who you'll never meet and probably would never be able to track down if something went wrong, you had better be certain of the service you will get. This means no last-minute fees you have to pay, or interest rate and down payment hikes right before the loan is due to be approved. It means whatever you were told at the time of qualification and loan application holds true at the time of loan approval and closing. More than anything, service means you get the loan just as you were told you would.

A bit of advice: If one online lender is offering an interest rate that no one else can come close to matching, be extremely cautious. Lenders' rates are based on established economic indicators. If one lender's rates are considerably better than everyone else's, it's making up for it some where else. Remember, it's in the business of loaning money to make money, not lose it.

When searching for a lender, there are certain things to look for. If you haven't been referred to a bank or mortgage company, the major home-buying sites and loan sites are excellent places to start. These sites offer reputable lenders with solid financing

119

packages. The service might be a little impersonal and detached, but that usually doesn't bother Net surfers. The strength and credibility of the financial institution should be checked into before committing to a lender. The number of loans it closes each month is something to consider. Your lender should do a healthy enough business to make you feel secure in its ability, but not so much that the service suffers and you get lost in a landslide of other unimportant customers.

Look for a lender that wants your repeat business down the road, not just this loan. A lender's employees should be well organized, efficient, detail oriented, and thorough. Your loan originator should be competent and knowledgeable about all the different types of loan programs. Strong listening skills are needed by loan originators to do their job well. If you are using an online lender, ask for a long list of references of satisfied customers. Contact these people to verify the lender's strength and service. If the contact is via email, scrutinize the comments carefully to make sure they are not rehearsed, similar to other feedback, or so overwhelmingly positive as to appear made up.

The following is a list of questions to ask prospective lenders:

➤ How long have you been originating loans and how long has your bank/mortgage company been in existence?

➤ What percentage of your bank/mortgage company's loans come from online clients?

➤ How many loans do you write each month?

➤ How long have you and your processor worked together?

➤ How is your working relationship with your underwriter?

➤ What type of loans do you offer?

➤ What is your current interest rate for a 30-year, fixed-rate loan?

➤ Are there points charged for that rate?

➤ What are the total application fees? How much for the credit report, appraisal fee, origination fee?

➤ Will I receive a good-faith estimate with all the closing costs itemized?

➤ Will mortgage insurance be charged?

➤ Can I float the interest rate and/or lock it in? What will it cost to lock the rate and how long will it last?

➤ Can I prepay the loan without penalty?

➤ When will my first payment be due?

➤ How much money will need to be set aside to start the escrow accounts?

➤ How long will it take for the loan to be approved?

➤ When are payments considered late, and what is the penalty?

➤ Who should be contacted if questions need to be answered?

Researching Histories of Target Houses

Another reason Realtors are valuable in the home-buying process is the access they have to data that cannot be found on the Internet. When you have narrowed your list of potential homes down to one or two homes, contact your agent and ask him to do a property archive search or history search of the target house or houses. This search consists of going back through the multiple listing service's records and finding all the activity of a particular home. Most MLS system's records go back eight to ten years.

If a home currently on the market was sold six years prior, your agent will be able to find the price the present sellers bought the house for, when they bought it, and how long it was on the market. This data will help you determine appreciation rates and to decide if the home is priced accurately and fairly for the neighborhood. (A comparative market analysis will do this too. Refer to Chapter 6, "Research Areas: Don't Get Stuck Living Next to the Addams Family," for online CMAs.) The history search also will show if the home was on the market in the past and withdrawn, or if it didn't sell and the listing contract expired. This data gives a more comprehensive picture of a target home's overall strength, resale ability, and future investment potential (wouldn't it be nice if we could do history searches before dating people?). Knowing a property's history enables you to write a better offer to purchase and helps determine what price you should pay for a home.

Getting Yearly Utility Averages

Whenever I am showing a client of mine a home and the seller has placed a work sheet of the average yearly utilities in the kitchen or dining room, my buyers always comment how handy the information is and how professional the other agent must be. Utility information not only helps buyers budget what their true costs will be after they're living in a home, but it tells a lot about the home.

Documents to Look For During a Showing

Sellers should have in their homes during a showing the following documents for buyers to review: MLS listing sheets with complete property data, sales disclosure sheets disclosing the condition of the home and all the mechanical systems in it, a lead–based paint disclosure form if the home was built prior to 1978, the utility averages and possibly flyers, and a survey of the home if the seller has one.

Utility information sheds light on the following questions. Is the home well built and well insulated? Are energy and the elements seeping out of the home or into the home because the doors, windows, fireplace, or basement aren't sealed properly? Are the furnace, water heater, and air conditioning systems functioning correctly? Should this home be put on a budget plan or pay as you go?

To get a true picture of what it will cost to buy a home and live there, the utility averages should be disclosed to the buyer before an offer to purchase is written. If the information is not in the home during a showing, your agent should request it prior to the second showing or writing the offer. Armed with this data, a home inspector can focus on specific mechanical systems to see if there are problems.

Researching Association Bylaws If Applicable

Some subdivisions have mandatory association memberships (all condominium communities do and most patio homes/zero lot line communities do). A large number of new-construction subdivisions have optional or mandatory memberships in their associations. If the existing home you are buying has a mandatory association membership, you will have to review the association bylaws and agree to abide by them. You can research the bylaws up front if you are looking to buy in only one or two subdivisions. If you are searching all over town or in various areas, it does not make sense time-wise to review the bylaws of many communities. These documents can be extremely lengthy (and boring). There's no point in reading hundreds of pages of bylaws when you're not even sure if you're going to buy a home in that community.

The purchase agreement contains a clause that states the buyer will have a designated period of time to review and approve the association bylaws if membership is mandatory. The buyer picks the time frame (typically five to ten days is allowed for the documents to be given to the buyer and then an additional week or two to review them). This is a contingency in the contract that must be removed for the transaction to close. If there is a covenant or restriction the buyer absolutely can not abide by and the association will not waive or change it, the buyer can get out of the contract and the deal dies.

If a buyer thinks there might be a potential problem with association bylaws and has narrowed his search down to just a few subdivisions, it might be wise to contact the association presidents of those subdivisions to request copies of their respective bylaws. Your agent can facilitate this. Other sources for information on association bylaws are the listing

Check This Out

Reviewing Association Data on MLS Sheets

MLS sheets contain information concerning the cost of association fees and how often it is paid (monthly, quarterly, semi-annually, or yearly). Examine this information carefully to see if the association has a mandatory or optional membership and what services are covered by the fee.

agents of homes for sale in those subdivisions or a subdivision's management company, if applicable.

Reviewing the Checklist of "Needs" and "Wants"

When you started the home-buying process weeks or months ago, you probably had an idea in your head of what you wanted. Whether you wrote your criteria down, or stored it in your computer or the computer between your ears, you know what that initial list had on it. During the process of house hunting, that list might have changed drastically or remained exactly the same. Either way, it's time to pull the list out and compare the home you've targeted with your checklist of needs and wants.

Let's say the top "need" features on your list when you started were three bedrooms, two full baths, at least a one-car garage, a fireplace, central air conditioning, and forced-air heating. The price range you wanted to search in was $100,000–150,000. Compare that checklist to what you found: a three-bed, one-and-a-half bath (half baths have a sink and toilet, no shower or tub) home with a fireplace, two-car garage, central air, and gas forced-air heat for $119,900.

The home you have targeted meets all your initial criteria except it does not have two full bathrooms. On the plus side you were willing to take a home with a one-car garage and the target home has a two-car garage. If you are comfortable with the price and all the "need" items, it's time to look at the "want" items.

The initial checklist for "wants" consisted of a separate dining room and kitchen, a fenced rear yard, a brick exterior, and a construction date of ten years old or newer. The target home you have found has a fenced rear yard and was built four years ago, but has wood and vinyl siding exterior and an eat-in-kitchen, not a separate dining room. You must weigh the pros and cons of your checklist and the target home's actual amenities to see if it is the right home for you. Can you live with items that are missing from your list? Does the home offer extra amenities that you didn't think you wanted or would get? Prioritizing the importance of items makes it easier to decide if you can live without something.

It's important to note there is no such thing as a perfect home. Even if you custom built a 20,000-square-foot mansion for $10,000,000, there would be items you wanted later that weren't built into the home. Existing homes are compromises of sorts. You want the tried and true conveniences of an established area or the charm and character of an older home, so you're willing to live with the decisions of the people who built the home (you can always change décor or add on and knock down walls).

The items on your checklist can change in importance as you hunt for a house. Some things can be added to the list while others can drop off. The list is a tool to help you prioritize and focus, not drive you crazy (it's not a things-to-do list or grocery list where everything has to be checked off). Use it as a frame of reference to gauge how much you like the final few homes you've narrowed your search down to. The checklist also is helpful in determining what price you should offer to buy the home. For instance, if the home you've found meets nearly all your needs and wants, offering a real lowball price doesn't make much sense unless the sellers are desperate to sell or the home has been on the market for an extremely long period of time and hasn't sold. Conversely, if a home only possesses half of the items you were searching for, you probably will write a lower offer and only buy the home at a certain price. More importantly, you might ask yourself if it's truly the right home for you or should you keep searching.

Tips for Making a Home-Buying Checklist

Your home-buying checklist should be broken down into two categories. The first category is "Needs" or "Must haves." The second is "Wants" or "Like to have." Keep the Needs or Must haves as short and general as possible. Put only the absolute must-have items down. If you are too specific, the number of available matching homes will be small and you won't have much to look at. Use the "Wants" or "Like to have" category to weed out the undesirable homes and rank your favorites.

Selecting a Home Inspector and Insurance Company

The Internet will probably not play a large role in picking a home inspector because the inspector will need to be a local outfit that is familiar with housing and construction codes and ecological issues pertinent to that region. Ask your agent or a trusted relative, friend, or co-worker for the names of two or three good inspection companies. Your agent should be able to provide you with a list of reputable inspectors. The real estate office your agent works out of probably has a list of inspection companies to use, and a list of companies to stay away from. You can verify the company with the Better Business Bureau if you have doubts or concerns.

Time might be an issue in selecting an inspection company. The home inspection should be completed within four to ten days after the offer is accepted (this is negotiated in the purchase agreement). When picking an inspector, ask for references from past clients and agents. Be sure to ask the inspector how long he has been inspecting homes and what his background training is. Look for inspectors with years of experience in the home inspection field as well as construction, home building, engineering, and contracting.

There are many poorly trained, shady individuals in the home inspection business. The industry is not well-regulated, so memberships in the ASHI (American Society of Home Inspectors), or NAHI (National Association of Home Inspectors) are important. Inspectors with these affiliations are practicing their trade by these organizations' guidelines.

Be wary of fly-by-night outfits trying to make fast or easy money. You want an inspection company that's been doing it for awhile and will be for years to come.

Your inspector should provide a written report detailing the entire inspection. An inspection company I work with a great deal takes Polaroid pictures of trouble spots (leaky roofs, rotten wood, termite damage) to document the problems to the owner. This makes it easier to get work done by the seller (video cameras can be used as well).

What Gets Fixed in a Home Inspection?

Major defects are items that directly affect the habitability of a home. Habitability issues are problems that compromise an owner's safety or well being. Major defects that affect habitability almost always get fixed unless the buyers negotiate a lower purchase price and agree to correct the problem themselves. Examples of major defective items that affect habitability are termites, roofs with no remaining useful life, furnaces and central air units that don't work, faulty electrical wiring, major plumbing problems, structural problems with the foundation, excessive radon or loose asbestos wrap, and severe moisture damage.

Insurance companies are easier to pick than inspection companies for two reasons. You probably already have a trusted insurance company handling your car, life, or renter's insurance, and insurance companies can't mess up as bad as inspectors can. Your insurance agent has a very simple job. A week or two before closing, contact him. He will prepare a declaration page showing you have homeowners insurance on the dwelling as of the day of closing. Your agent will ask some basic questions (address, sales price, square footage, size of garage, closing date) and prepare the document you need for closing.

Your agent might need to walk the outside of the home and take a photo. There is very little that can go wrong with obtaining homeowners hazard insurance. Just make sure you get it and the coverage begins the day of closing, not the day of possession. If lightning knocks a tree into your house the day after closing but you haven't moved in yet, your insurance will cover the damage. The seller has already conveyed title to you. Because the insurance company's job is so simple, look for a friendly, efficient agent with low rates who will make things as easy as possible for you. By carrying other lines of insurance with the same agent, you should be able to get a discount on your homeowners insurance.

You can use the Internet to find insurance companies, especially if you are shopping for prices. I advise staying with bigger, well-known agencies. Be sure the agency you pick on the Net will pay out if you file a claim, though. Some shakier agencies on the Net offer super low rates, but try to avoid paying on claims whenever possible. You want a legitimate, credible agency insuring your most valuable and important investment. Rates are important when buying insurance but service is vital, too. Ask anyone who has had their house destroyed by fire, natural disasters, or vandalized by burglars. Saving $50 to $75 a year on insurance is not worth the thousands of dollars you can lose if your insurance company doesn't pay a claim the proper way.

The Least You Need to Know

➤ HomeAdvisor is the easiest site to use when house hunting. Narrow your search down to ten homes or less.

➤ Virtual tours enable buyers to view the insides of homes from the comfort and convenience of their own home on their own time.

➤ Pick a lender who you trust, has competitive rates, and can close your loan on time. Close relatives, friends, and co-workers, as well as your Realtor, can recommend a good lender.

➤ When you find a home and want to write an offer to purchase, your agent can search the multiple listings records for all the activity on that house dating back about ten years. This past history search helps determine how much the home is worth and at what rate it is appreciating.

➤ Before writing an offer, get the home's utility averages and any association bylaws, if they exist.

➤ Review the checklist of items you need and want and compare them to the amenities in the home you're thinking about writing an offer on. This helps determine if you should write an offer and how much the offer should be for.

➤ Pick a home inspection company and insurance agent that will give solid, reliable service and charge fair, competitive rates for your home inspection and homeowners insurance.

Chapter 11

New Construction or Designing Your Own Home

In This Chapter

➤ Searching new-home listings and builders' Web sites

➤ Online touring of model homes, spec homes, and blueprints

➤ Search vacant lots and land

➤ Research building codes online

➤ Designing your own blueprints

➤ Finding contractors and specialty laborers online

Don't like older homes? Tired of all the maintenance problems your home is plagued by? Do you want control over the layout, floor plan, and design of the home you live in? New homes might be the answer. This chapter explains how you can search new-home listings and select a builder anywhere in the country.

Searching for New Homes

Start searching for new homes by typing the address www.newhomesearch.com in your search engine's search box. Then click **Go**. NewHomeSearch.com's home page will appear. This site is the leading new-homes site on the Internet with over 100,000 listings. In addition to size, NewHomeSearch.com is easy to move around on and is the official site of the NAHB, the National Association of Homebuilders.

What's a Spec Home?

Spec home stands for speculation or speculative home. Builders build these homes even though there is no buyer under contract to buy the house. Most homes are not built unless a buyer writes an offer to purchase and puts money down. Spec homebuilders gamble that there will be a buyer for the home when it is completed.

NewHomeSearch.com's home page will offer a Local Tools Menu. Possible selections are Featured Communities, Featured Builders, Free Housing Guide, and Relocating. You are given an option of searching for homes or builders (you must select one or the other). Click **new homes**. Next, click the prompt that says **U.S. Maps**. Select the state you want to build in. For instance, you might choose Colorado. Next, you are asked to select a metro area or county in Colorado. We'll pick the city of Denver (most people don't know counties unless they live there).

For a look at the NewHomeSearch.com Web site and the various menu items, see Figure 11.1.

Figure 11.1

The NewHomeSearch.com Web site lets you check out new-home construction in any area of the country.

The next step in your search of new homes is to input criteria for the home description. For instance, you might want to build or search for a spec home between the range of $150,000 and $200,000. Other requirements might be a minimum of three bedrooms, two baths, 2,000 square feet, a two-car garage, and a projected possession date of February 1, 2000.

After entering all these criteria click **Find Homes Now**. Sort through the matches that come up to see how many interest you. If you're not happy with the results, go back and adjust the search criteria. Remember, the more general and non-specific you are, the more matches you will find. Input too many requirements or make them extremely difficult (a four-bed, three-bath new home under $100,000, for example), and you will have very few options to choose from.

NewHomeSearch.com lets you tag homes as favorites and email matches to your agent or friends. There's also a financing menu that enables you to calculate what your monthly payment would be. Take a close look at the financing options available. Builders sometimes work deals with mortgage companies and banks as incentives to purchase that might result in lower interest rates and the closing costs being paid for you. Ask about these discounts when you contact individual builders if they don't offer them up front.

Other major new-home construction sites to consider surfing are www.newhomenetwork.com and www.homebuilder.com. These sites are similar to NewHomeSearch.com in many ways, but don't have the number of listings and builders NewHomeSearch.com has.

Searching for Qualified Builders and Contractors

Another way to search new-construction homes is through builders. To access a list of builders, click **Builders** instead of **Search Homes** at NewHomeSearch.com's main menu. A similar process of inputting data concerning geographic location and amenities requirements must be followed. A complete list of builders in that region will be generated after you click **Find Builders Now**.

NewHomeSearch.com also provides menu items titled *Featured Builders* and *Featured Communities*. These prompts enable you to quickly search pre-determined builders and communities. Click either of these prompts to speed search top builders and prime communities in the state and city you are moving to.

New-construction homes also can be found by logging on to individual builders' Web sites. If you were extremely satisfied with a particular builder in the past, have been referred to a company by a trusted relative or friend, or have done extensive research and have picked a particular builder, you can go directly to its Web site to review information on floor plans and model homes. For example, type www.ryland.com if you want Ryland to build your next home. This is a much simpler process than surfing new-home sites, but many people will not have settled on a builder already. Another potential problem arises if your favorite builder does not do business in the area you are relocating to.

Facts About New-Construction Deals

New-construction deals occur far less often than the sale of existing homes, but Boards of Realtors across the country usually see more arbitration, mediation, and grievances filed during new-construction transactions than during existing home sales.

Searching for contractors or custom builders to construct your future dream home is another option. If you do not have the Web address of a specific company, start your search by searching the key words **custom builder** or **homes** (use the search engine of your choice). Break down the list of matches according to their geographic location, reputation, and size. NewHomeSearch.com and the other major new-home sites offer lists of custom builders and contractors.

I would add a cautionary note about contractors. If you are considering a contractor to build your new home, make sure the firm is reputable, dependable, and large enough (has the personnel and resources) to complete the job on schedule. There's nothing worse than hiring a builder or contractor who promises the world and can't deliver squat. It's also incredibly frustrating to have your new home finished months late (particularly during the winter months and the holidays), or worse yet, have your builder file bankruptcy papers while your dream home is partially built. There are too many good outfits building excellent homes to pick a weak, inexperienced builder who will let you down.

After you have narrowed your list of new-home communities, homes, or builders down to a manageable number that isn't overwhelming, contact them and inquire about their quality building and service records. Ask if you will receive better financing terms if you finance your home through their lender instead of your own. Also, ask for a list of homeowners in the community or neighboring communities that built homes similar to the one you're considering building. See if the builder has won any awards in the past five years. Find out if the builder is in good standing with the local Board of Realtors.

A builder is only as good as its reputation. If the word on the street about a builder is good, chances are it is good. If the word is bad, count on it being worse than bad. A rule of thumb to follow in real estate is that a builder or contractor is usually a little bit worse than its reputation. So, if its reputation isn't good, odds are it's really bad.

Viewing Model Homes, Spec Homes, and Blueprints Online

Touring homes online has replaced open houses as "the way" for buyers to view a large number of homes on their own time. Online tours enable buyers to shop around on their own before they get serious and do homework without agents interfering. The best way to view model homes, spec homes, or blueprints is to go straight to a builder's Web site. Usually you can find a Web address (if you don't already have it) by typing www.*builder'sname*.com. For example, to find U.S. Homes on the Internet, type www.u.s.homes.com and click **Go**.

If you aren't successful finding the site that way, go to a search engine and type the builder's name, or input any of these key words: builder, new homes, home construction, home builder, new housing, housing construction. One final method to make contact with a builder in another city is to call information (dial #1411 on your phone) and get the 800 number or phone number. Call the builder, request its Web address, and have the builder email information to you. Now that you have the address, you can access their site.

Custom-Built Homes Versus Production Homes

Custom-built homes are designed and built with a buyer's individual wants and needs in mind. They are typically more expensive, better constructed, and designed in collaboration between a builder and the buying customer. Production homes are standard, assembly-line homes built in new subdivisions where buyers pick a pre-set floor plan and layout from one of a handful of options. Builders make money on production homes by building a lot of them in the same manner in a short period of time.

How you accessed a builder's site—directly, through a search engine, or by calling directory assistance—doesn't matter. After you're on the builder's home page, look for the menu option that enables you to tour model or spec homes online. Production homebuilders offer similar floor plans with slight variations, so you should be able to view floor plans quite easily. Not all builders are up to speed on Internet technology so the quality of this virtual tour might not match that of existing homes at www.ipix.com or www.bamboo.com. Nonetheless, you should be able to get a good feel for a spec home or model home from accessing the builder's Web site (spec homes can usually be found on IPIX and bamboo.com also).

Let's use a national builder, such as Ryland Homes, as an example when searching floor plans or doing a virtual tour. Access Ryland's Web site by typing www.ryland. com. The home page will offer a variety of menu options: Nationwide Home Search, About Ryland, Ryland Mortgage, Email Us, and Mortgage Estimators. Click **nation-wide home search**. After the second page appears onscreen, you are given a host of states to pick from (about 16). For instance, click **Arizona** if you are thinking about relocating to the West. The next page will present you with options of which city in Arizona you want to search in (I picked Phoenix), and the price range you want ($200,000 and above—Phoenix is pricey).

A list of matches will appear, typically categorized by community name. Ryland's site provides easy-to-follow instructions and simple screen prompts to help you move around. Alongside the list of matching communities is a menu function that enables you to check elevation, floor plans, video tours, and directions. Each listing will offer some of these options, but not all four. Most of the listings on Ryland's site offer information on elevation, floor plans, and directions, but don't let you take video tours.

To view Ryland Homes's Web page with city and starting price menu options, see Figure 11.2.

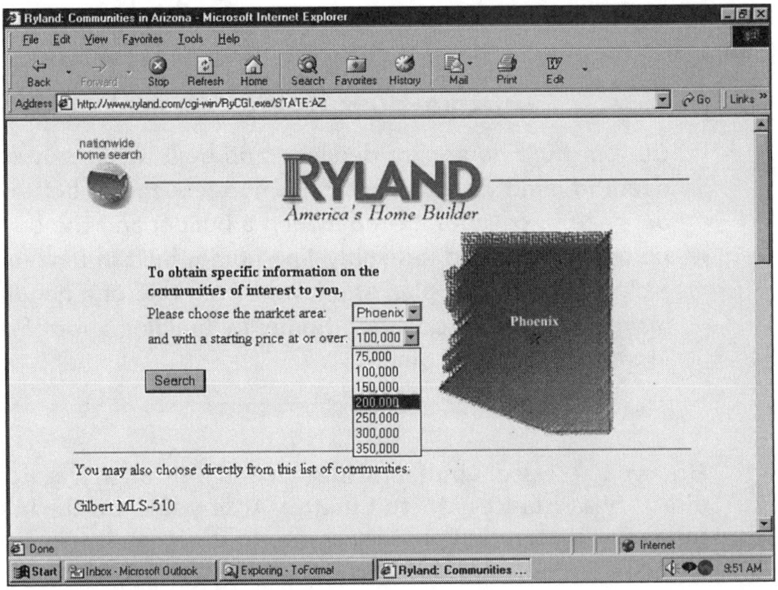

Figure 11.2

Ryland Homes is a national builder that lets you check out locations and floor plans on its Web site.

Along with data on price, bedrooms, baths, and the name of the floor plan, the status of each home is provided. Possible completion dates and move-in dates are listed as well as the type of unit, spec, or model home.

If you want Ryland to send you additional information there is a box at the bottom of the page where you can submit your name, address, phone number, and email address. Ryland will forward more data on its communities to you. This also is a tool to track who is using its site and to put you on its mailing list. Any time you give out personal information over the Net, especially with real estate–related sites, you will be bombarded by solicitors trying to sell their services. Be careful, because you have no control or idea where your personal data will end up.

One thing to remember is that this example deals only with Ryland builders. There are scores of national builders and regional builders who offer diverse floor plans, layouts, and amenities. Many of the larger builders are updating their technology to offer online video tours. Currently, the technology builders use is not as advanced as the online tour sites at www.ipix.com and www.bamboo.com. Viewing spec or model homes through the builders' sites can be a bit tedious and difficult. Most builders advertise their spec homes and eventually their models (when all lots in a subdivision are sold and built on) through the major home-buying sites such as www.realtor.com, www.iown.com, and www.cyberhomes.com. Real estate offices such as Century 21 and RE/MAX put all their listings online at their own sites and on www.realtor.com, so you will find spec homes there as well.

Searching exclusively through a builder to view floor plans of a model or spec home makes sense if you have already selected your builder. Going straight to that builder's site and checking out various floor plans is necessary and prudent. If you haven't picked a builder yet, going through individual builder's sites takes a bit longer and could be a slow way to view new homes online. Searching the major new-home construction Web sites (www.newhomesearch.com, www.newhomenetwork.com, and www.homebuilder.com) will probably save you time and trouble.

Why Models Are the Ideal Home

If you can buy a spec home that served as the model home for a builder, try to do it. A model home is usually built with better attention to detail and loaded with many extra features and upgrades because it is the unit all prospective buyers will walk through and view. Besides getting a higher quality of construction, you might be able to negotiate a lower price because models are typically a few years old by the time they are sold.

Currently, not many builders offer online copies of blueprints to potential customers. Part of the reason might be the industry's slow acceptance of the Internet. Technology has not been embraced by this "people industry." Therefore, a large number of builders haven't invested the necessary funds to offer virtual tours or online blueprints.

Other possible reasons more builders don't offer blueprints online are privacy and public domain issues. The Net can't be policed because it's cyber airspace. Anything

133

put out on the Net is open to public consumption, which means public ownership. Builders might fear they will lose customers if buyers everywhere have access to their blueprints. Why build with Ryland when you can build one of their floor plans or models with a contractor or independent builder for 10–15% less?

A more reliable way to get builder blueprints is to contact one of them via email or telephone, express interest in some of their communities, and request a copy of a blueprint they have built from in the recent past. Some builders are hesitant to give out this information too early in the ballgame, but if you show enough interest you should be able to view blueprints.

Unlike floor plans, which can be found in any model home in America, blueprints are a little more involved and show greater detail. Because of this, drawing them up requires more time, effort, and work. If you give a builder a reason to work hard for you, any company with good customer service will work with you to give you all the information you need and answer your questions or concerns.

Building and Closing on Time

Builders are notoriously slow in constructing homes and closing on time. You don't want your home built in less than four months because the quality will suffer. Make sure you and your agent get everything in writing from the builder—from every date you are told to every detail the builder promises to add or fix. Set target dates as early as possible and check the progress weeks in advance to make sure deadlines are met. You or your agent should go by the home site at least once a day, even if for only five minutes. This will keep everyone at the site working hard. Buy the contractors and laborers pizza or sandwiches to thank them. Get to know the construction supervisor. Ask lots of questions. Catch mistakes early so they can be repaired or replaced. You are the customer—you can't be wrong. Demand zero defects and no flaws from your builder.

Searching for Vacant Lots and Land

Hunting for vacant lots and land isn't as easy as house hunting because most of the major home-buying sites don't offer lots and land as search options. (By the time this guide hits bookstores that may have changed.) There are a couple of ways to search online for lots and land. The first and easiest involves using the Net to secure a Realtor or builder. Neither of these sources will have lots and land listings on their

Web sites. What you will have to do is email the agents or builders you like and ask them to electronically send these listings to you.

Agents' and builders' sites are designed to attract customers first and provide information second. A commonly held assumption in the real estate industry is that after they have your attention they can follow up with intensive information. Many in the field fear that too much data up front scares away or turns off prospective clients. The bottom line is agents and builders have access to the largest volume of information on lots and land. By contacting one or the other you will get the data you need and possibly secure an agent or builder in the process.

Agents' Commissions in New-Construction Deals

Many people are hesitant to use agents when they are building new homes. They incorrectly guess the home will cost more to build if they use an agent. Buyers do not pay the agent's commission in a new-construction deal. At the beginning of each year builders budget 2.5–3.5% for agents' commissions for every home they will build. If a buyer doesn't use an agent to build, the building company makes that much more profit.

Financing Vacant Lots and Land

When purchasing lots or land, it is difficult to finance the transaction because land is speculative and extremely non-liquid. Banks and mortgage companies typically won't loan money to buy land because there is no certainty it will sell if the borrower defaults on the payments. Most people have to pay cash to buy land or take out a second mortgage or equity line of credit to raise the funds to buy land.

After you have made contact with an agent or builder, request a list of all the lots and land in various areas you are interested in and the specific price range you want to search. They can send accompanying information on school districts, tax data, appreciation rates, and individual community amenities. Agents and builders make a living giving service to customers like you, so use these people to gather information and make your search easier and more effective. Until the Internet has sites dedicated to offering extensive information on lots and land, agents and builders are the best route to accumulating data.

If you want to avoid agents and builders as long as possible (some really are pushy), try logging on to your local town's Board of Realtors site, or the Board of Realtors site in the city you are locating to. You can obtain Board of Realtors Web addresses by accessing www.realtor.com or by contacting an agent in the new city.

For example, the Board of Realtors in Indianapolis is MIBOR (Metropolitan Indianapolis Board of Realtors). Like most boards around the country, MIBOR has an excellent site that is particularly helpful if you are searching for lots and land. To access this site you would type www.mibor.net. After the home page appears, click **property search**.

A prompt on the second page offers the choice between searching for residential or commercial properties. Click **residential**. The next page offers a menu of different residential property types based in select counties. Select the county and then select **vacant lots and land** in the Residential Property Type column. Now that you are in the search function, all that's left to do is input search criteria for the township you're looking in, a price range, and the amount of acreage you want.

If you're looking for larger tracts of land, another category to search under is farms and agricultural land. Going back to mibor.net as an example, after you click **residential property type**, select **farms and ag land** instead of **vacant lots and land**. Input similar criteria on township or county, price range, and acreage, and search away.

For an example of searching a Board of Realtors Web site for lots and land, see Figure 11.3, an image of mibor.net's site.

A third way to shop for land via a Board of Realtors site is under commercial listings. Commercial listings are vacant lots or land zoned for commercial or business use. At first glance you might wonder why this applies to your search for lots and land to build a home on. Commercial listings are applicable because land can be zoned for more than one use, or a variance can be granted to change the existing zoning that affects how land or a building will be used.

Land or the improved dwelling on it (that's a fancy way of saying a house or building) can sometimes be used for both residential and commercial purposes. The best example is a business run out of a home, such as that used by stylists, accountants, doctors, dentists, or attorneys. A building that is being used as a business can be torn down, a variance filed, and a new home built in its place. This isn't the traditional way to find a lot or parcel of land, but sometimes prime locations are corner lots or lots on main thoroughfares where multi-use structures can be built.

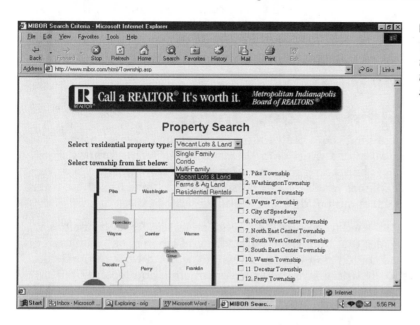

Figure 11.3

You can locate tracts of undeveloped land on many metropolitan realty sites.

What Are Zoning Laws?

Zoning laws determine the use of a property and its improvements. Zoning codes specify what a building will be used for when it is built. A variance is a legal exemption or waiver that changes the zoning code and allows for a different use then the original intended use. Certain buildings can be zoned for more than one use. A business run from a home can be zoned residential and commercial.

A final way to search for vacant lots and land online is through the use of list servers. This is a more sophisticated and complicated procedure that will not work for all homebuyers. You must be adept at surfing the Net and have a high comfort level online to use this technique. Those looking for an exact type of lot or parcel of land can sign up to join a list server.

Select a list server that is searching for lots or land, and input the criteria you want to search for. Pick the topic or category carefully so you don't get spam (junk information) that doesn't apply to your search. You will be contacted online by anyone who is trying to sell what you're attempting to buy. This certainly isn't the easiest way to find vacant lots and land, but because there aren't many simple, tried and true ways, this is an option for those of you who are searching for unique or hard-to-find parcels of land.

Researching Building Codes Online

Three sites to research building codes online are www.bocai.org, www.codecheck.com, and www.eren.doe.gov. All offer a variety of information in different formats. Checking building codes is one search procedure for which I recommend you review more than one site to gather as much data as possible. Before I dive into these three sites, let's talk for a second about building codes and why they exist.

Building codes were established to protect the public interest and health. If cities and counties did not have codes that builders, contractors, and laborers had to meet, or exceed, any knucklehead could pass himself off as an expert and work in the field. This would result in shoddy workmanship in the construction and repair of buildings, elevators, or bridges that the general public uses. The horrible stories we hear on the evening news about hotels or sports stadiums collapsing would occur once a week instead of once every few years.

There has to be a minimum standard of quality that is uniform, consistent, and known (people in the industry have to be aware of it or it does no good) to ensure the quality of construction and the well-being of the people who will use the facility. Building codes enforce this minimum standard of quality. If builders or contractors do not meet this level or standard, projects can be halted, fines can be levied, or the builder can be forced to make repairs.

Code Violations and Grandfathered Items

Home inspectors can point out code violations in a home inspection, but they can't make a seller fix a violation. City or county building inspectors can force owners to fix code violations. Many items in a home that are currently code violations were up to code when they were installed or repaired. These items might be grandfathered, meaning they met code at that time and do not have to be changed now.

It is vital that you and your agent take an active role in knowing what codes are for all the major mechanical systems in the home you are building. Don't blindly trust a builder because they can make honest mistakes, and don't hire contractors or subcontractors who have no affiliation with your builder or who don't share the builder's commitment to quality and service.

Bocai.org (Building Officials Code Administrators International) is an independent mega-site that promotes safe building worldwide. This site might offer the best information (certainly the most unbiased), but the site is a bit tricky to move around on. This site can be used on a national or international basis, and offers information on building codes of all types. Bocai.org is not trying to sell you anything, and is designed to help promote better, safer building. A cool feature on this site is the "Tips For Searching" function that assists you in searching key words or phrases.

Code Check provides a good deal of data, and the site is visually appealing and easy to navigate. However, you get the feeling it's really trying to sell you its products more then educate the public. Code Check presents two books that are designed to be used in the field (on a job site) and are quite helpful. Every major topic is covered in these two manuals, but you have to purchase the books to gain access to the data.

A host of industry-related books also can be purchased at this site. If you want fast, handy information on building codes at no cost, this is not the site for you. If you are willing to pay $15 to $25 for excellent information on almost any topic imaginable, Code Check might be your source of choice.

The final site to visit is eren.doe.gov (the Department of Energy's energy efficiency and renewable energy network). This is a government site that also promotes safe building and wise, efficient use of natural resources. This site offers information on many different types of technology. Data searches can be conducted and experts can be questioned. The information on this site is not as relevant as that on Bocai.org and Code Check, but there is some pertinent data and the site is easy to use and unbiased in its presentation of facts.

One additional source for researching building codes is city or county governments. Just as you searched government agencies to find information on property tax laws (refer to Chapter 7, "Property Taxes and What That Means for You"), you can research building codes on a state-to-state basis. Contact the city or county government agencies in the state you are relocating to and inquire about the agency that oversees building and construction. The agency should be able to email or fax information to you.

Create Blueprints

Blueprints are mechanical scale drawings that lay out the size specifications of the exact dimensions and measurements of a home, inside and out, level by level. They are the guidelines builders use to construct a new home. Every detail of a home, regardless how tiny or minute, must be planned and accounted for on the blueprints.

Any modifications to the home must be checked against the blueprints and approved.

Without blueprints in hand, builders can not even begin to construct a home, let alone finish it. In traditional building, buyers sit down with representatives of the builder and cost out a home detail by detail, dollar by dollar. Changes can be made in tract homes that deviate from established floor plans. In custom-built homes, buyers design from scratch what they want with the help of the builder.

Internet technology has changed the way many tasks are done. Creating blueprints is one of the areas in real estate that is slowing starting to change. Technology is being developed to put blueprint design in the hands of buyers. To date, the problem with this has been builders' reluctance to use blueprints other than their own. Other than time and man-hours saved, there are not many reasons for builders to use blueprints created by buyers online. Builders are notorious for wanting to maintain control of their product and the process by which they build. Simply put, buyers are not using the technology that currently exists because builders don't want them to.

Another concern of builders is the quality and consistency of blueprints. If they are done the wrong way or in a way that they are misinterpreted, specifications might be off and dimensions might not turn out the way the buyer envisioned. Builders don't want this liability.

There isn't much software available to create blueprints. The software that does exist is being used by small builders who can't afford to pay draftsmen to draw blueprints. Some Internet-intensive Realtors are using software that costs anywhere from $2,000–7,000 to market themselves to prospective buyers and have greater control over the building process (real estate is all about control).

Buyers are not yet using this technology. That is beginning to change, however. Instead of visiting bookstores and buying home-building books, buyers are purchasing software programs that create three-dimensional plans for building homes (at around $10–50) at stores like Office Depot and OfficeMax. The plans designed by this software are becoming increasingly more intricate. After the plans are devised, buyers are going to builders and asking them to expand on the plans and build that particular home.

Builders like this because it makes their jobs easier and less time intensive, but they retain control of the process and still have their own people draw up the plans. Buyers have more say in the process, save time, and get a better end product. The time is approaching when buyers will push harder for more control. This means additional online information and capabilities. Eventually, buyers will be able to completely design their own blueprints and builders will have to go along because the consumer is always right in real estate (remember, the real estate industry is slow to accept anything new).

Other Resources Found Online

Searching for information and listings on contractors and laborers of all types can be done in a variety of ways. Using a search engine, you can input the laborer's name. For instance, for plumbers or electricians go to www.yahoo.com and type plumbers, plumbing, plumbers unions, electricians, electrical unions. You can use this method for masons, framers, drywallers, landscapers, roofers, painters, carpet and flooring installers, and contractors. Other key words to search under are construction and contractors. Trade organizations like unions are another possible source to find laborers or contractors. Chambers of Commerce in cities also might provide names and information on contractors. www.digitalchambers.com and www.clickcity.com are the two sites with chamber of commerce data. The Better Business Bureau also can be contacted for listings on contractors and subcontractors.

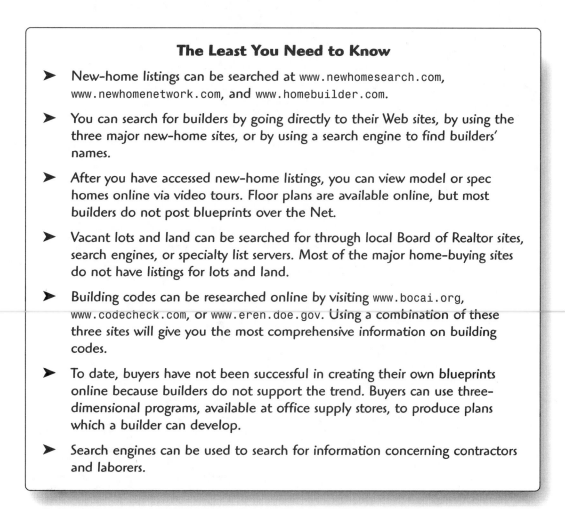

The Least You Need to Know

➤ New-home listings can be searched at www.newhomesearch.com, www.newhomenetwork.com, and www.homebuilder.com.

➤ You can search for builders by going directly to their Web sites, by using the three major new-home sites, or by using a search engine to find builders' names.

➤ After you have accessed new-home listings, you can view model or spec homes online via video tours. Floor plans are available online, but most builders do not post blueprints over the Net.

➤ Vacant lots and land can be searched for through local Board of Realtor sites, search engines, or specialty list servers. Most of the major home-buying sites do not have listings for lots and land.

➤ Building codes can be researched online by visiting www.bocai.org, www.codecheck.com, or www.eren.doe.gov. Using a combination of these three sites will give you the most comprehensive information on building codes.

➤ To date, buyers have not been successful in creating their own blueprints online because builders do not support the trend. Buyers can use three-dimensional programs, available at office supply stores, to produce plans which a builder can develop.

➤ Search engines can be used to search for information concerning contractors and laborers.

Chapter 12

Condominiums

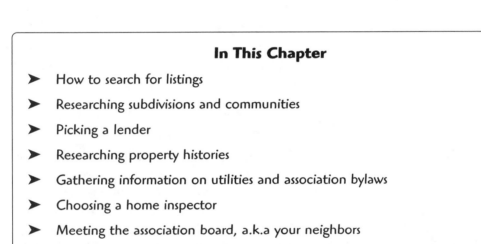

In This Chapter

➤ How to search for listings

➤ Researching subdivisions and communities

➤ Picking a lender

➤ Researching property histories

➤ Gathering information on utilities and association bylaws

➤ Choosing a home inspector

➤ Meeting the association board, a.k.a your neighbors

Searching for condominiums online is similar to searching for single-family residential homes. The same sites are visited and the research on areas and subdivisions is done in the same manner. The difference between the two is there are far fewer condo listings than homes and information is a bit harder to come by because there is less of it. With that in mind, let's move ahead into a discussion on finding condominiums online.

Searching Listings

Condos can be found online in an identical manner as residential homes. The easiest site to visit is www.homeadvisor.com. The same rules apply here as in Chapter 10, "Existing Homes," when we explored searching for homes online. HomeAdvisor is the simplest, most convenient site to house hunt on. REALTOR.COM has the largest number of listings and iOwn has the most thorough information. REALTOR.COM is a terrific source to shop for condos.

In any major city there are typically twenty times more residential homes than condos. In smaller cities and towns, that number jumps as high as a thousand to one. Some smaller towns and rural areas have no condos in their entire communities. Finding condo listings is complicated by the dearth of available units on the market. REALTOR.COM has far and away more listings than any other site, so the number of condo listings also is larger. CyberHomes is another site that has a nice display of condos on the market.

Unlike the residential home search where I recommended using one site exclusively (particularly to first time buyers and novice computer users), two or three sites might be needed to search for condos online. There simply will not be a large number of available listings on any one site, even REALTOR.COM.

What Do Condo Fees Pay For?

Condo fees or association dues cover the maintenance on the exterior part of the unit and the roof. They also pay for maintenance of common areas, any pools, tennis courts, clubhouses, or playground areas. Grass cutting, landscaping, snow removal, and special projects like road paving or erecting buildings or fences also are covered. A final item paid for by the condo fee is a master insurance policy that provides coverage for the building if fire, storms, or vandalism destroys the unit.

To access REALTOR.COM, type `www.realtor.com` in your browser's location field and click **Go**. After the home page appears, a menu will give you the option to **select a state** of your choice and **learning about buying**. Move the down arrow to the state you want (Georgia, for example), and select buying from the options available. The key difference with this search is the type of home you are searching for. Instead of shopping for house listings, you are hunting for condominiums. Click **Find a Home**. The next page will offer you a choice between searching by city, map, postal code, or MLS information. You can select whichever is easier for you (maps are provided for you). When the menu option for type of home appears, select **town home or condo** from the choices. This is an important step because failure to input condo will alter your search dramatically.

Now, that you have specified your search for condos, input the rest of the criteria you want to search for. REALTOR.COM offers an extensive list of criteria to search for. Be as general and non-specific as possible in the beginning to ensure a larger number of matches will come up. If you need to shorten the number of matches that you find, you can always go back and input more specific data. After typing in the required information on number of bedrooms, baths, price range, and so on, start the search. Depending on the number of available matches, you might need to adjust your search criteria to get more matches (widen or broaden your criteria) or less matches (narrow your criteria).

You can see an example of searching for condos on REALTOR.COM in Figure 12.1.

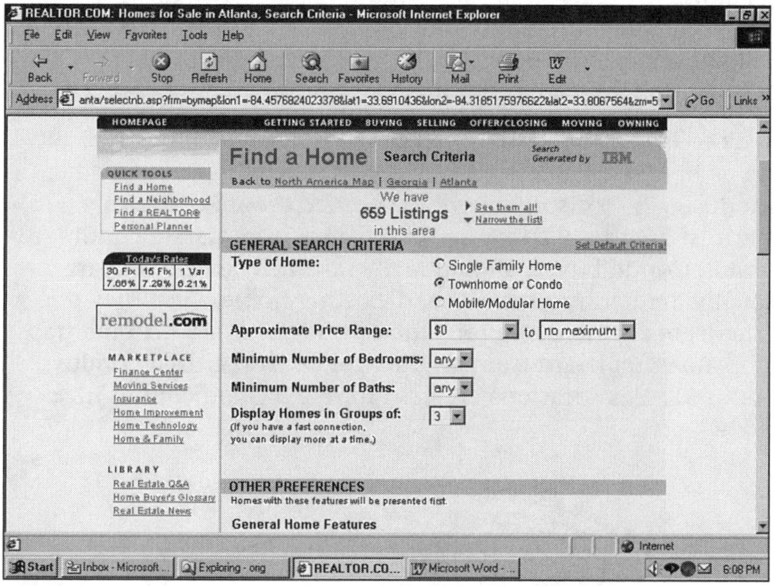

Figure 12.1

You can search for condos as well as single-unit homes on REALTOR.COM.

Other ways to search for condos online include accessing builders' Web sites and examining spec condos that might be available now or in the near future. Realtors also can be contacted directly online to see if their office has condos listed in the area and price range you are looking.

For Sale By Owner sites such as www.owners.com and www.fsbo.com also have condo listings you can sift through. A final way to search for condo listings is through a search engine of your choice. Type condominiums, condos, condo homes, or condominium homes and click **Go**. A long list of builders and real estate offices dealing with condos will appear as well as condo communities. This isn't the most efficient way to pinpoint condo listings, but it can be used.

Researching Subdivisions and Communities

Knowing demographic information about the area and subdivision that you are thinking about buying into might actually be more important for condos than for single-family homes. The reason lies in the stability of homes versus condos. Many people think condos are poor investments and homes always outperform condos in appreciation values and resale ability. The reality is location and supply and demand determine appreciation rates and resale ability, not the type of housing.

Here's an example. Condos in a hot location that are extremely desirable become popular. As more people learn about the community and want to buy into it, appreciation rates will increase. If there are not a lot of people selling these condos in this complex, but many people want to buy there, supply and demand will drive the prices up quickly. It doesn't matter if the homes are condos, single-family residential houses, or multi-family investment properties. If a lot of people want to own something and there's not a big supply of it, the price for that housing will sky rocket.

Because fewer people look to own condos than traditional housing, condos typically do not appreciate as fast as homes. Blanket generalizations should never be made in real estate because the industry is so disorganized. Market factors are constantly changing also. However, it is safe to say that researching areas and market conditions before any purchase is vital. Condo buyers should really take this advice to heart because condos traditionally are harder to resell than existing homes, and they don't appreciate as quickly. There are always exceptions though; so don't fall into the trap of discounting condos because you heard from an uncle or co-worker that condos can't be resold. Bad condos in weak locations are hard to resell. Good condos in excellent areas sell quickly.

Contemporary Living at Its Finest

Condos were designed to satisfy America's aging population and busy lifestyles. Most condo communities have been built within the last ten years, twenty years at the outset, so the architecture and floor plans are much more modern and contemporary. For buyers who like open rooms, vaulted ceilings, airy floor space, and light, bright colors, condos are appealing.

Condo communities are researched the same way existing residential home subdivisions are. Access www.homeadvisor.com, www.iown.com, www.realtor.com, or www.cyberhomes.com for demographic information. HomeAdvisor is the easiest to use, iOwn has the most information, REALTOR.COM has the largest number of listings, and CyberHomes has a clever mapping function to pinpoint communities in relation to your job, day care, and so on.

As stated in the discussion on researching areas and subdivisions in Chapter 6, "Research Areas: Don't Get Stuck Living Next to the Addams Family," pick one site you are comfortable with and stay with it. (For a recap of the various sites and what they specialize in, see Chapter 6.) Hopping from different sites can be beneficial, but if you are a first time buyer, or are unfamiliar with computers and the Internet the process can be overwhelming. Don't make it harder than it already is by jumping around from site to site (let your Realtor do that).

Factors to Consider When Buying a Condo

Just as when you buy a house, when shopping for a condo you need to keep several of the most important factors in mind. These factors include:

➤ How old is the condo?

➤ How satisfactory is the quality of service from the management company in charge of taking care of the community?

➤ How many units are in the community?

➤ What is the location of the unit within the community—near the entrance, parking lot, pool, tennis courts, clubhouse, playground, or on a lake or off the lake?

➤ Is the unit an end unit, or is it surrounded on both sides by other units?

➤ Is the unit on the ground floor, second level, or both?

➤ How large is the Association Board? Will you have a say in the community's politics?

➤ What is the condo association fee, and how often is it raised?

➤ How rigid are the association bylaws, and are they enforced?

➤ How well does the Association run the condo community?

➤ How much money is in the Association's emergency reserve account?

Selecting a Lending Institution

There is an abundance of online lenders just waiting to hear from you so they can loan you money, especially because the recent booming American economy has made lending a most profitable proposition. Unfortunately, not all of them are good lenders. Be careful of online lenders that offer nothing but low rates and low fees. A lender should back up their competitive rates with solid service. If a mortgage company can't get your loan approved and closed, it makes no difference what interest rate they were going to give you.

If you're planning to use an FHA or VA loan as your method of financing, make sure the condominium complex has been approved by the Federal Housing Administration or the Veteran's Administration.

Shopping for a low interest rate and small closing costs is perfectly fine, in fact it's advisable. Make sure the lender can and will do everything they promise. There's nothing worse than finding out the day before closing you are going to have to come up with an extra $5,000 to close the deal (believe it or not, it happens all the time).

What Are Closing Costs and Who Pays Them?

Closing costs are costs a buyer pays to have a loan originated and closed. Closing costs are made up of the origination fee (at 1% of the loan amount), discount points to lower the interest rate (if applicable), pre-paid items such as money deposited in escrow accounts, and settlement, and closing fees. Buyers can entice sellers to pay some or all of the closing costs, perhaps by offering concessions on the agreed price of the home. In effect, buyers bring less money to closing, but their loan amount is higher so the monthly payment is at $10–30 higher each month.

Shopping for rates is pretty straightforward. Visit as many sites as you like, and ask for quotes on rates and closing costs. If trusted friends, colleagues, or family members have referred you to a bank or mortgage company contact them first for a quote. Check with other lenders later to see how competitive the recommended lender is. If they're competitive, seriously consider ending your search and go with that lender.

When it comes to getting a mortgage, excellent service is priceless. Remember: Lenders don't have contracts with buyers. What they tell you up front is not guaranteed in writing for your closing three or four months later. Lenders are only as good as their word. The average to poor ones break it, sometimes at a moment's notice. A good lender will honor his word and deliver what he promised.

Security, privacy, and safety are the greatest challenges to online commerce. White-collar crime and illegal financial activity have flourished over the Internet because of its anonymous nature. Historically, the mortgage lending industry has had a less-than-stellar reputation (there's no licensing, testing, or training process to become a loan originator). The advent of Internet commerce has only made it easier for unethical conduct and loan fraud to proliferate.

Financing Differences for Condos

Surveys are not required for condo purchases. This exception saves the buyer between $100–500. Homeowner's insurance also is not required by lenders on a condo deal. The condo fee goes toward a master insurance policy that covers all the structures in the entire community. There is an additional $50–100 fee to change the condo association documents from the seller's name into the buyer's name. Condo owners should also carry contents insurance, sometimes called renter's insurance, to cover furnishings, personal belongings, and personal property within the dwelling. This runs about $100 per year.

Proceed cautiously if one online lender's rates are significantly better than all other lenders. Rates are based on economic indexes controlled by the Federal Reserve. If a lender's rates are considerably better than every one else's, chances are they're making hidden money on you somewhere else or they might not be able to honor the quote or close the deal.

If you haven't been referred to a bank or mortgage company the large home-buying sites and loan sites are terrific places to start. I recommend the following sites:

www.century21.com

www.cyberhomes.com

www.eloan.com

www.homeadvisor.com

www.homeseekers.com

www.iown.com

www.lendingtree.com

www.mortgage.com

```
www.quickenmortgage.com

www.realtor.com
```

These sites offer strong financial resources, solid service, and credible reputations. Some of these sites will compare your loan to various lenders or brokers. If this is the case, make sure to check the strength and credibility of the eventual lender. Net surfers typically look for convenience and efficiency more often than a warm, fuzzy feeling from interpersonal relations. Lenders at these sites will cater to the hard core wire-head (you know who you are), or the Internet rookie who is crawling down the information superhighway for the first time. There are literally thousands of online lenders, so take your time in selecting one. Like most things in real estate, you will need to trust your instincts. Do all the necessary research, and then make that leap of faith.

Traits of a Good Lender

As the number of potential lenders has proliferated, it has become more and more difficult to spot the best ones. A good lender should:

➤ Be someone who wants to earn your business for life

➤ Be efficient, organized, detail-oriented, and thorough

➤ Be competent and knowledgeable about all types of loan programs

➤ Possess strong listening skills

➤ Be patient, easily accessible, and hard working

➤ Put your needs ahead of his or his firm's

➤ Have good people skills

➤ Delegate well and be result-oriented

➤ Be honest, ethical, and forthright

If you are new to the home-buying process and/or a novice Internet user, you might not know what to look for in a lender or what to ask when you're interviewing one. Even the most experienced real estate investor had to start somewhere. Don't be embarrassed or feel bad for not knowing everything. Our heads can't possibly hold all the information we want to know. That's what computers and research are for. The following questions can be used to quiz prospective moneylenders to see if they are right for you:

1. How long have you originated loans? How long has your company been doing it?

2. Online loans make up what percentage of your total loan business?

3. What type of loans do you offer?

4. What is your current interest rate for a 30-year, fixed-rate loan?

5. Are points charged for that rate?

6. How many loans do you write each month?

7. How long have you and your processor worked together? How many other originators does she process for?

8. How is your work relationship with your underwriter?

9. What are your application fees? What does the credit report and appraisal cost?

10. When will I receive a good-faith estimate with a break down of all closing costs?

11. Will I have to pay mortgage insurance?

12. Can I float the interest rate and lock in a rate later? What does it cost to lock the rate, and how long will the lock last?

13. When will my first payment be due?

14. Can I pre-pay the loan or pay it off earlier without penalty?

15. When are payments considered late, and what is the penalty for late payments?

16. Will a slow payment hurt my credit as much as a late payment or non-payment?

17. How much money will be needed to set up my escrow accounts?

18. How long will it take for the loan to be approved?

19. What can I do to make the process go as smoothly and quickly as possible?

20. Who should I contact with questions or problems?

Researching Histories of Target Units

Realtors truly earn their commissions with the research they do via the multiple listings service and when they help clients negotiate better prices and terms. Only agents have access to the MLS database. The MLS (multiple listing service) has far greater data on homes than the Internet, or any other reference source. Every home sale in any given city or town is a matter of public record. The home you are thinking about buying might have sold two years before or twenty years ago. Regardless of when it sold the deed and mortgage was filed in the recorder's office of that town.

There are literally tens of thousands of recorded documents in every city's recorder's office. The multiple listing service stores the data online. The problem with the MLS is it only goes back five to ten years. It's easy enough to get the last transfer date of a property. Call the treasurer's office and ask for it. If your agent or the office they work out of saves old records long enough, they might be able to find the sales price of a property you are considering buying from ten or fifteen years ago.

Before you start digging through rows of boxes at the recorder's office, or have your agent climb up in her attic, consider one thing: Today's market conditions determine what a home is worth, not conditions from ten or twenty years ago. Realtors and appraisers will only use comparable sale prices from one year ago (two years at the absolute most).

Although data two years or older won't be a big help, sales prices within the last two years will. Ask your agent to do an archive history search on the property you're considering buying. This search consists of going back through all the multiple listing's records and finding all activity the home has had (homes could have been put on the market and withdrawn, listed, and expired because they couldn't sell, or the price reduced drastically to sell it). Knowing what the home sold for two years ago and what improvements the seller has made since will help determine if the current list price is accurate, high, or low.

Another benefit of an archive history search is to find out how long a home has really been on the market. The MLS sheet might show the time on the market as two months. The archive history search will show if the home was on the market a whole year prior with two other real estate companies before being listed by the current office. If the home has been on the market for a total of a year or a year and a half—and not the three months the present listing shows—there might be something wrong with it. Information from an archive history search might prevent you from buying the wrong home or save you thousands of dollars when negotiating price. The more you know about the history of a particular property, the more informed your decision to purchase will be.

Getting Yearly Utility Averages

A common question listing agents receive after buyers view homes concerns utility averages. Very few people will write an offer to buy a home without first knowing what the average costs for utilities are. The first reason utility costs are important is financial planning. When buyers estimate total monthly outlay of money during the house-hunting process, all financial obligations of a new home must be taken into account. Utilities in large homes, old homes, or poorly built or maintained homes can be incredibly expensive. Sometimes a home's utility bills can be so expensive the home is no longer economically feasible to a buyer. Utilities can run $100–500 per month so they must be factored into budgets and included in cash outlays when buyers are calculating expenses for a new home.

Another reason buyers should research utility averages is the information that can be deduced from them. Some key questions utility information can answer are: How well insulated and built is a home? Are poorly sealed windows, doors, skylights, fireplaces, or basements letting energy and the elements seep out of a home or into a home? Do the furnace, air conditioner, and water heater function correctly? Are water pipes exposed to dangerous temperatures that might cause expensive problems if unchecked? Is it economically sound for a homeowner to pay utility bills as they come in, or should the home be on a budget plan?

How Are Utilities Transferred from Seller to Buyer?

The transfer of utilities should be discussed at closing (a few days prior if posses-sion is the day of closing). With their agents help seller and buyer should exchange phone numbers and agree when utilities will be transferred. The seller should have a final reading done in her name, but not turn the utilities off as to avoid hook up or installation charges for the new owner. After the order for the final reading has been placed the buyer should call the utility companies and transfer the existing service into his name.

What Is a Budget Plan for Paying Utilities?

A *budget plan* is a payment plan where a homeowner pays the same amount each month regardless of what the actual utility usage was. The amount is deter-mined by past usage and agreed to in advance by the homeowner. Budget plans are popular for people who like to pay the same amount each month and those on fixed incomes. Money is refunded to the homeowner if the budget payment amount exceeds actual usage.

Utility costs provide a clearer and more comprehensive picture of what living costs in a new home will be as well as help to identify potential problem spots in a home's mechanical systems. If utility information is not in a home during the first viewing, your agent should contact the listing agent and request a copy of the utility averages before a second showing or offer to purchase is written. This data also is beneficial during the home inspection process. Inspectors can focus on certain mechanical systems that might be operating at less than 100% capability or malfunctioning alto-gether.

Researching Association Bylaws, Fees, and Services

All condominium communities have bylaws residents in the community must follow. Some communities have lots of bylaws, others have very few. Virtually all condo communities have associations that require mandatory membership (fortunately the boring association meetings aren't mandatory) and charge monthly fees. The association fees pay for the maintenance of common ground areas in the complex and the condos' exterior structures, fund new projects the community has agreed to undertake, and pay for a master insurance policy that covers all the units in the community.

Unlike bylaws in residential subdivisions that have a small to negligible affect on resident's lives, bylaws in a condo community can have a major influence on resident's day-to-day lives. The purchase agreement contains a clause that stipulates the buyer has a designated time period to approve the association bylaws if the community has a mandatory membership.

The buyer chooses the time frame (usually five to ten days) for the seller to provide the documents after the offer is accepted. This contingency must be satisfied for the deal to close. If the bylaws contain a covenant or restriction the buyer simply can not live with, and the association will not grant an exception waiver (they never do), the buyer can get out of the deal.

Why Do Associations Have Bylaws?

Bylaws ensure uniformity and consistency in the appearance and quality of individual units in a condominium community. Bylaws protect the overall community's value and guard against individual condo owners making changes or repairs to their unit that compromise the safety, value, or appearance of other units. Because each unit owner owns one share of the entire community, no one owner has more say or less say than others do.

Buyers should talk to their agent about bylaws before or during the first viewing of a condo. Don't attempt too much research up front. You might not like a particular community or unit at all, or it might slow down the process. Even worse, it might cause you to lose a terrific unit. The transaction is contingent upon the buyer accepting the bylaws, so the time to review the documents carefully and thoroughly is after the offer has been accepted.

An exception to this is when the buyer thinks there might be a potential problem with the bylaws, and time or competition from other buyers is not a major concern. In this scenario it might be wise to contact the association board or listing agent to gather information so you don't waste time and hundreds of dollars in appraisal, credit, and inspection fees. Consult your agent on what to do if you're not sure. The management company that oversees the community (cuts the grass, handles maintenance issues, and so on) is another excellent source for information on the community and the bylaws.

Condo homeowners own the interior of their individual units from the floor to the ceiling and every wall. Essentially, they own the air space inside the unit and the garage. The exterior portion of the unit, the ground space around the unit, mail-boxes, pools, tennis courts, clubhouses, driveways, and all other areas are known as *common areas*. All condo owners in the community own common areas equally. The monthly association fee pays for the maintenance of the common areas.

Condo owners are responsible for the upkeep and maintenance of the interior portion of their units. Doors, windows, and decks are usually the condo owner's responsibility. Pipes and heating/cooling systems that originate outside the unit but run into the condo also are the owner's responsibility.

Exterior maintenance items such as roof repairs or siding are covered by the association's master insurance plan and are maintained by the association's management company. Landscaping, upkeep of all common areas, and new additions in the community (fences, gazebos, walking paths) also are funded by the association dues and maintained by the association. An easy rule of thumb to follow is that everything inside the unit is the owner's responsibility, everything outside is taken care of by the management company that works for the association.

Reviewing Checklist of "Needs" and "Wants"

Most likely you had ideas of what you were looking for when you started the house hunting search months before. You probably saved your initial search list online, wrote it down, or simply memorized it. Usually that list will change into an amended list as you surf houses online. The list can really change and morph into a new list when you parade through homes. It's amazing how important

Check This Out

What Does a Management Company Do?

Management companies provide professional management for condo communities. Their tasks include financial record keeping and budgeting; building and grounds maintenance and repair; and enforcement of the community bylaws and rules.

155

a fourth bedroom can become or how unimportant an attached garage can be after you look at ten or fifteen homes and haven't found the right one. Regardless of how different your final list looks compared to your initial one, it's wise to compare the two when you are close to writing an offer to purchase.

Buyers should weigh the pros and cons of their checklist against your target home's actual amenities to gauge if it is the right home. Questions to ask yourself are: Can you live without the items that are missing from your list? Does the target home have other features you didn't expect to get or have amenities you like more than you thought you would? How do the missing items or extra features affect resale and appreciation? How much enjoyment will you lose or gain because of missing items or additional features? Prioritizing the significance of amenities helps determine if you can live without something.

Developing "Needs" and "Wants" Checklists

Start your home-buying checklist with a needs or must-have section. Keep this category as small as possible in the beginning so you'll have more homes to consider. Make a wants or like-to-have section that is larger. You'll be able to weed through the matching homes with the wants list. As you whittle down the list of homes, the wants section will rule out a lot of homes. The wants list normally is the category that determines which home you will buy.

There is no perfect home in existence. Even Bill Gates has to make periodic changes and repairs to his $60-million dream home. Condominiums are bought by people who want a lifestyle of ease and convenience. Buying a condo means you are agreeing to follow the rules of an association and live in a community of fellow owners.

A certain amount of freedom and control is lost owning a condo. Your checklist of wants and needs should reflect this. For example, a large lot size, fenced back yard, or privacy should not be items on your checklist if you're considering buying a condo. Location, price, number of bedrooms and baths, year built, and community amenities (lake, pool, tennis courts) should be. Understand before writing an offer that you can change only interior items of a condo. If you want an extra garage, mini-barn, or different color siding on a condo, you're not going to be able to change it down the road. Checklists have to be scrutinized more closely with condos than with single-family residential homes because you are severely limited in what you can change.

All About Association Dues

Association dues are paid once a month to a management company that manages the complex for the association board and condo owners. They are due the first of the month, are not tax deductible, and can be considered a lien against the title if unpaid. Association dues pay for insurance on the structure of the unit, cover all maintenance and repairs on the exterior and common ground areas, and enable you to gain access to amenities such as pools, tennis courts, and hot tubs.

The "Wants" and "Needs" checklist is an instrument to help prioritize and focus, not drive you insane. Use it as a reference point or compass to measure which condo you like the most when you've narrowed down your search to two or three units. Because condos are so similar on the outside and have many common features, it's sometimes harder to distinguish and pick between two or three units (residential homes tend to be extremely different).

The checklist also is beneficial when deciding what price to offer a seller. For example, if a condo meets nearly all your requirements or exceeds them you probably won't want to offer a significantly lower price than what the owner is asking. Conversely, if you've had to settle for a unit that does not have some of the amenities you desired, chances are your offer price will reflect this. Sometimes the checklist can move a buyer off the fence if the decision to buy is that agonizing. If a condo has only half the features desired or is missing one or two of the major must-have items, buyers might opt not to write the offer to purchase. The checklist is the manual or map buyers use to find their way to the right home. It should be referenced throughout the entire home-shopping process, specifically at the time of writing an offer.

Selecting a Home Inspector

Condos should be inspected just as residential homes are, especially if the buyer plans to occupy the unit as her primary residence. Because most condominium complexes are twenty years old or newer, and not terribly large in size, condo inspections turn up fewer problems than home inspections do. Another reason condo inspections usually go smoothly is because the roof and exterior of the unit are maintained by the association. Condo owners have less to take care of, so the condition should be better than residential homes.

Condos can and do have repair problems that inspectors will find. A typical problem in condos is the age and remaining useful life of the mechanical systems and appliances. A large number of condo communities have electric heat pumps instead of gas forced-air furnaces. Heat pumps last eight to twelve years on average. Air conditioning units, water heaters, ovens, refrigerators, and dishwashers are near or at their remaining useful life in condos that are ten to fifteen years old. These are common items that appear on condo home inspections. In large part though, home inspections for condos are easier than single-family homes.

What's on an Inspection Report?

Home inspectors should provide a written report of the entire inspection to the buyer and the seller. The report should list all items not functioning properly as well as explain the difference between major defective items that directly compromise habitability, less significant defective items that do not affect habitability, and minor maintenance issues that result from normal wear and tear. Good inspection reports also make suggestions as to how problems can or should be fixed.

The Internet will probably not play a significant role in choosing a home inspector for a few reasons. Home inspectors have been slow to jump aboard the online bandwagon, so few advertise over the Net. Inspectors need to be local outfits that are well versed in housing construction, environmental issues, and building codes in the area you purchased in. I don't recommend a fast food approach to having your condo or home inspected. The investment is too large to trust it to an amateur, or an outfit that isn't familiar with housing conditions in your city or town.

Ask your Realtor or a trusted friend, family member, or work colleague for the names of two or three reputable inspection companies or individual inspectors. The real estate office your agent works out of might have a list of good inspectors and companies and bad inspectors and companies.

Time might be a factor in selecting your inspector. Short time frames on purchase agreements are attractive to sellers. Home inspections should be done within seven to ten days after the offer is accepted. I routinely write three to four days in contracts to make the offer more appealing to the seller. If your time frame is this short the inspector will have to set up the inspection and complete it pretty quickly. Inspectors that work evenings and weekends make the process considerably easier.

When picking an inspector, request references from past clients and agents. Oftentimes you'll never have to contact the people. The inspector's reaction and willingness to comply, and the speed in which they can comply will provide the answer. Look for an inspector with years of experience in the field. Backgrounds in construction, building homes, contracting work, and engineering make excellent home inspectors. Be careful of start up companies with little experience or references. Inspectors should have plenty of experience and be in the business for years to come. A recent feature that some inspectors offer is Polaroid pictures or videotapes of problem areas. These can be used to negotiate repairs with the seller.

The Least You Need to Know

➤ There are fewer condominium listings online than residential homes, but the same home-buying Web sites can be used to search for condos.

➤ Researching condo communities is more important than residential home subdivisions because condos require mandatory memberships in associations that set and enforce bylaws and rules.

➤ Select a trustworthy lender with competitive rates, who will close the loan on time for the exact costs you were quoted. Trusted relatives, friends, and co-workers, as well as your agent, can recommend good lenders.

➤ Have your agent search the multiple listing service for the history of all activity on the home you're thinking about buying. This archive history search will help determine how fast the home is appreciating and what your offer price should be.

➤ Review utility averages, and try to review the association bylaws before writing an offer, but don't let the bylaws slow you down or prevent you from getting a condo before someone else does. You'll have time to review them after the offer is accepted.

➤ Review the checklist of items you based your search on, and compare it to the condo you are thinking of buying. Your checklist will help determine if you should pursue the unit and what price you should offer.

➤ Choose a home inspection company or individual inspector that provides reliable, quality service and charges competitive rates.

Chapter 13

Patio Homes/ Zero Lot Lines: What Are They?

In This Chapter

➤ Descriptions of patio homes and zero lot lines

➤ Searching the Internet for listings

➤ Researching communities and subdivisions for data

➤ Picking a moneylender

➤ Researching histories of target units

➤ Getting utility averages and association bylaws

➤ Reviewing checklist of "needs" and "wants"

➤ Choosing a home inspector

Builders and developers are constantly changing the homes they build to change with the times and meet the demands of clients. Two examples of this are patio homes and zero lot lines. Both types of housing feature small lots designed to limit the amount of yard work owners must do. As peoples' lives get busier and busier, and homeowners want to do less and less around the home, patio homes and zero lot lines provide an alternative to the traditional single-family house and condominiums. They are happy mediums between owning your house and yard and living in a condo community. Read on to find out how to research and find these hybrid forms of housing online.

Part Home–Part Condo: Planned Communities

To meet the ever-changing demands of buyers' needs, developers started building residential homes with smaller lots. The idea was to limit the amount of yard work and ground maintenance owners would have to do. Many buyers don't want to give up control or privacy, so condominium complexes are not options. The answer: hybrid housing that offers most of the benefits of single family residential homes coupled with the ease and convenience of condos.

In the 1980s and '90s, builders realized Americans were living longer and longer, and their lives were becoming more hectic. The need for convenient housing with little or no yard work became a major buying issue. Developers responded with patio homes and zero lot lines.

Patio homes provide most of the normal single-family housing benefits. The new twist on an old idea was making the entire subdivision a planned community and creating an association to oversee landscaping work and common area maintenance. With patio homes owners get to own and take care of the interior and exterior portions of the dwelling and enjoy a yard of their own without having to do the work. A small association fee is paid to have yard work done. Many patio home communities also have pools, tennis courts, and clubhouses similar to condominiums.

Zero lot lines are single-family subdivisions where all the homes are shifted to one side of the lot. The homes are built right on the property line. Zero lot lines were devised by developers who wanted to sell people on smaller lots. By moving the home over to the property line instead of centering it in the middle of the lot, the homeowner has more yard to enjoy, and visually there appears to be more space between homes.

These communities are extremely uniform. All homes in the subdivision are built on the property line. If some were centered in the middle of the lot and the rest pushed over to the property line, the result would be disastrous. Owners are responsible for upkeep of their homes' exterior and the yard. The yards are small so there isn't much maintenance to do on the outside.

There are advantages and disadvantages to patio homes. The following is a list of "pros" of patio homes and zero lot lines:

➤ Little to no yard work

➤ Not much exterior housing maintenance

➤ Contemporary floor plans and easy upkeep because they are twenty years old or newer

➤ Subdivisions commonly offer amenities like swimming pools; tennis, volleyball, or basketball courts; clubhouses; and work out facilities

➤ Provides top features of single-family housing along with benefits of condominiums

A list of "cons" of patio homes and zero lot lines includes the following:

➤ Lack of individuality in architecture and appearance

➤ Reduced privacy and control

➤ Association fees

➤ Subdivisions usually have little landscaping in place, and warmth and charm are absent because community is brand new

Searching Listings

Searching online for listings of patio homes and zero lot lines is done the same way you would search for single-family residential homes (refer to Chapter 10, "Existing Homes"). Both are single-family dwellings and are categorized as homes, not condominiums. Compared to traditional houses, patio homes and zero lots make up a miniscule amount of listings on the Internet. There are tremendously fewer listings for these types of homes because the number of patio home and zero lot communities is tiny in relation to the number of traditional homes.

What's a PUD?

PUDs are *planned unit developments*. Developers build a community of houses complete with entertainment amenities such as swimming pools, clubhouses, ponds or lakes, and recreational facilities. An association fee is charged to homeowners to maintain common areas and perform landscaping duties. A professional management company normally supervises the community.

The mega-sites are the best sites to use to search for patio homes and zero lots because they have more listings to sort through. Expect to find considerably fewer listings than traditional homes and even condominiums. www.realtor.com is the best site to surf. Use the site in the same manner you would if you were searching for a regular house. Patio homes and zero lot lines will be grouped in the category of homes (real estate Web sites are not very specific in grouping properties, whereas MLS systems have separate search functions for patio homes and zero lots).

On REALTOR.COM and other sites you will have to search for patio homes and zero lot lines just as you would a regular house. The type of housing should be noted under the property description. If a site offers patio homes and zero lots as an option on their menu list, choose it and input your required data. For instance, you might be searching for a two-bedroom, two-bath home with a two-car attached garage on a lot smaller than one quarter of an acre. Of nine matches that fit your criteria three of them might be patio homes or zero lot lines.

Any of the major home-buying sites can be used (refer to Chapter 3, "Picking a Home-Buying Web Site," for a laundry list of sites), but try to stick to the bigger sites that have more listings to save time. You might need to check multiple sites if your search doesn't turn up a large enough number of matches. When surfing through listings make sure you check the description part of the listing to see if the match is in fact a patio home or zero lot line.

Fortunately, REALTOR.COM, the largest site with the most available listings, is affiliated with the National Association of Realtors. REALTOR.COM lists homes that are patio homes or zero lot lines as such, thereby setting them off from traditional single-family houses.

www.homeadvisor.com is once again the easiest site to use. The problem with HomeAdvisor is the drastically low number of listings on its site compared to REALTOR.COM. Search REALTOR.COM or the Board of Realtors Web site in the town you are moving to. Either way, don't expect to find an abundance of listings. There simply aren't a lot of patio homes and zero lot lines in existence.

Another way to perform a search of patio homes and zero lot lines is through builders' Web sites. Because these two types of housing are so new, and the need for convenient, low-hassle housing is doing nothing but increasing, developers are continuing to build new subdivisions. Patio homes in particular are being built all over the country in record numbers. Retirees and empty nesters are finding patio homes a wonderful happy medium between residential homes and condominiums. If you've lived in a home for 30 or 40 years, it's incredibly difficult to move into a condo community with no yard and neighbors all around you.

The best builder sites to check are www.newhomesearch.com, www.newhomenetwork.com, and www.homebuilder.com. Search these sites the way you would normally hunt for new construction houses (refer to Chapter 11, "New Construction or Designing Your Own Home"). If you have a list of favorite builders, contact those handful of builders (make sure they build in the region, state, and city you're moving to). You can view the home page of NewHomeNetwork.com in Figure 13.1.

You also can search patio homes or zero lot lines directly through a search engine. Go to www.yahoo.com or any search engine and type the key words patio homes, zero lot lines, and click **Go**. This type of search will either provide you with a list of subdivisions or builders' names. You can then use the builders' names to search under builders for new construction subdivisions where patio homes and zero lot lines are being constructed.

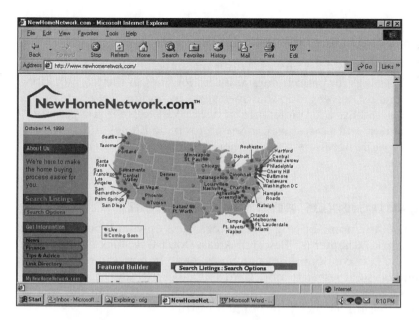

Figure 13.1

Among the top builder sites currently online is NewHomeNetwork.com.

Pick a Realtor if you haven't already, and give them the criteria you're basing your search on. They have access to the multiple listing service. This is the most comprehensive and detailed way to search for patio homes and zero lots. You are going to need an agent to help you gain access to the homes, do demographic research on the area and subdivision, determine the value of the home, and write and negotiate an offer. You might as well use the services of an agent to find home listings. You can see an example of a Realtor's home page review in Figure 13.2.

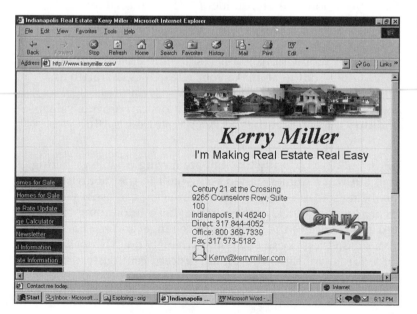

Figure 13.2

You can have a Realtor check listings for you. An example of a Realtor's home page is shown here.

At the very least, check the Board of Realtors Web site. There might be listings that did not get posted on REALTOR.COM that you will want to see.

A final way to search is specialized list servers. This is recommended only if you are having trouble finding listings for patio homes and zero lot lines in the town or city you are moving to. Join a list server group that specializes in finding real estate or unique types of housing and list your preference or need. Wait to see if you get any matches. This is the hardest and slowest way to search for patio homes and zero lots, but in some cases it might be necessary because there are not an overwhelming number of listings available.

Researching Complexes and Subdivisions

Research is a vital part of the home-buying process regardless of what type of housing you are purchasing (refer to Chapter 6, "Research Areas: Don't Get Stuck Living Next to the Addams Family"). Like condominium purchases, patio homes and zero lot lines might actually depend on solid research more than single-family purchases. Simply put, in a patio home or zero lot line you are what you neighbors are. Your home will be worth what the subdivision dictates your home is worth.

There is very little difference in value in a planned community. With single-family houses there can be a huge range in value within a subdivision or even on a street. With patio homes and zero lots, the exterior housing looks the same, the size and square footage is generally similar, and all the homes abide by the same bylaws. The homogeneous nature of this housing prevents large swings in value.

The downside to patio homes and zero lot lines is this narrow range of appreciation. Your home will not outperform the neighborhood by 5–8%. The subdivision can hold it back. On the other hand, your home will not under perform and sell for 5% less than the neighborhood (unless there are some real problems on the inside with condition or décor).

Any way you slice it, research on subdivisions is a necessary and crucial part of the home-buying process. Use various sources to make your research as thorough as possible. www.iown.com is the best mega-site to do your research on (www.cyberhomes.com and www.realtor.com are strong also). Realtors can provide valuable data and little-known industry information that you won't get from surfing Web sites.

If you find a subdivision or builder you really like, but are having trouble gathering research, here's a tip. Find out when homes started being built in the subdivision and research how fast lots are being sold and homes built. Your agent can assist you with this. When subdivisions are sold out quickly buyers are saying a resounding "Yes!" to the location, quality, and appearance of the housing, price range, and reputation of the builder. Just because a subdivision doesn't sell out extremely quickly doesn't mean it should be discarded from your list. You should proceed cautiously and gather more information.

Using Agents for Research

Always employ the help of an agent during or after the research process. Even if you have already done your research online, compare your findings to your agent's. Realtors typically have access to additional statistics via the multiple listing service and oftentimes can dig up well guarded or hard-to-find industry information on builders, subdivisions, or the history of a community. The cost for the agent's assistance is nothing, and the time and legwork you are saved is substantial.

Selecting a Lending Institution

As mentioned in Chapter 5, "The Mortgage Process: Getting Your Ducks in a Row," and Chapter 10, "Existing Homes," quality service should be weighed heavily when considering what moneylender to use. You are a valuable commodity: a qualified buyer intent on obtaining a loan to purchase a home. You should be treated as such. Gone are the days when securing a mortgage was a two- or three-month ordeal. Lenders today have loosened their guidelines and streamlined the process. Some transactions I do take a total of two weeks from the time the offer is written to the day the deal is closed (I'm fortunate to work with an outstanding loan originator and terrific clients).

There are more banks and mortgage companies lending money today (online and otherwise) than can be counted. There is no excuse for selecting a lender that provides poor service or loans money at excessively high rates. But how do you know if a lender is good? How do you determine which lender is right for you?

What Factors Determine the Interest Rate You Get?

Current economic market conditions and the credit history of the borrower have the biggest influence on the interest rate. Other factors that impact the rate are the size of the loan (loans under $50,000 and over $240,000 will get a higher rate), if the borrower was referred to the lender by a Realtor (rates are usually lower), and the integrity and ethics of the loan originator.

Questions to Ask Prospective Lenders

A standard list of questions can help you interview two or three lenders to find one that suits your needs. The following are important questions to ask prospective lenders:

➤ How long have you and your company been originating loans?

➤ How many of your loans each month originate from online contacts?

➤ How many loans do you write each month? How many does your company?

➤ What type of loans does your company offer?

➤ What is your rate for a 30-year, fixed-rate mortgage?

➤ Are points charged with that rate?

➤ How long have you worked with your loan processor?

➤ What is your work relationship with your underwriter like?

➤ How much are your application fees, and what will my total closing costs be?

➤ When will I receive a good-faith estimate itemizing all my closing costs?

➤ Will I have to pay mortgage insurance?

➤ Can I float the interest rate and lock it in later when rates are better?

➤ What will it cost to float the rate, and how long will it last?

➤ Can I pre-pay the loan without penalty?

➤ When will my first payment be made?

➤ How much money will be collected from me to set up my escrow accounts?

➤ When will the loan be approved?

➤ When are payments considered late? What's the late penalty?

➤ Who should I contact if I have questions, concerns or needs?

Where to Find a Good Lender

Ask trusted relatives, friends, and co-workers if they can give you the name of a reputable loan originator that provided great service and competitive rates for them. Your Realtor also should be able to provide a short list of strong lenders.

Try to find a lender that will not just service this loan, but future business down the road. Qualities to look for in a good lender are patience and listening skills. Your lender should be competent and knowledgeable about economic markets as well as all the programs his company offers. He should be organized, detail-oriented, and thorough. Above all your lender should be genuinely interested in helping you close the loan and have the best experience possible. Desire and motivation are great qualities for a loan originator to possess. It means he will work their hardest for you and handle any obstacles or problems that arise.

If you are considering using an online lender expect its service to be weaker than banks or mortgage companies in your home town, but its rates should be the same if not better. Online lenders specialize in fast, easy, no-hassle transactions. Because their work is primarily or completely done online, the time and expenses incurred are less than standard lender's. Some of the money saved should be passed on to you in the form of lower interest rates and closing cost fees.

Be extra cautious with online lenders that have incredibly lower rates or fees compared to everyone else. They might fish for clients with empty promises then raise the rate or closing costs right before closing. Also be wary of lenders that have been in the business less than a year. Lenders are popping up all over the Internet every week. Many of them are poorly funded, poorly managed, poorly staffed, and have no expertise or experience to loan money. Online crime is growing exponentially, and no one knows how to curb it, let alone stop it. Anytime you are giving out sensitive personal information over the Net, you must have a high level of trust that the recipient of the information will use it with discretion and integrity.

Presenting Your Team of Mortgage Experts

Lenders are companies (banks, mortgage companies, credit unions, or savings and loan institutions) that loan you money to buy a home. *Loan originators* provide borrowers with all information regarding the lending company, the lending process, interest rates, and fees. Originators also walk buyers through the good-faith estimate and application process and originate the loan. *Loan processors* process the entire loan, verify data, collect information from borrowers, and provide backup service to the originator. *Underwriters* review the complete loan package and approve or deny the loan using company guidelines or any applicable government guidelines. *Closing department personnel* prepare the approved file for closing and send it to the title company with instructions on how to close the loan.

Researching Histories of Target Units

The archive history search will not be as helpful with patio homes and zero lot lines as it is with single-family dwellings and condominiums. Because patio homes and zero lots are typically young in age or brand new, there will be little to no history in the multiple listing service detailing past activity. (When new construction homes are first built the price and closing date does not usually get inputted in the MLS system.)

One useful item to consider that an archive history search provides is the true list date, not the current list date. Have your agent check to see if a patio home listed for sale has been on the market longer than the current list date shows on the MLS sheet. You might be able to negotiate a better price if you have information that shows a home has been on the market for nine months instead of just three. Sellers tend to be more confident the first three months of a listing, and then lose leverage and confidence as the months pass.

When your Realtor does an archive history search on a home you are thinking about buying, look for patterns of activity. Has the home been put on the market and withdrawn many times? How many times has the home been sold? Did the home go on the market in the past and the listing expire without selling? If you can find no information on a target property, have your agent do an archive history search for the homes around it or most of the subdivision. Then compare the square footage, amenities, and condition of those other homes with the one you're thinking about buying.

Tips for Conducting an Archive History Search

When your agent is doing an archive history search on a specific property through the multiple listing service, have her search for part of the address, not all of it. For instance, if you're trying to find all past activity on a home at 5533 Main Street in Jefferson County, Springfield, Illinois, have your agent type in 55 Main Street, instead of 5533. This will bring up all activity for any house on Main Street. More importantly, it will bring up all activity for that particular home, not just information on the current MLS listing. The first two digits of an address and the street name should be entered to obtain complete history data, instead of just data pertaining to the current MLS listing.

Getting Yearly Utility Averages

Patio homes and zero lot lines are newer in age, and subsequently are built with energy efficiency in mind. Typically the floor plans are not huge (most are not over 2,000 or 2,500 square feet). Reviewing the utility bills before writing an offer is still advised. Budgeting your monthly costs in advance is reason enough to know the utility averages.

Another reason to request utility information if it isn't provided is to make the home as energy efficient as possible. Very few people have so much money they're willing to throw it out their windows and doors. That's exactly what happens if a home is not properly insulated and energy seeps out windows and doors. Reviewing the utility averages will show if the home is energy efficient, or if there are problem areas that need to be corrected.

Having said that, most owners find utility bills at patio homes and zero lot lines less expensive than the homes or apartments they're coming from. This is due to the size of patio homes and zero lots, their young age, and the fact that many are built on concrete slabs instead of over crawl spaces or basements. Slabs are more energy efficient than crawl spaces and basements because less energy can seep in and out. Regardless of what type of foundation the home is built on, it's always a good idea to know what the utilities will be before you purchase.

Researching Association Bylaws, Fees, and Services

Patio home and zero lot owners enjoy the benefits of owning their own home, and the services and amenities of condominium living. Because there are characteristics of condo living, owners must abide by bylaws set forth by the association. Researching bylaws for this type of housing is more important than for new-construction housing subdivisions because associations play a greater role in the day-to-day operation of these communities.

Check with your Realtor to gather information about the bylaws of the association that you are seriously considering buying into. The best online sources for information are iOwn and the builder's Web site if the target home you're looking at is a new-construction home, or new homes are still being built in the complex.

Other sources of information are the listing agent, the management company that manages the complex, and association board members. Keep in mind where you got the information. Association boards, builders, and listing agents trying to advertise their communities always give the rosiest information designed to promote the subdivision. Your agent, iOwn.com or other online house sites, and the management company should provide the most unbiased information.

Fees for patio homes and zero lot lines are generally not very expensive. Fees might range in price from $20 per month to over $100. The owner owns and maintains the entire dwelling, inside and out, so money does not have to be collected for roof and exterior housing repairs.

Association Bylaws Review and Approval

The purchase agreement contains a clause where buyers can request a copy of the bylaws within a certain number of days (about five) after the offer is accepted. There is a second provision in the purchase agreement that states buyers must approve or reject the bylaws within a certain number of days (about five) after receiving them. If the buyer cannot live with the bylaws, the transaction will be dissolved, and both parties will go their separate ways.

Builders typically turn control of the neighborhood association over to the homeowners when the community is 70–80% built. Homeowners have the same goals in mind: Keep the cost of running the community (the association fee) as low as possible, yet get the necessary work done to maintain the highest monetary value for the community. A board of officers is usually elected or appointed by the homeowners. This board oversees the work or the hiring of a management company that manages the needs of the entire community.

Because the homes, common areas, and facilities are younger in age, there are few maintenance issues, so the association fee is minimal. In addition, patio homes and zero lots do not offer as many amenities and services as condominiums. The association fee reflects this. Some patio home communities have master insurance policies that cover liability issues, the lot, and all common areas. The premiums for these policies are paid out of the association fees that are due either monthly, quarterly, semi-annually, or annually.

Patio home and zero lot owners typically own the inside and outside of their dwellings. They usually own the lot their home is built on as well. The differences between these types of housing and traditional houses are yard maintenance, common areas, and mandatory membership in an association. Patio homeowners normally don't take care of their own yard. They pay the association fee, and the landscaping is done for them (zero lots handle their own landscaping).

Both patio homes and zero lots have common areas that are maintained by a contractor hired by the association. Association fees fund this work. Common areas include but are not limited to parking spaces, signs at entrances and exits, playgrounds, walking paths, lakes, clubhouses, recreational facilities, and open areas where no structures are built.

Mandatory membership means you must be a member of the association and pay dues for services performed and use of facilities. Whether you use the facilities or not, you still pay the same fee. (Might as well use that pool because you're paying for it.) Residential home subdivisions rarely have mandatory memberships in associations. Many zero lot line communities do, and nearly all patio home subdivisions do.

Homeowner responsibilities, amount of common areas, services provided, and association fees vary from subdivision to subdivision. There is no hard and fast rule that applies to every community across the country. Essentially, the builder picks what the bylaws will be when the community is built. From that point on it's up to the association board and the concerned members of a housing community to decide what rules will be in place.

Reviewing Checklist of "Needs" and "Wants"

Just as you would pull out and review your checklist before writing an offer on a home or condo (refer to Chapter 10 and Chapter 11), you should examine your initial search criteria for patio homes and zero lot lines.

Did you initially start your search with patio homes and zero lot lines in mind? Are you looking at condos, residential homes, and patio homes? Does the target home you've found meet the criteria you started with? How does it match up to the location, price, condition, amenities, and décor you want?

Make sure you have broken your checklist into separate categories. The needs list, or must-have, gets the search started. This category dictates what area of town you'll look in, what price range you'll search, how many bedrooms, baths, and garages you'll need, and any other features you absolutely must have in a home. Keep the needs list as small as possible so more matching listings will be found. If too many matches come up, you can always add one or two things to your needs list (a fireplace, screened porch) to narrow the list down to a manageable number.

Your wants list, or like-to-have, finalizes the search. These are the items that differentiate one patio home community from another or homes within a community. This list can be more detailed and specific. In fact, it should be. The wants list will typically help a buyer choose between two properties if everything on the needs list is met.

The items on your checklist can change in significance as you shop for a home. Some things will be added, and others might drop off. The checklist is a tool to keep you focused on the criteria that are most important. Use it as a frame of reference to measure how much you like the final home or two you have left on your short list of favorites.

The checklist also is helpful in determining how much your offer price should be. For example, if the house you've found meets all your wants and needs, going in with a lowball offer isn't appropriate unless the sellers are desperate to sell, or the home has been on the market for over a year. On the other hand, if a home only meets some of your criteria, you should offer a lower amount than the asking price. In this situation the home isn't your dream home, it's the right home for you at the right price.

Prioritizing "Wants" and "Needs" Checklists

Start your needs checklist by listing in order the things you must have. For example, your list might resemble this. 1. Location 2. Price 3. Number of bedrooms and baths 4. Any other features. Your wants list also should be prioritized in order of importance. 1. Brick exterior 2. Fireplace 3. Gas heat 4. Two-car attached garage 5. On a lake or pond. Prioritizing your list from the start will make it easier to refer to it as you hunt for homes.

Sometimes homes only have half the criteria on a buyer's wish list, but those matching items are extremely attractive or compelling. The checklist is an excellent reminder of the big picture. Typically, buyers are not swayed by the outstanding features. Instead, they refer back to the checklist and rationally decide the home doesn't have enough of the needs on their list—so it isn't the right home.

Selecting a Home Inspector

The Internet will not have a major impact on your selection of a home inspector. To date, most inspection companies and individual inspectors don't advertise online. Inspectors also need to be familiar with local customs and knowledgeable about housing and construction codes and environmental issues relevant to that city or town. Odds are you will have a local outfit inspect your home, and they will do the best job because of their familiarity with codes and legislation in that area.

Ask your Realtor for the names of two or three good inspection companies. Inquire as to how many inspections the company has done for clients of the Realtor. The real estate office your agent works out of should have a list of good and bad inspectors. Trusted friends, family members, and co-workers also are good sources of information. Try to get the name of one or two good individual inspectors, not just inspection companies. Inspection companies can have as many as 10 to 15 inspectors, and not all of them may be good. If your agent has worked with one individual inspector many times in the past and knows the quality of the work and service, have that person do the inspection—not someone else from the company.

It is wise to ask the prospective home inspector a series of questions before making a commitment, such as the following:

➤ How long have you been doing home inspections?

➤ How long has your company performed home inspections?

➤ How many inspections do you do a week? A month?

➤ How much do you charge for a complete inspection?

➤ Do you perform other inspections like termites, radon, water, and asbestos?

➤ Do you work nights and weekends?

➤ What is your background in? What qualifications do you have to be a home inspector?

➤ How well do you know my agent? How many inspections have you done for clients of hers?

➤ When will I receive a written report of your findings?

➤ Will you explain problem areas to me or my agent if we don't understand them?

➤ How long will the inspection take?

➤ What areas of the house will you inspect?

➤ Do you provide a reference list of past clients I can contact? Past Realtors you've worked with?

➤ Are you licensed and insured?

What's a Sphere of Influence List?

Your *sphere of influence* is all the people in your life that influence you and vice versa. Generally this consists of your family, friends, co-workers, business associates, and sometimes acquaintances. Your sphere of influence is vital when looking to buy or sell a home. These people can refer you to a good Realtor, builder, mortgage company or loan originator, home inspector, contractor, tradesman, title company, and insurance agent. Smart selections on these decisions can ensure a pleasant, efficient, successful real estate transaction. Poor decisions can lead to a nightmare experience.

The Least You Need to Know

➤ Patio homes and zero lot lines are newer homes that sit on small lots. They provide convenience, low-hassle living, and ease of maintenance while offering owners the benefits of owning a single-family home.

➤ Advantages of patio homes and zero lot lines include little to no yard work and exterior maintenance, a contemporary floor plan, and extra amenities in the subdivision. Disadvantages include a lack of individuality, privacy, control, small lots, and association fees.

➤ Search for homes through REALTOR.COM and other major Web sites or through your Realtor's multiple listing service.

➤ Researching communities, subdivisions, and association bylaws are vital because planned living communities are greatly affected by these factors.

➤ Select a moneylender and home inspector with an excellent track record, who comes highly recommended from trusted friends or family members.

➤ Research utility averages and the history of all activity concerning the property you're thinking about buying so you can make the most informed decision on whether to write an offer and for how much.

Part 5

Playing a Game of Tug of War

Ever watch a tennis match where both sides continually strike the ball, sending it back into the other person's court? Have you participated in a tug of war where first one side seems to have the advantage, and then the other team takes the lead? Negotiating is somewhat similar. Unlike a tennis match or tug of war, negotiating can and should end with both parties coming out ahead.

Sellers have a home they want to sell. Buyers want to buy a home. When the offer is written, both sides scramble for leverage. This chapter explains how both sides can come out ahead, but also how sellers and buyers can gain leverage. Read this section before writing an offer and negotiating the sale of a home (hopefully the other party in the transaction hasn't).

Chapter 14

Writing an Offer and Negotiating the Terms

Do you love to shop for a bargain? Do you enjoy the process of settling on a price almost as much as the item you're buying? Or do you hate discussing money and find the whole process uncomfortable? Do you pay whatever someone is asking and end the discussion as quickly as possible? Some people are negotiators, and others aren't. When it comes to writing an offer to purchase, you can't escape the negotiation process unless you pay the seller's asking price. (I rarely recommend that.)

Regardless of whether you love or hate to negotiate, we have to do it every day of our lives. Good negotiators have an advantage in life. They are able to get what they want simply by negotiating better. The goal of this chapter is to learn how to write an effective offer, understand the value of negotiating, and become more comfortable and adept at negotiating.

The Purchase Agreement and Other Forms

Now that you have found the right home it's time to make an offer to purchase. This is done on a purchase agreement.

The most important form in real estate is the contract to purchase. Without it no homes would be bought or sold. All terms and conditions of the sale must be included in the contract, or they will not be binding. Realtor Boards all over the country distribute purchase agreements for agents to use. These forms are standard within each town, but might vary from one city to another. For Sale By Owners can find purchase agreements at office supply stores like Office Depot, CopyMax, and Staples.

The purchase agreement or sales contract contains several pre-written sections with blanks to be filled in and a Further Conditions section where buyers can write in additional relevant information.

For an example of the front page of a purchase agreement, see Figure 14.1.

Figure 14.1
Here's the form you'll use for a purchase agreement—the first page, anyway.

PURCHASE AGREEMENT
(IMPROVED PROPERTY)

Sample

Date: ____________

1. **BUYER:** ____________ ("Buyer") agrees to buy the following property from the owner ("Seller") for the consideration and subject to the following terms, provisions, and conditions:

2. **PROPERTY:** The property ("Property") is known as ____________ in ____________ County, ____________, Indiana, and legally described as: ____________

together with any existing permanent improvements and fixtures attached **(unless leased)**, such as, but not limited to, electrical and/or gas fixtures, heating and central air-conditioning equipment and all attachments thereto, built-in kitchen equipment, sump pump, water softener, gas grills, central vacuum equipment, window shades, curtain rods, drapery poles and fixtures, ceiling fans and light fixtures, towel racks and bars, storm doors, windows, awnings, TV antennas, satellite dishes and controls, storage barns, all landscaping, mailbox, garage door opener with control(s) AND THE FOLLOWING: ____________

All items sold shall be fully paid for by Seller at time of closing the transaction.

3. **PRICE:** Buyer will pay the total purchase price of $ ____________ for the Property.

4. **EARNEST MONEY:** Buyer submits $ ____________ as earnest money which shall be applied to the purchase price. The listing broker shall deposit the earnest money into its escrow account within two (2) banking days of acceptance of this Agreement and hold it until time of closing the transaction or termination of this Agreement. If Buyer fails for any reason to submit earnest money, Seller may terminate this Agreement. Earnest money shall be returned promptly in the event this offer is not accepted. If this offer is accepted and Buyer fails or refuses to close the transaction, without legal cause, the earnest money shall be forfeited by Buyer to Seller as liquidated damages, and Seller may pursue any other legal and equitable remedies. The Broker holding any earnest money is absolved from any responsibility to make payment to the Seller or Buyer unless the parties enter into a Mutual Release or a Court issues an Order for payment. If the parties do not mutually consent to the release of the earnest money, then they agree that the Broker holding the earnest money may file an interpleader action with a Court regarding disposition of the earnest money and that the payment of the Broker's resulting costs (including attorney's fees) incurred in connection with such interpleader are a priority claim against the earnest money regardless of the Court's apportionment of the balance of the earnest money.

5. **METHOD OF PAYMENT: (Check appropriate paragraph letter)**

☐ **A. CASH:** The entire purchase price shall be paid in cash and no financing is required.
☐ **B. NEW MORTGAGE:** Completion of this transaction shall be contingent upon the Buyer's ability to obtain a ☐ **Conventional** ☐ **Insured Conventional** ☐ **FHA** ☐ **VA** ☐ **Other:** ____________ first mortgage loan for ________ % of purchase price, payable in not less than ______ years, with an original rate of interest not to exceed ________ % per annum and not to exceed ______ points. Buyer shall pay all costs of obtaining financing, except ____________.

Notwithstanding any other provisions of this Agreement, any inspections and charges which are required to be made and charged to Buyer or Seller by the lender, FHA, VA, mortgage insurer, or closing agent, shall be made and charged in accordance with their prevailing rules or regulations and shall supersede any provisions of this Agreement.

☐ **C. ASSUMPTION: (Attach Financing Addendum)**
☐ **D. CONDITIONAL SALES CONTRACT: (Attach Financing Addendum)**
☐ **E. OTHER METHOD OF PAYMENT: (Attach Financing Addendum)**

6. **TIME FOR OBTAINING FINANCING:** Buyer agrees to make written application for any financing necessary to complete this transaction or for approval to assume the unpaid balance of the existing mortgage within ______ days after the acceptance of this Agreement and to make a diligent effort to meet the lender's requirements and to obtain financing in cooperation with the Broker and Seller. No more than ______ days after the acceptance of the Agreement shall be allowed for obtaining favorable written commitment(s) or mortgage assumption approval. If a commitment or approval is not obtained within the time specified above, this Agreement shall terminate unless an extension of time for this purpose is mutually agreed to in writing.

7. **CLOSING:** The closing of the sale (the "Closing Date") shall be on or before ____________, or within ______ days after ____________, whichever is later or this Agreement shall terminate unless an extension of time is mutually agreed to in writing. The closing fee shall be paid by ☐ **Buyer** ☐ **Seller** ☐ **shared equally.**

____________ **(Office Use Only)**

Page 1 of 5

Produced with ZipForm™ by Vertisoft Inc. 18025 Fifteen Mile Road, Clinton Township Michigan 48035, (800) 383-9805

Your Real Estate Company 18025 15 Mile Road Clinton Twp. MI 48038 Phone:(800) 383-9805 Fax: (810) 293-3950

Every blank line in a purchase agreement should be filled in, even if just to say *Not Applicable*. The further conditions section might be filled in, left blank, or a line drawn through it.

For an example of the back page of a purchase agreement, see Figure 14.2.

Sample

20. FURTHER CONDITIONS: ____________________

____

____

____

21. EXPIRATION OF OFFER: Unless accepted by Seller and delivered to Buyer by __________ ☐ **A.M.** ☐ **P.M.** ☐ **Noon** ☐ **Midnight**, the _____ day of ____________________, this Purchase Agreement shall be null and void and all parties shall be relieved and released of any and all liability or obligations.

22. CONSULT YOUR ADVISORS: Buyer and Seller acknowledge they have been advised that, prior to signing this document, they may seek the advice of an attorney for the legal or tax consequences of this document and the transaction to which it relates. In any real estate transaction, it is recommended that you consult with a professional, such as a civil engineer, environmental engineer, or other person, with experience in evaluating the condition of the Property.

23. ACKNOWLEDGEMENTS: Buyer and Seller acknowledge that each has received agency office policy disclosures, has had agency explained, and now confirms all agency relationships. Buyer and Seller further acknowledge that they understand and accept agency relationships involved in this transaction. By signature below, the parties verify that they understand and approve this Purchase Agreement and acknowledge receipt of a signed copy.

This Agreement may be executed simultaneously or in two or more counterparts, each of which shall be deemed an original, but all of which together shall constitute one and the same instrument. The parties agree that this Agreement may be transmitted between them by facsimile machine. The parties intend that faxed signatures constitute original signatures and are binding on the parties. The original document shall be promptly executed and/or delivered, if requested.

BUYER'S SIGNATURE — DATE	BUYER'S SIGNATURE — DATE
PRINTED	PRINTED
BUYER'S SOCIAL SECURITY #/FEDERAL I.D. #	BUYER'S SOCIAL SECURITY #/FEDERAL I.D. #
MAILING ADDRESS — ZIP CODE	MAILING ADDRESS — ZIP CODE
(Area Code) TELEPHONE NUMBER	(Area Code) TELEPHONE NUMBER

____________________ **(Office Use Only)**

Page 4 of 5

Produced with ZipForm™ by Vertisoft Inc. 18025 Fifteen Mile Road, Clinton Township Michigan 48035, (800) 383-9805

Figure 14.2

Your purchase agreement form may run several pages, but you sign it on the last one.

Many forms are used during a real estate transaction. Some of the more common ones include the following:

- The counter offer
- The addendum to the purchase agreement (adds to the contract)
- The amendment to the purchase agreement (changes the contract)
- The inspection amendment
- The mutual release waiver (dissolves the contract)

All of these forms tie into the purchase agreement. Without the sales contract there would be no need for any other forms.

How to Write an Offer

After you have a purchase agreement form in hand (your agent will provide one), sit down with your Realtor to write the offer. I don't advise doing it online, or over the phone or fax machine unless you've bought and sold numerous homes. Real estate laws and customs vary from city to city and state to state. Your agent will explain customary practices and procedures in your region.

Purchase agreements should be as clean, straightforward, and concise as possible. The point of writing the offer is to buy the home. The offer should reflect that. The offer should be written in a manner that is easy to read and understand. Offers can be typed, handwritten, or computer generated. As long as the material is legible it truly doesn't matter. All the seller cares about is the price and terms on the contract, not what it looks like.

Many items make up the complete purchase agreement. Some are more important than others are, but they all serve a purpose and should be filled out the correct way. Failure to do so could result in thousands of dollars being lost or someone else buying the home you wanted. All offers should include the following components:

➤ Listing broker and agent's name, and buyer's broker and agent's name

➤ Date of the contract

➤ Address and legal description of property (subdivision name, block, section, and lot recorded by city)

➤ Offer price the buyer agrees to pay

➤ All items that will stay in the home that are not already attached (appliances, window coverings, shelving, shed)

➤ Method of payment (cash, new mortgage loan—VA, FHA, or conventional—or conditional sales contract)

➤ The time period during which the buyer will apply for the loan and be approved

➤ The date for closing the transaction

➤ The date on which the buyer will take possession

➤ Liquidated damages amount if the seller is not out of the home on the possession date

➤ Disclosure forms that state the condition of the home and all the improvements on the lot

➤ An inspection section where buyers reserve the right to have the property inspected or waive their right and accept the home in the "As Is" condition they viewed it

➤ Payment of property taxes

➤ Title insurance requirements and when it will be ordered

➤ Which party is responsible for the settlement closing fee

➤ Which party will pay for the survey

➤ Amount of earnest money the buyer offers as a deposit

➤ Number of days buyer has to review and approve association bylaws (if applicable)

➤ Additional terms or conditions can be written into the further conditions section

➤ Time and date the seller must respond by

➤ The buyer's legal signature

What Price Should You Offer?

Many factors influence what a buyer should offer a seller. There is no hard and fast rule or universal truth in making an offer. Every transaction is different because every buyer, seller, house, and situation is different. Luckily, there are some very good guidelines to follow.

When you are buying a home, you are in a bartering situation. The seller has made the first offer (their listing price), and you respond to it. How do you respond? Do you offer their asking price or close to it, or do you offer much less than what they're asking?

The most frequently asked question I get as a Realtor is, "What should I offer the sellers?" My answer is always the same: Look at a few important factors and then tell me what you should offer. Those factors are the recent sale prices of comparable homes in the same subdivision or immediate vicinity, how much you can afford to pay, the motivation level of the seller, and how motivated you are as a buyer.

Reviewing comparable sale prices is probably the best way to determine what you should offer a seller. It's certainly the most objective. Your agent can tell you what the average sales price in the neighborhood is for homes that are comparable in size, bedrooms, baths, and so on. Decide if the condition of the home you are trying to buy is in above-average or below-average condition. Factor this into the equation as well as appreciation for the homes on the list that sold a year or two ago.

Also, consider what the average time to sell a home in the neighborhood is—anything under 60 days is good—and the difference between list price and sales price. If sellers are averaging over 96% of the list price, the area is selling well. These statistics along with the average sales price numbers will help you determine if the seller's asking price is fair, high, or low. If the statistics indicate the seller's price is fair to low, and the home has been on the market for less than a month or two, you might be wasting your time and the seller's by offering 85–90% of the list price.

What Factors Influence Seller Motivation?

When sellers are motivated to sell their home, buyers tend to get a better price. Factors that make owners motivated to sell are job transfers, divorces, having to pay two mortgages, rising interest rates, kids going back to school, winter and holiday seasons approaching, and sickness or death. A final factor to consider is how long the home has been on the market. The shorter the time, the less motivated a seller will usually be. Typically, the longer a home has been on the market, the more leverage a buyer has. Therefore, she can be expected to offer less money.

On the other hand, if the statistics show a home is priced high compared to the other homes around it, and the home has been on the market for five months, you probably should go with a low offer. Every home, seller, and transaction is different. Time of the year and market conditions greatly influence what buyers should offer and what a seller will accept. The statistics your agent provides from the multiple listings can help you make the best informed, unbiased decision. Remember, the seller used the same information from the multiple listings to set their asking price. If you're not sure how to interpret the statistics, ask your agent to explain them.

What you are pre-qualified for and can afford to pay has a significant bearing on what you will offer. For starters, you should not tour homes that are out of your price range. (Bad agents are notorious for this.) Be careful about viewing homes that are at the very upper limit of your price range. For instance, if you are approved up to $120,000, don't look at homes listed at $124,900 in hopes you can get them down in price. Even if you're lucky enough to convince the owner to sell for $120,000, you're still stretched to the limit on what you can afford. I don't recommend being house poor (making your mortgage payment and having no money left to furnish the home or go anywhere).

Using the same $120,000 example, the right way to search for a home and write an offer is within a comfort zone. (Your lender should help you with this.) If you can run 20 miles before passing out, you wouldn't really run 20 miles would you? Most people would run 17 or 18 miles before calling it quits shy of their outer limit. The same logic applies to house hunting. If $120,000 is your outer-most limit, you might want to search up to $120,000 or even $115,000 and then attempt to get the seller to come down in price. This way you're not a slave to a certain price. Instead, you have the power to say, "I will pay this price," or "I won't."

The seller's motivation and your motivation are the final two elements that determine what your offer price should be. If the seller is not highly motivated, or even slightly motivated, it will be hard to get them to come down in price. Some sellers fish for buyers by putting their home on the market at a high price just to see if they'll catch a sucker. Conversely, if a seller is highly motivated to sell, buyers stand a good chance of getting a better price.

Buyer's motivation has a lot to do with the offer price. If you like a home but aren't ga-ga over it, you might offer 10% less than the asking price just to see what the seller will do. On the other hand, if you find a home that blows your socks off (meets and exceeds all your criteria on your checklist), you might be willing to offer close to list price. There are only a few situations where I advise buyers to pay full list price or above it.

To begin with, the buyer must love the home and have an incredibly high motivation level. Without this strong desire it doesn't make sense to pay the list price or above. Secondly, if you know there is another offer already presented to the seller or have knowledge that other offers are being written, you should write a strong, high purchase price or not bother writing an offer at all. You're simply wasting your time and the seller's, and you risk getting emotionally attached to a home you're not going to get.

Finally, if both these factors are in place—strong buyer desire and a competitive situation with multiple offers—and the listing is only a few days old, you might consider writing the offer for $100–1,000 *over* the list price. Homes are sometimes priced at or below market value. Buyers, not agents, determine what a home is worth. If multiple buyers want to buy a home that quickly then paying more than the asking price is justified. Remember, an additional $1,000 on your mortgage will only cost approximately $7–10 more a month. Is your one-of-a-kind dream home worth losing over that amount?

Hints to Make the Offer Stronger

The only perfect offer is a buyer showing up at a seller's door with a suitcase full of cash. The buyer pays the seller $10,000 over the seller's asking price, and allows the seller six months to find a new home. (Even this might not be perfect because the seller has to explain to the bank where the money came from.) All other offers have some sticking points that have to be worked out. I can't help you make a perfect offer, but I can help you write the best offer possible. This is important because it gives you a better chance of getting your dream home, and possibly for less money.

First things first. The most effective way to make an offer to purchase strong is to offer a high price. That's simple enough. Give the seller what he's asking and you'll get the house, right? Usually, but not always. Other terms in the contract could scare the seller. The other terms provide opportunities to make an offer strong without offering a super high price.

When to Offer the Full List Price

When demand for an area, neighborhood, or subdivision is through the roof, buyers sometimes have to write offers at or even above the seller's asking price, or they won't stand a chance of getting a home. This is especially true during busy real estate months and when interest rates are low. Examples of this are Silicon Valley in California, the South Beach area in Miami, and parts of Colorado such as Vail and Aspen.

Buyers are also well served to check the prices of homes in subdivisions and areas around the neighborhood they're searching in. If a home has everything you desire, comparing it to other homes in surrounding neighborhoods might serve as a barometer to gauge how well priced your target home is. After looking at the prices of homes in nearby neighborhoods, you might realize what a bargain your target home really is. In such a case, you can feel good about a full-price offer. But be careful not to look too far away from the neighborhood in question because location is the single most significant factor that influences the value of homes.

Gauging Seller Motivation

There are a few ways to play sleuth and try to figure out the sellers' motivation. Have your agent directly ask the listing agent why the sellers are moving, where they are going, and if they've found a place yet. Are they building a home and doing a double move into an apartment then a home? Check the closets, cabinets, refrigerator, and garage to see if the sellers are already packed? Talk to neighbors and see if they have information about the sellers. Have your agent subtly ask the secretaries and receptionists at the listing agent's office about the sellers' plans. Review the time on the market data to determine if the sellers might be losing leverage and getting antsy.

One of the best ways to strengthen your offer is to make sure your financing is completely in order. Make the seller feel so good about how you will pay for the home it becomes a non-issue. Paying cash does this most effectively but most of us can't buy houses that way. There's another way to be a cash buyer, however, and that's getting pre-approved for a mortgage. After you are pre-approved for the mortgage, the lender promises to loan you the money. You're as good as a cash buyer. Another way to show your strength as a buyer is to put more money down for the down payment and the earnest money.

Sellers love short time frames on a sales contract. Fast deadlines show you are a serious, competent buyer who is fully committed to the deal. To make yourself more attractive to a seller, set short time frames to complete your home inspection and a fast closing date. What sellers want more than anything is a proceeds check in their hand at closing. Offer to give this to them in two weeks instead of a month or six weeks, and you stand a much better chance of getting a better price.

Don't rush them on a fast possession, though. Closing and possession are vastly different. Nearly all sellers want a fast closing, but many don't want to give up possession of the home quickly. If the seller is building a home or can't gain possession of their next home for two or three months, they won't want to give up their home any time soon. Consider giving them a super-fast closing and a long possession time frame to get a better sales price. Have your agent find out what the seller is looking for in the way of possession time frames, and structure your offer accordingly. Done the right way, you may separate yourself from other buyers because you are willing to give the seller something they need.

One of the most important things you can do to make a strong offer is write one without a lot of contingencies. Contingencies are clauses written into a contract that stipulate certain things must be done in order for a deal to close. If contingencies are not removed from the contract, the deal can't close. Sellers like contracts containing as few contingencies as possible. Fewer contingencies means fewer things can go wrong.

Some contingencies are necessary (financing and inspection contingencies are present in most offers, as well as approval of bylaws in all condo deals). One you want to avoid is the contingency of having to sell your current home to purchase the next one. Sellers are oftentimes extremely wary of buyers in this predicament. If you've already sold your home you will make a better impression. Try to include as few contingencies as possible and your offer will be much more attractive to sellers.

One more way to catch a seller's eye is to waive your right to a home inspection. Home inspections might be the hardest contingency to overcome. Sellers lose sleep at night wondering how inspections will go and what will be found. This technique isn't recommended for everyone, or even for many people, but it is effective. If you have an excellent background in home repair, you might consider writing an offer to buy the home As-Is. Sellers love this because all that's needed to close is approval of the mortgage.

How Much Should Earnest Money Be?

The amount of earnest money deposits differs from city to city. They range from 1% of the sales price to as much as 10% of the gross sales price. Your agent will recommend what the standard practice is in your region. Sometimes a high earnest deposit can entice a seller to accept your offer over another. Be careful because you also stand to lose a lot more if you breach the contract and have to forfeit your earnest money.

One trick to buying a home As-Is follows. Write in the further conditions section: Buyer reserves the right to have all inspections done within five days after the acceptance of the purchase agreement. At the end of the five-day period buyer must either buy the home in As-Is condition or sign a mutual release dissolving the transaction. If the buyer signs the mutual release, earnest money will be promptly returned to the buyer. The seller can continue to show the home and accept back up offers during the five-day period.

What Does Buying As-Is Mean?

Buying As–Is means purchasing a home in the exact condition it's in when you viewed it. The seller will make no repairs or improvements. In addition, the seller offers no warranties or guarantees, expressed or implied, to the condition or function of any item in the home. What you see is what you get.

This type of As-Is clause enables the buyer to have a home inspection and protects him from losing his earnest money. If there's a major problem, the buyer can walk away and not be out anything other than time and the inspection costs. At the same time the seller knows she will be selling her home in As-Is condition or still be showing it and accepting back-up offers if something turns up bad in the inspection. There's no downside to the seller, so they love it. If they buyer wanted out because of an $800 termite problem, the seller could agree to pay for the termite treatment to keep the deal alive. This is an excellent way to make your offer stronger to a seller, but you have to be prepared to purchase a home in As-Is condition.

Setting Time Limits

Purchase offers require time limits. If time deadlines were not set offers would hang in limbo forever.

Sellers could sit on your offer and wait until another one came in. When you write an offer submit a time for the seller to respond to it. This time is usually 24 hours to 48 hours, unless the offer is presented over a long holiday weekend where the seller is out of town. Buyers should always set short time frames to respond. Don't give the sellers days and weeks to respond because they will wait for another offer and play them against each other (sellers should always give long time frames to buyers).

Dates to have the home inspection completed and to have the mortgage loan approved are included in the offer. Your agent will help you with these time frames. Closing dates and possession dates must be inserted in the offer. Mortgage and title companies need target dates to shoot for, or the work will be put off and never done. Closing usually takes three weeks to forty-five days. Possession in most large cities is at closing (always at closing if the house is vacant), or possibly a few weeks later if the seller still occupies the home.

Time frames keep buyer, seller, agents, and all vendors focused and working hard toward a goal. Without them transactions would languish and not move forward. Ask your agent how you can use time frames to make your offer stronger, or review that section earlier in this chapter.

Presenting the Offer

The code of ethics Realtors follow stipulates that buyers' agents must present offers as soon as they are written. Offers should be accompanied by an earnest check (typically 1% of the offer price) or a copy of an earnest check. The original check usually has to be delivered within 48 hours of the offer being accepted. Most offers are presented via the fax machine because of the hectic world of real estate.

Your agent will present the offer for you. She will contact the listing agent and inform him that an offer is coming in. This contact might occur over the phone, email, or voicemail. This is the time for your agent to sell the offer to the list agent. This means play up the strengths of the offer and downplay any weaknesses. Essentially, the agent makes a case to explain why the offer should be accepted. Your agent should do this regardless of how strong or weak the offer is.

A buyer should make sure his agent made "live contact" with the listing agent via a direct phone conversation or in person. Part of the buyer's agent's job is to gather as much information as possible about the listing agent's response to the offer. A buyer's agent should try to read, or get a feel for the listing agent's attitude to see how it will be presented to the sellers. It is important that the seller understands the buyer's position and the reasons the offer was written the way it was. Faxes and voicemails don't convey this—direct, live conversations do.

One of the worst things an agent can do is present an offer and not sell it. Worse still, some agents actually sound apologetic or embarrassed by the offer their clients wrote. Agents should sell the offer no matter what's in it. Many times this is the difference between a deal getting done and falling apart. This is also the time for your agent to explain any unusual clauses or terms in the contract. The seller shouldn't have to guess as to what your plans or intentions are. Have your agent convey them so the offer can be considered thoroughly and carefully.

After your agent has contacted the listing agent and faxed, or dropped off the contract offer, you must wait for a response. Along with the offer your agent should present verification of your financing, the copy of your earnest check, and any additional documents pertaining to the offer.

Who Communicates and Negotiates the Offer?

Agents present and receive offers for their clients. Listing agents must present all offers to their sellers regardless of how bad the offer is or when it came in. Agents cannot make decisions for their clients without first consulting their clients. Agents should not tell clients what to do; they should inform and advise. Buyers and sellers ordinarily don't communicate during a negotiation. Agents act as a buffer between parties, helping their clients negotiate, remaining somewhat unemotional and objective. Offers are not reviewed in a sequential, first come, first serve basis. Listing agents present all offers, and sellers choose the one they want to respond to based on the merits of the contract, not the time frame in which it was written.

Basic Rules and Protocol of Negotiating

The first and most important rule in negotiating real estate is there are no rules. Buyers cannot purchase real estate without sellers, and sellers have to sell to buyers. There are always at least two parties involved (four if Realtors represent both parties). Whenever there are multiple parties involved, anything can happen and usually does. Buyers can't control who the owner of a home is, and they certainly can't control how reasonable, ethical, or intelligent the seller is. Clients also cannot control who the other agent is and how they negotiate. One thing is certain in real estate negotiating and negotiating in general: You don't get what you deserve; you get what you negotiate.

Good-Faith Negotiating

Good-faith negotiating refers to two parties engaging in a fair, open negotiation where both parties genuinely seek a resolution that benefits both sides. Complete honesty is almost never present in negotiating—even in good-faith negotiating—but all parties have the mindset to reach a conclusion that is mutually beneficial.

Hopefully all parties in your transaction will negotiate in good faith. This means they will actively pursue a resolution that benefits all parties. If one or more parties has absolutely no regard for their counterparts the negotiations can be strained, nasty, and incredibly difficult to work out. This adversarial relationship normally doesn't benefit anyone.

Do not look for the other party to be completely honest; you shouldn't feel compelled to be completely honest either. I'm not recommending you engage in treacherous or deceitful conduct. I am acknowledging that part of negotiating is holding back information and presenting data in a manner that gains leverage and improves your bargaining power. There is a big difference between trying to achieve the best terms possible for you and attempting to harm someone else. Your agent serves as a guide to instruct you if you are asking for too little or too much. Ideally, your agent will also make sure you don't get carried away and go too far, or give up too much.

Here are some tips to negotiating. Use them as a reference when you are negotiating the price of your home. Know what the home is truly worth and what it is worth to you. Use comparable sales prices to reasonably arrive at a price range the home is worth. You can tell a seller the home is worth $10,000 less, but there's no excuse to not know what the value of the home truly is. Find out what the other party wants and what's most important to them. After you know this give it, or a portion of it, to them to get what you want. Know what you want as well (usually it's the lowest price possible).

Give yourself more room to compromise (come up in price) by offering a lower amount as opposed to opening with a reasonable price. As long as there isn't another offer on the table or one coming in, make your initial offer lower and you stand a better chance to get the seller down in price.

Avoid making the largest concession. If you come up in price in small increments, you will usually get a better price. Try to force your counterpart into making the largest concession. In addition, your chances improve if you can force your counterpart into making the first concession or the first bigger concession. Finally, make smaller concessions as deadlines approach, or the pressure increases. Negotiators that stay detached, unemotional, and poised as pressure increases usually fare better than those who come unglued do.

Constantly seek the counsel of your agent. They negotiate on a regular basis and should be able to advise you throughout the process. One of the most important roles agents play is that of negotiator and advisor (this is why it's vital you trust your agent and they act in your best interest). Besides being the conduit of communication that passes information and decisions on to the other side, your agent is an excellent sounding board for ideas and suggestions.

Agent's Role in Negotiating

Agents present the offer to purchase to the seller's agent. During this initial contact they should highlight the strengths of the offer and downplay the weaknesses. Agents also should justify why the price and terms were written and point out all the negatives in the home. Agents counsel buyers about their options, make suggestions, and receive all counter offers and submit new counter offers. At no time can agents tell a client what to do, make a decision for the buyer without consulting them, or disclose information to the listing agent without the buyer's consent.

Most Important Traits of a Good Negotiator

As you can see, the negotiator's role is a very important one, so she should be chosen with care. A good negotiator should possess the following traits:

1. Ability to think clearly under stress
2. Planning skills
3. General practical intelligence
4. Verbal ability
5. Product knowledge
6. Ability to perceive and exploit power
7. Personal integrity

8. Inner desire to achieve

9. Strong faith in one's own self

10. High tolerance for ambiguity and uncertainty

Counter Offers

After buyers submit an offer, sellers can do only one of a few things. They can accept the offer as it is written (Congratulations!). They can reject the offer outright (this rarely happens unless the offer is pitifully bad). The sellers can not respond. After the deadline expires the offer is null and void. The final option is to counter the initial offer with a new proposal. This is known as a *counter offer*.

Counter offers in theory are neither good nor bad. They involve a rejection of a proposal, and the submission of a new counter proposal. Anyone who has ever gone through a negotiation to buy a house will tell you that counter offers can range from really good to really bad, depending on what the previous offer was. For instance, if a seller was asking $100,000 a buyer might offer $90,000, and the seller might respond with counter offer #1 for $99,000, the buyer would feel he got a bad response. If the buyer counter offered with $91,000, the seller could either come down significantly in price or send a counter #3 for $98,000 and stay firm and final. At this point the buyer should either walk away and pursue another home or accept the counter #3 for $98,000. If the buyer attempted another counter offer, the seller probably wouldn't respond or would simply reject the bid.

There is no rule to the number of counter offers that can be exchanged. (The highest I've been through is nine—it's not fun.) There are some rules as to how they're exchanged. The listing agent usually faxes the buyer's agent the counter offer. Only items the seller disagrees with are put on the counter offer form. All the terms and conditions the seller accepts are not mentioned in the counter offer. For an example of a counter offer form, see Figure 14.3.

For instance, if a seller wants to change the sales price, move the date the buyer will take possession, and take the refrigerator with him, those are the three items that will appear on the counter offer form. All other items are agreeable to the seller (buyers and sellers can go back later before the deal is accepted and change terms previously agreed upon). The seller inserts a time frame for the buyer to respond within, and the listing agent faxes the counter back to the buyer's agent. If the buyer does not respond to the offer within the time stipulated, the deal is null and void. If the buyer rejects the counter outright, the deal is null and void. If the buyer accepts the counter offer, they have bought themselves a home.

Figure 14.3

You might present a counter offer on a form like this.

COUNTER OFFER # _____

1
2 ☐ A.M. ☐ P.M. _____
3 The undersigned makes the following Counter Offer to the Purchase Agreement dated _____
4 concerning property commonly known as _____
5 _____ in _____ Township,
6 County, _____ Indiana between: _____
7 _____ as Seller(s) and
8 _____ as Buyer(s).
9
10
11
12
13
14
15
16
17
18
19 Note: Seller has the right to accept any other offer and buyer has the right to withdraw any offer prior to written
20 acceptance and delivery of such offer/counter offer.
21
22 All other terms and conditions of the Purchase Agreement and all previous Counter Offers shall remain in effect except
23 as modified by this Counter Offer.
24
25 This Counter Offer # _____ is void if not accepted in writing on or before _____ ☐ A.M. ☐ P.M. ☐ Noon
26 ☐ Midnight on _____
27
28 This Agreement may be executed simultaneously or in two or more counterparts, each of which shall be deemed an original, but
29 all of which together shall constitute one and the same instrument. The parties agree that this Agreement may be transmitted
30 between them by facsimile machine. The parties intend that faxed signatures constitute original signatures and are binding on the
31 parties. The original document shall be promptly executed and/or delivered, if requested.
32
33
34
35 ☐ SELLER ☐ BUYER SIGNATURE   DATE   ☐ SELLER ☐ BUYER SIGNATURE   DATE
36
37
38 PRINTED   PRINTED
39
40
41 SOCIAL SECURITY/FEDERAL I.D. #   SOCIAL SECURITY/FEDERAL I.D. #
42

_____ (office use only)
Page 1 of 2

Produced with ZipForm™ by Vertisoft Inc. 18025 Fifteen Mile Road, Clinton Township Michigan 48035, (800) 383-9805
Your Real Estate Company 18025 15 Mile Road Clinton Twp. MI 40038   Phone: (800) 383-9805   Fax: (810) 293-2050

The last option the buyer has in this scenario is to counter that counter offer with another counter offer. This time the buyer might agree with the possession date and the refrigerator going with the seller, but not the price. The buyer and his agent will discuss different options, and then the buyer's agent will write up another counter offer form and submit the new price proposal to the listing agent. This bargaining goes back and forth until a counter offer is accepted, or one or both parties gives up or walks away.

One important side note is this: If another offer comes in from buyer #2 during the counter offer process, the seller can respond to the second offer and shelf the first offer if the ball is in the seller's court. In this situation the seller essentially has two offers on the table at the same time. It doesn't matter that buyer #1's offer came in first. However, if the seller has made a counter offer to buyer #1 and the ball is in his court, the seller must wait for buyer #1 to respond, even if buyer #2's offer is considerably higher.

How Long Do Negotiations Take?

There is no standard or rule of thumb as to how long a negotiation might take—offers may be accepted by sellers in the exact form they are written. Sometimes one or two provisions need to be cleaned up or changed, and the counter #1 is accepted. Other times negotiations will be extremely long and protracted. It is not uncommon for some negotiations to take five, six, or even eight counter offers before an agreement is reached, or the parties go their separate ways.

Verbal Counters

All offers and counter offers must be in writing and signed to be enforceable in a court of law. Verbal offers are not binding and should not be used. Any time someone makes a verbal offer tell them to put it in writing and you'll consider it. If they are not willing to do so they're admitting they are wasting everyone's time. Counter offers can be written on any form or paper. Putting the terms in writing and signing the paper makes it valid.

Agents' Role in Negotiating

Agents receive counter offers for their clients and should present them immediately. As you come closer and closer in price and terms, remember your checklist of wants and needs. This list will help you decide if you should raise your price an extra $1,000–2,000. Don't let your emotions get the best of you when negotiating gets intense. Buying a home is an emotional and economic decision. Be careful to make decisions for the right reasons, not to "get the last word in," "show the seller who's the boss," or decide something for "the principle of it." In the end, the process is about money so keep your head clear and focused, and don't let side issues or petty emotions distract you from your goal of buying a home.

Your agent should soften counters when you're too tough or strengthen counter offers up when you're too meek. This doesn't mean they change what you want to do on the form. Rather, they phrase their verbal responses in the most positive way to help you get the best price and terms. For example, if you say the seller is being a real stubborn SOB, your agent should say the buyer appreciates the seller's position but feels these other factors are extremely important and affect the price tremendously. Couching or phrasing responses is part of an agent's job. The good ones do it effectively and help their buyers get lower prices and better terms.

Negotiating Without an Agent

If you are buying or selling a home without an agent this entire chapter applies to you, not just this section. Take heart in the fact that you probably have saved money already because agents are not involved (buyers should get better prices on For Sale By Owner homes because sellers aren't paying 6–7% in commissions). One of the most important things to remember when negotiating for yourself is this: Never let your physical expressions or voice give away your true feelings. If you're good at poker, chances are you'll negotiate well. If you are a poor poker player or don't play at all, don't put yourself in a position where the seller can see your reaction. Communicate via email. Fax information and use voicemail so you can control information and how it is presented.

If you get nervous or uncomfortable discussing money, let alone negotiating, don't get caught talking directly to the seller where you have to make an immediate decision or could possibly show your strong desire to buy the home. Keep your true intentions to yourself. Don't be open and forthright about how lovely and wonderful you think the home is. Express interest in the property but give the seller a long list of problems or concerns that trouble you. Be as courteous, polite, and pleasant as possible (no one wants to negotiate with a rude, obnoxious jerk). Criticize the home itself and state objections—don't criticize the seller personally.

Use a trusted family member, friend, or co-worker to help you when you are negotiating without an agent. Persons with backgrounds in real estate, law, or any type of negotiating can be helpful.

Even if you don't know a Realtor or attorney who will give you free advice, utilize someone close to you who you know to be honest, forthright, and reasonable. Don't necessarily ask for their advice on what to do. They might know less about buying a home than you do. Instead, ask them to serve as a sounding board to toss ideas at and offer suggestions. You want to make sure you are being as objective and unemotional as possible. This can be difficult when negotiating and purchasing your first home or your dream home without an agent. Ask the person for ideas, and make sure you're not missing something because you are so close to the action.

Criticizing a Home During the Negotiation Process

Moderation is the key to criticizing a home during a negotiation. Never directly or personally criticize the seller. Always speak in terms of the home's deficiencies or flaws, not the seller's. Low offers should be justified, or the seller won't take you seriously. List the reasons the home falls short of your original expectations or other homes in the area, particularly those priced the same or below your target home. Don't attack the home or make the list too negative or condescending. Stating problems in a courteous, professional way is much more different than mercilessly ripping apart a home or the seller's asking price. Stay detached and unemotional, if possible. Remember to acknowledge some of the home's obvious strengths, but not too many. Remind the seller that other buyers will probably agree with you and deduct value from the home's asking price.

Pain from Losing a Negotiation

An excellent question to ask yourself when negotiating the price of a home is how much pain will I feel if I don't get the home? If not buying the home or losing it to another buyer doesn't bother you very much, you shouldn't go up in price to get the home. Conversely, if losing the home will truly upset you and cause emotional pain and stress, this is an indication that you really want the home. Paying an extra $7–10 per month on your mortgage to get a home you really want is most likely worth it. It's hard to predict how much we'll like something, but we usually know how much we'll dislike it.

When communicating with the seller be direct, polite, and firm. Show confidence in yourself and your decisions even if you don't feel that way on the inside. Don't feel the need to apologize for your thoughts or decisions. The trick to negotiating is showing the other party one thing while privately thinking another. Remain silent when engaged in a tense, pressure-filled moment. It's amazing what the other party will give up or concede simply because the silence is uncomfortable. Don't be afraid to ask for something you want. In addition, when you have been turned down don't be afraid to make the exact same request again or modify it only slightly.

You must have a little bit of courage when negotiating. In order to really get a terrific outcome sometimes you have to risk losing what you want. Think before you speak. Take time to analyze options before responding. Understand the other party's position as well as possible. Be patient and don't try to get everything accomplished immediately. Negotiations sometimes take time.

How Aspirations and Goals Affect Negotiating

Aspiring to more in a negotiation gives you a better chance of being successful. If you are content paying a seller full list price or close to it, that's exactly what will happen. If you love a home but your goal is to get it at the lowest price possible, you stand a significantly better chance of accomplishing this simply because you had these aspirations. Most things in life, as well as in real estate and negotiating, cannot possibly happen unless we first want them to and then take steps to achieve them.

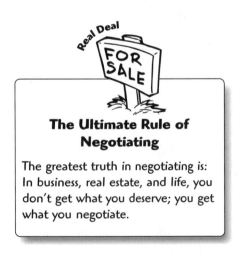

The Ultimate Rule of Negotiating

The greatest truth in negotiating is: In business, real estate, and life, you don't get what you deserve; you get what you negotiate.

He Who Has Leverage Usually Wins

What is leverage? Leverage is bargaining power. It's playing ball on a playing field that is tilted in your favor. Leverage is having the power to influence someone or an outcome. How do you get leverage is obviously the next question. Leverage can be obtained naturally, or it can be inherently present. Some situations in real estate automatically dictate who has leverage. Other times it is fought over and won in the negotiation process. As the title of this section suggests, the person with leverage usually comes out ahead.

Sellers have leverage when they initially list their home. For no reason other than their home is brand new on the market, sellers are in a position of strength. Buyers who have looked through all available listings and haven't found the right home will stampede over each other to view the new listing.

If one or more of them likes it and wishes to make an offer on it, the seller is in a huge position of strength for many reasons. First of all, if more than one buyer writes an offer, the seller can use the offers against each other. Secondly, there is always a chance a buyer will write an offer in a few days given the high number of showings taking place. Finally, because the home has only been on the market for a few days to a week or two, the seller can afford to be pickier and stick to his guns. Most sellers would correctly reason that if the home is attracting so much attention quickly from so many buyers, he will probably be able to sell it soon and for a high price.

Through no fault of the buyer or by no talent of the owner, the seller enjoys a significant advantage in this negotiation. The playing field is not level when a seller first puts their home on the market. On the other hand, if a buyer starts looking for homes in September and finds a nice home that was listed eight months earlier in January, the buyer enjoys a huge advantage for no reason other than lucky timing.

Homes that have been on the market for a long period of time (compare the average days on the market in that subdivision to the target home's days on the market) suffer from a perception problem. What's wrong with it? Why hasn't anyone bought it in eight months? There must be something wrong or someone would have bought it by now. Sellers must fight this perception not only in getting a buyer to write an offer, but in negotiating the offer.

Who Usually Loses a Negotiation?

The person who speaks first or makes the first offer usually loses a negotiation. After an initial offer is made, it's difficult to take it back. Oftentimes the other party will give you what you want right off the bat. Sellers make the first offer by stating a listing price. Rarely do homes sell for their full asking price or above. Responding to the other party's initial offer gives you a big advantage. Make them speak first.

Leverage can be gained by making the other party want or need what you have to offer, or by making the other side believe you don't want what they have. This can be tricky. One way to make a seller want you is to write an offer that is phenomenal in every way except price. If you are willing to buy a home in As-Is condition and close in two weeks the seller might be willing to concede a couple thousand dollars in price so as not to lose you.

Another option would be to write a clean offer that has few contingencies and have your agent stress every negative about the home to the listing agent. The seller might start to doubt the value of the home and worry every buyer will feel the same way. If the seller likes the rest of the offer he might be inclined to sell for less because the home is now damaged goods in his eyes.

An additional option is being adamant about your price and not budging until the seller caves in. It might sound overly simplistic but often people get worn down and simply give in. If a seller doesn't have a rock-hard reason for selling at a certain price, you might be able to get them down in price through persistence, firmness, and endurance.

A final technique that is risky and somewhat of a gamble involves writing a low offer, waiting a few weeks or months and then re-submitting the same low offer or an even lower offer on the same house. If the home hasn't sold the owner might be more motivated to sell. Sometimes sellers' opinions of their homes change, and they don't feel so confident about them. If sellers' opinions of their homes decrease, buyers stand a much better chance of getting reduced prices.

Other factors that influence leverage are interest rates, market conditions, reasons the seller is selling, reasons the buyer is buying, and the time of the year. For example, if a buyer is re-locating to a new city and has only a few weeks to buy a home he doesn't have a ton of leverage when negotiating with a seller. On the other hand, if a buyer has a month-to-month lease that can be easily broken, and Christmas and the cold winter months are approaching, the seller has little leverage. Depending on what is happening with these elements a buyer can exploit a seller's weaknesses to receive a better price or vice versa.

Believing in Your Own Negotiating Skills

One of the most important attributes needed in a negotiation is self-confidence and a belief in one's own ability. You have to believe in your ability to affect a positive outcome and be able to see it happen, or it will not happen.

Negotiating Where Everyone Wins

I started this chapter by stating that the best negotiations occur when all parties come out ahead. In good-faith negotiating this is the goal. Most real estate transactions operate under good-faith conditions. For the purpose of this discussion, we will assume (that's always dangerous) all parties are negotiating in good faith.

Someone has a house to sell. Someone else wants to buy a home. Neither person can satisfy his goal without the other. Both persons are equally important and necessary for satisfaction to occur. They need each other. This is the nature of good-faith negotiating. Both parties want the best for themselves, but they must be respectful of the other party's needs, or they won't get what they want themselves.

Sellers typically have a range in price they will sell for. Buyers usually have a top dollar they will pay. If the seller's bottom dollar amount overlaps with the buyer's top dollar, a deal will be consummated. Often sellers have to give up something to get the price they want. By leaving the washer and dryer sellers might make an extra $500 or $1,000 on the sales price. Likewise, buyers can give in one area to receive consideration in another. Price isn't the only issue that needs to be negotiated (just the biggest).

If a seller is building a new home, they might ask the buyer for a long possession date so they will not have to make a double move into an apartment, store their belongings, and move again into the new home. Many sellers will sell the home for less money because they'll save considerable time, stress, and inconvenience by avoiding the double move. The buyers will not get to move into the home they bought at the normal time, but it might be worth it to them because they got a better price on the home.

Seller A might ask $200,000 for his home, but be willing to take $190,000 or above. Buyer B might be approved for a loan up to $210,000, but only be willing to pay $195,000 for seller A's house. There is an overlapping range of agreement or mutual benefit of $5,000. This deal should get done unless the agents or clients act unreasonably. Buyer B might offer $186,000 initially. Seller and buyer might send counter offers back and forth until buyer B stops at $191,000.

Don't Ever Let Them See You Sweat

In a negotiation don't let the other party see your anxiety, fear, doubt, or hesitation. Show no emotion or reaction, but look for tell-tale signs in them. If you have trouble hiding your emotions, control the situation so you aren't negotiating with them over the phone or in person. Use email, faxes, or voicemail.

When seller A accepts the counter offer for $191,000, both parties have won. Seller A sold his home in the range he wanted, and buyer B bought in the range she wanted. This is an example of both parties mutually benefiting. In reality, nothing is exactly perfect or even. In this scenario buyer B came out ahead because she won $4,000 of the common-ground money and only gave up $1,000. Both parties are satisfied after this negotiation, but buyer B probably feels better.

Knowing the Top Dollar You'll Pay

Buyers should always have some idea what their top dollar is. For starters you are qualified up to a certain amount so you can't go above that point. Most buyers have a self-imposed limit they don't want to exceed that is lower than the lender imposed maximum. Different homes should have different self-imposed maximums. A home that meets all your criteria and requires very little to no work when you move in should have a higher max. You might be willing to pay up to $99,000 of the seller's $100,000 listing price. Another home that doesn't meet all your criteria and needs new carpet and paint might interest you enough to pay $95,000 at the most.

Buyers don't necessarily have to confide this top dollar amount to their agent when the offer is written. If your top dollar is really low you should. The agent might caution you against writing the offer at all if it is an unwise use of everyone's time. Sometimes it's better to not disclose the top dollar amount to your agent. When negotiating with the listing agent your Realtor can honestly admit he doesn't know your top dollar and use that as a negotiating ploy. It is important for you to have an idea how high you'll go. As negotiations progress that number might go up or down slightly as your motivation level goes up or down.

Counter offers can fly back and forth quickly, so it helps to have an idea of where you're willing to go. The process will be easier and more comfortable if you've thought about it in advance.

A seller cannot be forced down off her price. Sometimes a seller doesn't budge no matter how good a negotiator you or your agent is. Maybe the seller is that good of a negotiator or the home just wasn't meant to be yours. The seller might not be doing the smart thing by not coming down. Nice homes sometimes languish on the market for many months because sellers are unreasonable or stubborn. Just because you can't get a seller off her price doesn't mean you or your agent failed. The home probably wasn't meant to be yours.

Going in Low

There is a perception among buyers that all sellers price their homes high to leave room or a cushion to come down and sell for the price they really expect to. There is some truth to this theory, but it is dangerous to believe unconditionally because every home, seller, and transaction is unique and different. Some sellers going through a divorce or job transfer must sell within 30 days, so they price the home at or even below the market price range. If a buyer arbitrarily offered 15% less than list price, the seller certainly wouldn't take the buyer seriously, or might be so offended they wouldn't respond. Having your agent do a comparative market analysis will help you determine how accurate the listing price is.

What Does House Poor Mean?

House poor is not a place any new buyer wants to be. When a buyer has bought a home at the uppermost level of his price range and stretched himself so far financially he can barely make the mortgage payments, he is said to be house poor. This situation does not have to happen and shouldn't. Buyers' lives should not have to drastically change after they buy a home. They should still be able to spend money and have fun while enjoying their new home.

There is only one universal truth in real estate: There are no universal truths that *always* hold true. I read articles in newspapers all the time by so-called real estate experts that say buyers should write their initial offer 15% lower than the listing price every time. This is fine advice unless there are two other offers coming in at the same time, or the home has been on the market for two days. By the time your offer was accepted (after 7 counter offers) the seller could have sold the home twice.

The very best properties in top neighborhoods go extremely quickly. There is an area in Indianapolis where homes usually sell in five days or less on the average throughout the summer months. Many homes sell in one or two days. If a buyer offers 10–15% less than listing price every time she writes an offer in this area, she might find an okay house by Christmas time.

Time of year, interest rates, the buyer's motivation, and seller's motivation all influence what a buyer should write an offer for. There is no one right way or blanket rule to writing purchase agreements. Consult your agent and look at the situation you are in to determine if you should go in low and just how low to go.

The advantages of going in with a low offer price are substantial. If the offer is strong in all other areas and your agent does an excellent job selling it to the listing agent, the seller might accept it. If you like the home, but aren't crazy about it, you give yourself much more room to negotiate and get it at the lowest price possible. I don't recommend writing offers unless you are serious about a home and are intent on buying it, but sometimes making an offer will help a buyer solidify her feelings and motivation level. If you go in low you protect yourself from buying a home that you might not adore. At certain low price points, homes that are nice can become great simply because the price is so great.

Writing an Aggressive Offer

There are times when buyers don't want to mess around with negotiating or don't have the luxury of time to negotiate. In these situations buyers can be aggressive and write their best or near-best offer right out of the gate. If you are re-locating and have a week to buy a home, you should consider writing a high-price offer to make sure you get the right home for your family. In this scenario the buyer has to decide which is costlier. Spend a few thousand dollars more ($20–50 per month), or buy the wrong house for you and your family. Often companies will pay moving costs or closing costs, so buyers aren't really out any money by writing a high offer.

Another situation where buyers might want to write an aggressive offer is when they find the perfect home, and there is another offer already in, or one or two coming in (your agent will help you find this out). I advise clients to either forget the home and move on to another one or write the best offer possible (this might include offering more than list price). Buyers can get emotionally attached to a home. Damage can be done if they don't get the home they wanted. Agents should protect clients' interests. Sometimes agents have to say walk away, or go after it with everything you've got. Taking a middle-of-the-road attitude in this situation would put the buyer in a bad place.

Writing a high-priced offer leaves less room to negotiate. You're basically showing your cards to the seller and asking him to accept your offer. I don't recommend it often (it's not the most desirable situation to be in), but occasionally it's the only way to buy your dream home. Agents should give buyers all their options, and this is certainly one of them. Unfortunately, only the top homes in the best areas present this problem for buyers (why are most good things in life this way?). A final comment about writing high-priced, aggressive offers: Most buyers don't regret doing it. There's more regret from buyers who didn't give their best effort and didn't get their dream home because of it.

Low Balling Your Chances Away

There are times when low-ball offers make sense and should be employed by buyers. There are other scenarios where writing a low-ball offer can cause a buyer to lose a home. *Low-ball offers* are purchase agreements written far below the listing price. If a home has been on the market for a long time (at least five months or longer, but check with your agent for the statistics in your area), they might be ripe for a low offer. Another low-ball candidate is a home that has not been maintained well, where the cost to rehabilitate the house is high. Potential buyers might go in extra low in hopes they will be rewarded for taking on the time and trouble of fixing up the home.

Multiple Offer Situations

Sellers can only respond to one offer at a time. They must pick one of the offers to respond to (usually the higher priced one; it doesn't have to be the first one in) and accept or counter offer that offer. If the seller counters the buyer that buyer can accept the counter (and buy the home), or they can send counter offer number 2 back to the seller. The seller can then go to the other buyer and counter their initial offer or continue dealing with the buyer that sent counter number 2. Sellers can have only one counter offer out at any given time.

Buyers should consider low-ball offers any time a seller is highly motivated to sell a home and is having trouble doing just that. This might be caused by current market conditions like high interest rates, seasonal downturns in the market (winter and the holidays), or poor conditions in an area.

When a buyer has no competition for a home, or likes a home but does not love it, a low-ball offer might be appropriate. Make sure you don't waste your time making one unsuccessful low-ball offer after another though.

The problem with low-ball offers is most sellers are more educated in today's real estate market and don't have to accept seriously under-priced offers. Buyers who continually try to low ball sellers might end up never buying a home, or worse yet, buying a below-average to poor home they don't enjoy or can't resell a few years down the road.

Situations where low-ball offers are not recommended are: new listings or homes on the market for 30 days or fewer, homes in terrific condition, homes that have many buyers interested in them, and a house that you love and have an incredibly high motivation level to buy. Be careful to exercise good judgement when writing low-ball offers. Use your agent as a guide on when to consider it and just how low to go. Fifteen percent to 25% below list price are standard low-ball ranges. Remember, in today's sophisticated real estate market, with competition fiercer than it's ever been, buying homes through low-ball offers is harder than ever.

What Designates a Low-Ball Offer?

Sellers and buyers usually disagree on what a low-ball offer is because they're both biased for opposite reasons. Any offer written 15% below the seller's asking price is generally considered a low-ball offer. If a home is in a strong area, an offer 10–15% below the asking price would be considered a low ball.

The Least You Need to Know

➤ Your agent can provide all necessary documents to write an offer and advise you on an offer price. He will present the offer to the listing agent, serve as a buffer between you and the seller when negotiating, present and receive counter offers, give advice based on the data in the multiple listing service, and assist buyers in remaining as detached and unemotional as possible.

➤ Strong offers include few or no contingencies and might or might not be high price offers.

➤ Negotiate in good faith with respect for the seller's wants and needs as well as your own, and everyone comes out ahead. To negotiate better terms for yourself you have to go in with that in mind, be able to see yourself doing it and fully commit to obtaining the best price and terms possible.

➤ Try to learn the seller's motivation and what they want, and then give it to them to get what you want. Some leverage can be won; other leverage is natural and results from things out of your control.

➤ Have the top dollar amount you'll pay in mind before you write an offer and continually refer to it while negotiating. There are also situations where buyers should write low-priced offers or be aggressive and write high offers. Market conditions, interest rates, time of the year, amount of competition, and seller and buyer motivation levels dictate this.

Congratulations Mr. & Mrs. Jones, They've Accepted Our Offer: Now What?

In This Chapter

➤ Officially applying for the mortgage

➤ Having the home inspection done

➤ Getting homeowners insurance

➤ Doing the final walk-through

➤ Closing the transaction from A to Z

Time to take a deep breath. Whew! Way to go. You did your homework on homes and neighborhoods, found a good Realtor and mortgage company, wrote an offer and got it accepted. You've been through a lot in the past few weeks and months. I hope you're not ready for a break just yet, because you've still got a ways to go. It's time now for the people you diligently researched and selected to *really* go to work. This chapter will steer you from the time your offer is accepted through the day of closing.

The Work Has Just Begun

When an offer gets accepted, the buyer's agent and listing agent usually congratulate each other out of professional courtesy. One of the most common things said is "We're looking forward to working with you and your buyer." When I first got into the real estate business, I thought this was an odd thing to say considering all the work already done. My buyer and I might have been looking at houses for two months, finally found the right home, written an offer, negotiated it, and got it accepted. That's a lot of time and work. So what did agents mean by this? I thought we were already working together.

I learned very quickly what agents meant when they said this. Writing an offer and getting it accepted only *starts* the home-buying process. Everything prior to this is preparation, research, and leg work (this is why buyers should use an agent to help them buy a home, especially because it's free).

Now that your offer is accepted the real work begins. By real work I mean carrying out the terms of the contract that you and the seller have agreed to. Every term and condition in the contract must be met or the transaction will not close. Don't worry. If you wrote a relatively clean offer (and read the chapters in this guide concerning getting pre-qualified and selecting a good agent, lender, and inspector) you will be fine.

The first thing to do after the offer is accepted is make sure all documents are signed. Contracts are not considered fully executed until all documents (and there are usually a lot of them) are signed. Your agent should give you copies of all the paperwork, send all the signed documents to your mortgage company, and start a master file at her office. She also should send the earnest check deposit to the listing agent's office within 72 hours of the offer being accepted. Until the paperwork has been signed and the earnest money received by the list office, the home cannot be marked as a sale pending in the MLS computer system. Your agent also should watch the time deadlines in the contract and advise you when things need to be done.

Why Do Deals Fall Apart?

The two main reasons transactions fall apart after an offer is accepted and before closing is a buyer's inability to obtain financing and problems in the home inspection that can't be worked out. Other possible reasons are a low appraisal, lender incompetence, and buyer disapproval of mandatory association bylaws, bad surveys, and a seller's inability to convey clear and marketable title.

Formally Applying for Financing

The first thing you should do after celebrating the accepted offer is contact your mortgage company or bank and set up an appointment with your loan originator to formally apply for the mortgage. Your agent should fax or email the signed purchase agreement and any counteroffers, the MLS listing sheet with property tax information, a copy of the earnest check, and the residential sales disclosure form to your loan originator. In the contract you stipulated when you would meet with your originator to apply for the loan. Meet the originator as soon as possible to get the mortgage ball rolling.

When you set up the appointment the originator will tell you what to bring. A list of those items follows:

➤ Most recent pay stubs

➤ Copies of last two years' W-2s and federal tax returns

➤ Names and addresses of employers (past 24 months)

➤ Last three months' bank statements or addresses and account numbers

➤ Names, addresses, and account numbers for all monthly debts

➤ Name and address of landlord (past two years)

➤ Copy of purchase agreement (if agent hasn't already sent it) along with earnest check copy and MLS listing sheet

➤ Copy of divorce decree, separation, or child support papers (if applicable)

➤ Social security number and picture I.D.

➤ Checkbook/money to pay for credit report and appraisal fees

During your appointment the loan originator will have you fill out an official loan application form. You will decide and put in writing the type of loan (conventional, FHA, VA), and the amount of your down payment. Usually an interest rate is locked in and the total costs to close the deal are given to you. You also will be given a ballpark estimate of what your monthly payment will be (this estimate should be extremely accurate). These items make up the good faith estimate. For an example of a good faith estimate, see Figure 15.1.

Make sure you have all the information your lender requests, or the process can be slowed down considerably. If the lender requests additional information, gather the data as quickly as possible and get it to the originator or his processor rapidly.

Mortgage loans used to take 30 to 45 days to close. Now they can be closed as quickly as two weeks. This is advantageous because sellers want a proceeds check right away (you'll get a better price if you close quickly), and you get to move into your new home sooner. Cooperate with your lender in getting things done in a timely manner. Also, remember that you are the customer and should receive excellent service from your lender.

Figure 15.1

A good-faith estimate gives you an idea of your monthly mortgage payment.

FT MORTGAGE COMPANIES, D/B/A MNC MORTGAGE

Applicants: Scott Hasch	Sales Price: $ 112,000.00
123 Brownstone Drive	Mortgage Amt. Requested: $ 105,400.00
Property Location:	Mortgage Amt. with MIP/FF: $ 106,400.00
Loan Type: ☐ FHA ☐ VA ☐ CONV. ☒ INS-CONV.-LTV 95.0000 %	Interest Rate Requested: 8.500 %

ESTIMATES OF CLOSING COSTS, PREPAID ITEMS AND MONTHLY PAYMENTS

The information provided below reflects estimates of the charges which you are likely to incur at the settlement of your loan. The fees listed are estimates – the actual charges may be more or less. Your transaction may not involve a fee for every item listed. The numbers listed beside the estimates generally correspond to the numbered lines contained in the HUD-1 settlement statement which you will be receiving at settlement. The HUD-1 settlement statement will show you the actual cost for items paid at settlement. The below listed figures are estimates provided in good faith by the Lender and based upon the sales price, mortgage amount, interest rate and discount points in effect or reasonably assumed at the time of preparation. The actual interest rate and discount points charged will be determined by the terms of the Financing Agreement.

ESTIMATE OF CLOSING COSTS

801. Loan Origination Fee (%)	$	
802. Loan Discount (%)	$	
803. Appraisal Fee	$	
804. Credit Report	$	
805. Final Inspection Fee	$	
806. Mortgage Broker Fees	$	
807. Loan Document Preparation Fee	$	95.00
808. Application Fee	$	360.00
809. Underwriting Review Fee	$	175.00
810. Tax Service Fee	$	65.00
811. Flood Certification Fee	$	22.00
902. FHA/PMI Ins. Prem. (%)	$	
VA Funding Fee (%)	$	
1107. Attorney's Fees (includes title examination, title binder, notary fees, etc.)	$	
1101. Settlement/Closing/Escrow Fee	$	300.00
1108. Lender's Title Insurance Policy	$	100.00
1109. Owner's Title Insurance Policy (optional)	$	
1303. Commitment Fee	$	
1201. Recording/Filing Fees	$	42.00
1202. Recording Tax Stamps (1/2 or all)	$	
1203. Transfer Tax (state & local) (1/2 or all)	$	
1301. Location Survey	$	110.00
1302. Pest Inspection	$	
1304. Well/Septic Certification	$	
Other ERIE INS.$388.00 POC-B		
COURIER FED EX FEE	$	22.00
	$	
	$	
	$	
TOTAL OF ITEMS PAID BY LENDER	$ –	22.98
TOTAL ESTIMATED CHARGES	$	1,288.02
Less: Items paid prior to closing		
Closing Costs paid for by Seller	$	1,119.15
NET TOTAL ESTIMATED CLOSING COSTS	$	168.87

$ 22.98 LENDER CREDIT APPLIED TO CLOSING COSTS

PREPAID ESCROW AND ADJUSTMENTS

903./1001. Hazard Insurance	14	mos.	$	452.82
1003. Real Estate Taxes (st. & local)	3	mos.	$	172.74
1002. FHA/PMI Insurance Premium		mos.	$	
1006. Flood/Wind & Hail Insurance	/	mos.	$	
1007. Ground Rent		mos.	$	
1005. Special Assessments	2	mos.	$	7.99
901. Interest @ $ 25.13 per day				
15 days equals			$	376.95
TOTAL PREPAIDS AND ADJUSTMENTS			$	1,010.30

DETAILS OF PURCHASE

Purchase Price of Property	$	112,000.00
Add: Closing Costs	$	168.87
Prepaids		1,010.30
Total of Above Items	$	113,179.17
Less: Mortgage Amount	$	106,400.00
Deposit on Contract		
Other Credits		
CASH REQUIRED FOR CLOSING	$	6,779.17

ESTIMATED MONTHLY MORTGAGE PAYMENTS

Principal and Interest	$	818.13
Hazard Insurance		32.33
Real Estate Taxes	$	57.58
FHA/PMI Premium		66.27
Flood Insurance	$	
Ground Rent		
Special Assessments	$	2.67
Condo/HOA Fee		
	$	
TOTAL ESTIMATED MONTHLY PAYMENTS	$	976.98

These estimates are provided pursuant to the Real Estate Settlement Procedures Act of 1974, as amended (RESPA). Additional information can be found in the HUD Special Information Booklet, which is to be provided to you by your mortgage broker or lender.

SETTLEMENT AGENT

In connection with this loan application, the undersigned applicant(s): (Check One)

1) ☐ Have no preference as to who conducts settlement and issues the required Mortgagee Title Policy.

2) ☐ Recommend the following attorney or title company to conduct settlement and issue the required Mortgagee Title Policy:

(NOTE: Lender requires such settlement agent to provide at no cost to Lender an "Insured Closing Service Letter" from a reputable title insurer. Lender must be notified in writing of any change in above selection. Lender reserves the right to disapprove the recommended title insurer and/or settlement agent for reasonable cause.)

NOTICE: Each loan Applicant must personally attend settlement or obtain advance approval from Lender for Special Power of Attorney.

ACKNOWLEDGEMENT

Date Mailed _____   BY: Ted Sherfick, Branch Manager
FT MORTGAGE COMPANIES, D/B/A MNC MORTGAGE

I/We acknowledge receipt of a copy of this completed form and the following booklets/disclosures, as applicable:

☒ HUD's "Settlement Costs and You"   ☐ Consumer Handbook on Adjustable Rate Mortgages prepared by FRB/FHLBB
☐ Adjustable Rate Disclosure

Date _____   Applicant _____   Applicant _____

Date _____   Applicant _____   Applicant _____

PP02 10/96

Setting Up the Home Inspection

The other appointment that needs to be set up immediately after the offer is accepted is the home inspection. Call the inspection company you want to use (refer to Chapter 10, "Existing Homes") and set up a time where you can be there for the entire inspection (two to three hours). The inspector will call the listing agent's office and schedule the inspection for the agreed upon time. Your agent might or might not be at the inspection depending on the time you pick.

I recommend at least one of the buyers be present at the inspection (ideally the handy one in the family) for a couple of reasons. You will learn more about the home you are buying, how components work, and where certain items are located. If there are defective items, you will have a much better understanding of the severity of the problem if you're there. You can also quiz your inspector about maintenance tips, home improvement ideas, and sources to get work done. You will get a better, more thorough inspection if you are there. Finally, many inspectors require payment at the end of the inspection. To get your money's worth, it helps to be at the inspection for at least part of it. They take two to three hours and can be somewhat boring and tedious (if the home is in good condition).

The inspector will be able to gain access to the home via the lockbox whether your agent is there or not. Be sure to ask questions if you don't understand something. Have the inspector note in his report all deficient items no matter how small or insignificant they might be. While the inspector is examining the home, feel free to ask questions on home improvements that you plan to make in the future, such as adding a deck or painting the exterior. Inspectors aren't experts in all fields, but they can usually steer you in the right direction. You're paying the inspector a lot of money that day so get your money's worth.

At the end of the inspection the inspector should give you a written report detailing the condition of all mechanical systems and the housing structure (some companies mail a slick, fancy report a few days later). To see an example of an inspection report, see Figure 15.2.

Negotiating Inspection Repairs: Another Tug of War

After you and your agent have looked over the inspection report, discuss any items that might be major defective issues. Normally you will have seven days from the time you received the report to respond to the seller in writing. If you need to call contractors or laborers to price jobs or take bids, your agent can help you with this.

When you have discussed the report in detail and researched the costs involved in making repairs, your agent will write a response to the inspection amendment and send it to the listing agent. Negotiating the home inspection is similar to negotiating the price of the home. Sellers typically want to repair as little as possible and buyers want as much fixed as possible.

Figure 15.2

The home inspection report details any problems with the house.

Negotiating home inspections can be a very difficult and tricky endeavor. Most standard purchase agreements state that any item the buyer reasonably believes to be a major defect could be grounds for the contract to be dissolved. Sounds easy enough, right? Inspections are rarely black and white. Getting sellers and buyers to agree on what is a major defect and what isn't is difficult. Getting them to agree on what is the proper way to fix the defect is even harder.

Inspection responses are sent to the listing agent who presents it to the seller. The seller can accept the inspection amendment thereby agreeing to make the repairs the buyer requested, reject the amendment outright, or send a second inspection amendment back to the buyer (essentially a counter offer). Responses can go back and forth until an agreement is reached or the deal falls apart.

If a home fares less than perfect in an inspection, where many major items come back defective, requiring thousands of dollars in repairs, the buyer might consider giving the seller options as to what items must be fixed or a dollar amount the seller will pay the buyer in lieu of making any repairs. Lowering the sales price is another option (check with your lender to make sure this is okay). Sellers don't like to make repairs because they'll never enjoy the improvement and buyers see the home in a more realistic, cold manner so they want to get everything fixed that they can. While negotiating the inspection, sellers should remember they would have to fix nearly all if not all the same items with another buyer so they might as well make the repairs now and move on. Buyers need to remember the home is probably not brand new and even new-construction homes aren't perfect.

Are Major Defects Grounds for Ending a Deal?

Major defects found in a home inspection are not always deal breakers. If the seller is willing to correct the defect, lower the purchase price, purchase a warranty plan insuring the item, or give money in the form of an allowance at closing, the transaction can proceed. Only if a seller is unable or unwilling to correct a major defect to the buyer's reasonable satisfaction will the purchase agreement be deemed null and void.

What Is a Major Defect?

Any item that affects the habitability of a home is considered a *major defect*. If a homeowner's safety is compromised, or the housing structure's integrity is compromised, the problem is considered a major defect. Problems with the furnace or the roof are two examples, but are by no means the only ones.

These potential problems illustrate why sellers might consider having a home inspection of their own done before they put their home on the market. The downside to this is spending $200 to $500 for an inspection you don't have to get. The upside is you know in advance what you will be dealing with. Sellers that fear their homes might have major problems or numerous defects of unknown severity should seriously consider a pre-inspection to avoid losing a buyer and valuable market time down the road.

Good inspectors not only point out defective items, they also explain their findings and interpret them to buyers. Many buyers don't know what is serious and what is a

213

minor repair problem that costs less than $100 to fix. Inspectors should explain the difference.

The following guide, which is used by many home inspection companies, explains the various conditions of disrepair in homes:

Major Defect   Any item that is identified as harmful or dangerous due to its presence or absence. A major defect usually significantly affects habitability and may be an expensive repair/replacement cost. The age of the item can be a concern. Professionals in appropriate trades should be consulted immediately.

Minor Defect   Any item identified that does not significantly affect habitability and can be considered an inexpensive repair/replacement cost. The item might function properly, but age is a concern. Professional trades people might be consulted.

Maintenance Issue   Any item identified as normal or routine to maintain a home. A maintenance issue is generally considered the soon-to-be owner's responsibility.

Deals can not close until the inspection process has been completed and buyer and seller agree on what will be repaired. This process can be so difficult many agents feel they have to sell the home a second time. Negotiations can be extremely intense. The loser in the first negotiation (sales price of the home) often tries to make up for it during the inspection negotiation. Buyers want to buy homes and sellers need to sell their homes, so reasonable heads usually prevail, but the process can be as difficult as negotiating the sales price of the home.

Differences Between Home Inspections and Appraisals

Home inspections examine the condition of a home and do not address monetary value at all. *Appraisals* focus on the value or worth of a home but also might consider the condition if the buyer is financing the home with FHA or VA financing.

Inspections are contingencies inserted into the contract to protect the buyer from any unseen problems. They're insurance policies designed to show the truer condition of a home than what is seen during a one-hour tour. Sellers should address legitimate problems found in the inspection, and buyers should not expect to get a perfect home or have every item fixed.

Complying with Government and Lender Guidelines and Environmental Laws

FHA and VA mortgages are government-insured loans. Mortgage companies and banks underwrite these loans, but the federal government guarantees them. The guidelines imposed on buyers who use FHA or VA financing are actually imposed on lenders by the federal government. The government tells lenders what to do and lenders must obey. If you want to obtain an FHA or VA loan, you must also comply with these guidelines. Two inspections that must be completed when FHA or VA financing is used are wood destroying insect infestation (termite) reports and a well and/or septic report, if applicable. Both inspections must come back clear for the deal to go through.

Buyers using FHA or VA financing are seen as greater risks because they are not making a large down payment. Because they have less money to put down, the government and lenders want to protect these buyers (and protect their own investments). Guidelines have been established to save these buyers from costly repairs of big-ticket items like roofs, furnaces, air conditioners, and so on. The theory is FHA and VA buyers don't have thousands of extra dollars to make these expensive repairs. By requiring homes to pass more stringent guidelines during the appraisal and inspection processes, buyers are shielded from high dollar repairs. Lenders don't want homeowners faced with major repair bills so they won't default on the loan.

Some examples of these tougher guidelines are

➤ Roofs must have a minimum amount of useful life left (three years or more)

➤ Clear termite/wood destroying insect reports must be made

➤ Lead-based paint disclosures must be explained and signed

➤ Water, well, and septic tests must pass acceptable standards

Buyers using insured conventional (5% down), or conventional financing (20% or more down) do not have to meet such stringent guidelines from the government or mortgage companies. They are viewed as smaller risks with larger capital reserves to handle problems if they occur. Lenders usually have few or no guidelines for conventional buyers, but local environmental laws still apply.

VA, FHA, and Conventional Mortgage Guidelines

VA guidelines are the strictest of all financing types. VA loans have more guidelines that must be met and they are the hardest to pass. FHA guidelines are the next toughest. Buyers are protected by FHA guidelines, but not to the extent VA buyers are. Conventional loans have almost no inspection guidelines to be passed. Buyers receive little to no protection from conventional financing, and sellers like buyers with this type of financing considerably more than FHA and VA buyers.

Obtaining Homeowner's Insurance

As you near the date of closing your lender and agent should review the checklist of items needed at closing. One of the most important items will be homeowner's insurance. Your lender will require you to pay the first year in advance. Contact your insurance agent and give him the address of the property you have purchased and the date you will close the transaction (condo buyers aren't required to have hazard insurance). If you have other lines of insurance with him, he should give you a 10% discount on your homeowner's insurance.

Your insurance agent will give you the declaration page of your policy and a receipt showing you paid the first year premium. Take both items to the closing. Your hazard insurance will begin the day of closing, because that is the day title is passed to you. If the home you bought caught fire the day before closing the seller's insurance company would be responsible. If the home caught fire the day after closing (and you weren't set to take possession for two weeks), your insurance company would be responsible.

Lenders require the first year to be paid up front because at the time of closing, buyers do not yet have a mortgage in place to escrow the money. (Escrow accounts are set up the day of closing.) If lenders didn't require the first year to be paid in advance, some buyers might gamble and not get insurance—immediately resulting in a gap between the closing date and the time at which the escrow account has accumulated enough money to pay the yearly insurance premium. This is crucial to lenders because they have much more money invested in a home than buyers do at the day of closing. If buyers make a 5% down payment, the bank has invested 95% of the purchase price and buyers only 5%. If the house burnt down the day after closing, the bank would be out a whole lot more than the homeowner, so insurance is required to close the deal.

When Is Homeowner's Insurance Paid?

The first year hazard insurance is paid prior to closing because lenders want to make sure the property is insured. Additional money is collected the day of closing to set up an escrow account to pay the insurance premiums for upcoming years. Each month a portion of your mortgage payment goes into the escrow account. Once a year your lender pays the insurance premium for you to keep the home insured.

The Final Walkthrough

The purpose of a final walk through, which is done one to two days prior to closing, is to make sure the home is in the same condition as when you bought it. The time and place to ask for a final walk through is in the purchase agreement. The other reasons to conduct walkthroughs are to see if all the items that are to remain in the home (for example, refrigerator, oven, drapes, and mini-barn) are still in the home or on the property. If the seller is supposed to be out of the home the day of closing, walkthroughs also help gauge if this is going to happen or if there is going to be a problem. Another reason to do a walk through is to check any repairs done during the inspection process. The repairs should be done the correct way, but should not affect any other systems in the dwelling.

When Final Walkthroughs Turn Up Problems

Leave enough time between your final walk through and closing to deal with problems. If during the walk through you find mechanical systems are not working, the condition of the housing structure has changed, or the sellers are not ready to vacate the home when they should, postpone the closing until these problems are rectified. Do not close with problems unresolved because there is no guarantee they will ever be resolved after closing.

Use the final walk through to avoid a messy, complicated closing. All issues should be resolved after the walk through is completed. If there are unresolved issues, do not go to the closing table. Demand the problems be corrected or refuse to close. After the seller has their closing check, getting them to fix a problem can be next to impossible.

If everything goes smoothly during the final walk through it's time to close the transaction.

If the final walk through turns up problems, the buyer and seller can put into writing what items still need to be fixed, who will fix it, and a deadline for it to be corrected. The title/escrow company can hold money (usually 1.5 times the estimated cost or whatever amount buyer and seller agree to) back from the seller's proceeds check until the unresolved items are corrected. Once this is done, and the buyer and seller agree in writing it is done correctly, the remaining balance of money is returned to the seller.

Closing the Transaction

Real estate professionals constantly talk about closings. Closings are the events where everything happens: Buyers sign the mortgage documents, sellers pass title to the buyer and receive a proceeds check, and agents get commission checks. Closings are the "show me the money" day.

There is a perception that closings are grueling, ultra serious meetings that last for hours. They shouldn't be, but occasionally are. If the agents and lender have done their jobs the right way and everything is in order, closings are pleasant, hour-long meetings where everyone gets what they want. The key is to have all tasks completed in advance, not at the closing table or an hour before closing (sometimes things do come up at the very end that can't be avoided).

Closing day is the most important day in the home-buying process. Let's debunk all the rumors and myths by walking through the key components of closing a transaction.

The Title Company's Role

In most cities, title companies host closings and oversee the proceedings (attorney's offices are sometimes used). Usually sellers and their listing agent get to pick the title company because they pay the larger title insurance premium guaranteeing clear title for the buyer. Title companies also order the survey and prepare the settlement statement and financing package for the buyer. Lenders send the buyer's closing packet to the title company and they prepare all the documents for the buyer and seller.

What Is Clear and Marketable Title?

Sellers must provide title insurance for buyers guaranteeing clear and marketable title at closing. *Clear and marketable title* means there are no liens, judgments, or encumbrances against the properties' title. When the buyer receives the title the only lien against it is the new mortgage loan used to finance the purchase.

During the closing proceeding an escrow officer from the title company explains all documents to the buyer and seller, collects signatures, all required paperwork, and money from the buyer and disperses money to the seller and both Realtors. All terms of the contract must be met to close the deal.

After the closing the title company couriers a payoff check to the seller's old mortgage company (satisfying that loan in full), sends the deed and mortgage downtown to be recorded in the county recorder's office, returns the signed documents to the lender, and might even file the property tax exemptions for the new buyer.

Where, When, and How to Close

In most cities the closing is usually held at a title company chosen by the listing agent. Because the seller pays the larger title insurance policy for the buyer, the seller typically gets to select a title company. Most sellers follow their listing agent's choice because they don't know title companies well and the listing agent can usually get them a discount on the title work.

The closing also can take place at a title companies' branch office near the newly purchased home or at the listing agent's office. If there is a major problem with logistics and scheduling any office will work. There isn't a home court advantage with closings. All the work should be done and the proceedings should simply be a signing party.

Closing usually takes place on the agreed upon date in the purchase agreement. Occasionally, closings can be moved up if all contingencies are removed and both parties want to close sooner. Conversely, if all conditions and terms are not met the closing can be moved back a few days, weeks, or even months if all parties agree to the change in writing. Closings should occur as soon as possible after the buyer gets mortgage approval and the inspection process has been completed. There is no reason to wait after the contingencies have all been removed. Close the transaction as quickly as possible so problems do not arise or economic conditions change adversely.

Check This Out

Standard Time Lines to Close Deals

Transactions are closed much faster today than ten or twenty years ago. Cash deals can close in three days to a few weeks depending on how quickly the title work can be completed. Conventional loans can close in ten days to a few weeks depending on how fast the appraisal can be done and the loan approved. FHA deals can close in two to six weeks depending on the speed of the lender and the buyer's cooperation. VA deals close in three to eight weeks. Transactions should close as quickly as possible because everybody comes out ahead.

Closing a transaction does not have to be a difficult procedure. You won't be tied to a chair and blood drained from your arm. Show up on time if not a little bit early. Your agent should have already faxed you a copy of the settlement statement detailing your costs and expenses. Bring all the items requested of you. Review the documents to ensure the interest rate, monthly payment, mortgage due date, and closing costs are all accurate. Listen to the escrow officer's explanations and instructions carefully. Ask your agent or the escrow officer to explain anything you don't understand.

The buyer is the key person in this proceeding. Make sure you are comfortable with everything that is being discussed and signed. Buyers sign twenty to forty documents depending on their type of financing (sellers sign approximately ten to fifteen documents). Do not sign any document that is incorrect, inaccurate, or not part of the contract. Now is the time to speak up and contest mistakes or errors. If you wait until after closing you will not be able to get the mistake changed.

Estimating Monthly Payments and Closing Costs

Good lenders will budget high when they go over the good faith estimate with you. When you get the actual monthly mortgage amount and the closing costs the day before closing, the figures should be the same as you were told when you applied for the loan if not slightly less. Bad lenders quote inaccurate estimates that result in higher mortgage payment amounts and closing costs then expected.

Buyer's Closing Responsibilities and Costs

Your agent should give you a list of items to bring to closing. All are important and necessary to close the transaction. The dollar amount you need to bring to closing consists of your down payment plus the closing costs. This money should be brought in the form of a cashier's check, certified check, or money order (title companies usually don't accept personal checks or cash over $200). The cashier's check should be made payable to the title company, or to the buyer. The buyer would then have to sign and endorse the check at the closing table before presenting it to the escrow officer.

If the property is a residential home (anything but a condominium), the buyer must show proof of homeowner's insurance, which can be done by presenting an insurance policy's declaration page and a paid receipt for the first year. Buyers also must bring picture identification verifying they are who they say they are. Driver's licenses and work photo IDs suffice.

Depending on the type of financing the buyer is using, there can be additional items needed at closing. One of the most common items is a clear termite/wood destroying insect report (FHA and VA loans). Satisfactory water, well, and septic tests also are commonly required at closing. Any extraneous items the lender has requested that have not yet been provided by the buyer also will be collected at closing. Examples of these are updated bank statements, credit card statements, letters of explanation for late or unpaid bills, and verification that outstanding debts have been paid off.

The buyer is responsible for anything the lender has requested that hasn't been turned in. If these conditions are not met the title company will follow the lender's instructions and not allow the transaction to close. Money for any unpaid fees also will be collected at the closing (appraisal and credit report). The amount of money and the documents needed to close should not be surprises to the buyer. They should have been made aware of these items weeks or months before by their lender and Realtor.

When Closing Figures Are Late

Don't panic if you haven't received your settlement figures by the morning of the closing and don't know how much money to bring. Contact your lender and ask for a ballpark figure approximately one or two hundred dollars above the estimated amount. Get a cashier's or certified check for the higher amount. At the closing the title company will give you a check back for the overage or excessive amount you brought. This saves time, stress, and hassle trying to pick up a check right before closing.

Seller's Closing Responsibilities

Sellers have far less to bring to closing and fewer documents to sign. Sellers also must bring picture identification. The biggest responsibility sellers have is making sure all repairs have been made and the home is in the same condition now as when the buyer bought it. If possession is at the closing table the seller must be packed and out of the home, and ready to turn over house keys to the buyer.

Sellers should bring original receipts of all work done to the closing. Any repairs that have not been paid for must be paid at the closing. Money can be collected from the seller or deducted from the seller's proceeds check. Any other special terms or conditions in the purchase agreement that have not yet been met by the seller must be satisfied at closing. An example is money paid to the buyer in lieu of repairs being made. Sellers and buyers should also coordinate the utilities being switched out of the seller's name into the buyer's, especially if the buyer receives possession at closing. For details on closing responsibilities and duties, see Chapter 16 "Tying Up Loose Ends."

No terms and conditions should survive the closing. Everything should be done with the possible exception of possession. Sellers have it easy at closing. They have less to sign and get a check at the end of the proceeding. Other than making sure the figures are accurate, sellers have very little to do at closing.

Standard Seller Closing Costs

Mandatory seller costs depend on local custom. Typically sellers must pay all real estate commissions, property taxes through the date of closing, title insurance for the buyer, FHA or VA financing fees if applicable, courier fees to overnight the loan payoff, and the balance of their current mortgage. Sellers occasionally have to pay attorney fees to review the closing documents and any other closing costs they agreed to pay per the purchase agreement.

Understanding the Settlement Statement

Along with the purchase agreement the settlement statement is the most important document in real estate. The settlement statement is an itemized breakdown of all expenses and credits given to the buyer and seller. The transaction is closed from the figures shown on the settlement statement. In simple terms, this document shows what the buyer owes and what the seller gets.

The settlement statement is a two sided, legal size document that is separated into two columns. The buyer's charges are on one side, the seller's on the other. To view an example of a settlement statement, see Figures 15.3 and 15.4.

Figure 15.3

The all-important settlement statement...

A. **SETTLEMENT STATEMENT** U.S. DEPARTMENT OF HOUSING AND URBAN DEVELOPMENT HUD-1 Rev.3/86 OMB NO.2502-0265 (Exp. 12-31-86)			

	B. TYPE OF LOAN
OLD REPUBLIC TITLE COMPANY OF INDIANA	1.( )FHA 2.( )IHFA 3.(X)CONV.UNINS. 4.( )VA 5.( )CONV.INS
	6.File Number 96-43850
	7.Loan Number 0117250538
	8.Mortgage Insurance Claim Case Number

C.NOTE: This form is furnished to give you a statement of actual settlement costs. Amounts paid to and by the settlement agent are shown. Items marked "(p.o.c.)" were paid outside the closing; they are shown here for informational purposes and are not included in the totals.

D.NAME OF BORROWER:	E.NAME OF SELLER:
F.NAME AND ADDRESS OF LENDER:	G.PROPERTY LOCATION:

H.SETTLEMENT AGENT: Old Republic Title Company of Indiana	PLACE OF SETTLEMENT: 10401 N. Meridian Street, Suite 115 Indianapolis, IN 46290	I.SETTLEMENT DATE October 31, 1997 DISB. 10/31/97

J. SUMMARY OF BORROWER'S TRANSACTION		K. SUMMARY OF SELLER'S TRANSACTION	
100. GROSS AMOUNT DUE FROM BORROWER:		400. GROSS AMOUNT DUE TO SELLER:	
101. Contract sales price	164462.00	401. Contract sales price	164462.00
102. Personal Property		402. Personal property	
103. Settlement charges to borrower (line 1400)	1210.19	403.	
104.		404.	
105.		405.	
Adjustments for items paid by seller in advance		Adjustments for items paid by seller in advance	
106. City/town taxes to		406. City/town taxes to	
107. County taxes to		407. County taxes to	
108. Assessments to		408. Assessments to	
109.		409.	
110.		410.	
111.		411.	
112.		412.	
120. GROSS AMOUNT DUE FROM BORROWER	165672.19	420.GROSS AMOUNT DUE TO SELLER	164462.00
200.AMOUNTS PAID BY OR IN BEHALF OF BORROWER:		500. REDUCTIONS IN AMOUNT DUE TO SELLER:	
201. Deposit or earnest money	2500.00	501. Excess deposit (see inst.)	2500.00
202. Principal amount of new loan(s)	140000.00	502. Settlement charges to seller (line 1400)	10181.17
203. Existing loan(s) taken subject to		503. Existing loan(s) taken subject to	
204.		504. Payoff of first mortgage loan First Ind.	131400.00
205.		505. Payoff of second mortgage loan	
206.		506.	
207.		507.	
208.		508.	
209.		509.	
Adjustments for items unpaid by seller		Adjustments for items unpaid by seller	
210. City/town taxes to		510. City/town taxes to	
211. County taxes to		511. County taxes to	
212. Assessments to		512. Assessments to	
213.		513.	
214.		514.	
215.		515.	
216.		516.	
220. TOTAL PAID BY/FOR BORROWER	142500.00	520. TOTAL REDUCTION AMOUNT DUE SELLER	144081.17
300.CASH AT SETTLEMENT FROM/TO BORROWER		600. CASH AT SETTLEMENT TO/FROM SELLER	
301. Gross amount due from borrower (line 120)	165672.19	601. Gross amount due to seller (line 420)	164462.00
302. Less amounts paid by/for borrower (line 220)	142500.00	602. Less reduction in amount due seller(line 520)	144081.17
303. CASH (X)FROM ( )TO BORROWER	23172.19	603. CASH (X)TO ( )FROM SELLER	20380.83

I have carefully reviewed the HUD-1 Settlement Statement and to the best of my knowledge and belief, it is true and accurate statement of all receipts and disbursements made on my account or by me in this transaction. I further certify that I have received a copy of the HUD-1 Settlement Statement.

_____   _____
Borrower   Seller

_____   _____
Borrower   Seller

The HUD-1 Settlement Statement which I have prepared is a true and accurate account of this transaction. I have caused or will cause the funds to be disbursed in accordance with this statement.

_____   _____
Settlement Agent   Date

Warning: It is a crime to knowingly make false statements to the United States on this or any other similar form. Penalties upon

The escrow office starts on the back page of the document, usually with the buyer. Beginning at the top of the document the closing agent reads line by line every expense charged to the buyer. The total expenses are added up at the bottom of the back page and carried over to the top of the front page. The officer brings this number down from the top of the front page, reads the remaining expenses and totals all the buyer's expenses.

Figure 15.4

...and its itemized list.

-2-

		PAID FROM BORROWOR'S FUNDS AT SETTLEMENT	PAID FROM SELLER'S FUNDS AT SETTLEMENT
L. SETTLEMENT CHARGES			
700. TOTAL SALES/BROKERS'S COMMISSIONS based on price $ 164462.00@ 3.50% = 5756.17			
Division of Commission (line 700) as follows:			
701. $ 5756.17 to Century 21 at the Crossing			
702. $ to			
703. Commission paid at Settlement			5756.17
704.			
800. ITEMS PAYABLE IN CONNECTION WITH LOAN			
801. Loan Origination Fee 1.000 % Ritchie Financial Services			1400.00
802. Loan Discount 2.000 % Ritchie Financial Services			2800.00
803. Appraisal Fee to Ritchie Financial Services		275.00	
804. Credit Report to Ritchie Financial Services		60.00	
805. Lenders's Inspection Fee			
806. Mortgage Insurance Application Fee to			
807. Assumption Fee			
808. Underwriting Fee Ritchie Financial Services		250.00	
809. Commitment Fee			
810. Document Preparation to D.P.S., Inc.		80.00	
811. Messenger Service			
812. Tax Service Contract			
813.			
814.			
815			
816.			
900. ITEMS REQUIRED BY LENDER TO BE PAID IN ADVANCE			
901. Interest from 10/31/97 to 11/01/97 @ $ 28.19000/day Ritchie Financial Services		28.19	
902. Mortgage Insurance Premimum for months to			
903. Hazard Insurance Premium for years to POC			
904. One-Time FHA Insurance Premium			
905. VA Funding Fee			
906. Flood Insurance Premium for years to			
907.			
1000. RESERVES DEPOSITED WITH LENDER			
1001. Hazard insurance months @ $ per month			
1002. Mortgage insurance months @ $ per month			
1003. City property taxes months @ $ per month			
1004. County property taxes months @ $ per month			
1005. Annual assessments months @ $ per month			
1006. Flood Insurance months @ $ per month			
1007. Solid Waste months @ $ per month			
1008. Aggregate Escrow Adj months @ $ per month			
1100. TITLE CHARGES			
1101. Settlement or closing fee to Old Republic Title Company		205.00	
1102. Abstract or title search to			
1103. Title examination to			
1104. Attorney's fees to Fred L. Jones			35.00
(includes above items numbers:)			
1105. Title insurance to Old Republic Title Company		130.00	130.00
(includes above items numbers:)			
1106. Lender's coverage $ 140000.00			
1107. Owner's coverage $ 164462.00			
1108. Construction policy Old Republic Title Company			50.00
1109.			
1110.			
1111.			
1200. GOVERNMENT RECORDING AND TRANSFER CHARGES			
1201. Recording Fees: Deed $10.00 ;Mortgage $30.00 ; Releases $10.00		40.00	10.00
1202. City/county tax/stamps: Deed $;Mortgage $			
1203. State tax/stamps: Deed $;Mortgage $			
1204. Assignment Hamilton County Recorder		11.00	
1205. Auditor Fee/Deed Hamilton County Auditor		1.00	
1300. ADDITIONAL SETTLEMENT CHARGES			
1301. Survey to Benchmark Surveying		85.00	
1302. Pest inspection to			
1303. Auditor Fee/Disclos. Hamilton Cty Auditor		5.00	
1304.			
1305. Nov-Dec Assoc. Dues Lantern Ridge Owners Association		40.00	
1306.			
1307.			
1308.			
1309.			
1310.			
1311.			
1312.			
1313.			
1400. TOTAL SETTLEMENT CHARGES (enter on lines 103, Section J and 502, Section K)		1210.19	10181.17

Buyer's Initials _____ Seller's Initials _____

Items paid for on the buyer's behalf are then totaled. The escrow officer then subtracts the items credited to the buyer from the expenses charged. The balance is the amount the buyer has to pay. After the buyers side has been explained the escrow agent goes through the seller's figures in the same manner.

The settlement statement does more than show the money the buyer has to bring and what the seller gets. It also details the commissions paid to the real estate offices, the money paid to the mortgage company, the payoff amount of the seller's current mortgage, the payment of property taxes, the amount of money collected to set up the escrow accounts, all lender fees, earnest money deposit, title and survey fees, and any closing costs the seller paid for the buyer.

The settlement statement is normally the first document reviewed and signed. If buyer and seller agree on all the costs and who pays what the documents are signed and the escrow agent moves on to the next phase of closing.

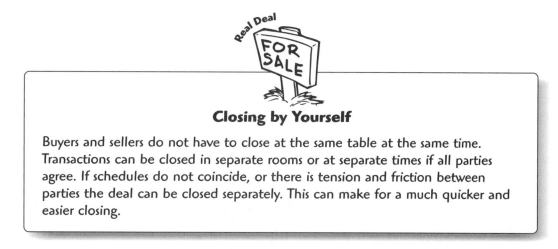

Closing by Yourself

Buyers and sellers do not have to close at the same table at the same time. Transactions can be closed in separate rooms or at separate times if all parties agree. If schedules do not coincide, or there is tension and friction between parties the deal can be closed separately. This can make for a much quicker and easier closing.

Signing Documents and Dispersing Funds

After the settlement statement has been signed (usually six copies) the escrow agent will start pulling papers out of a thick file. The buyer must sign the majority of the forms, especially if the buyer's financing is FHA or VA. The escrow agent will place one document after another in front of the buyer or seller and briefly summarize its content. Remember to slow the escrow officer down and ask questions if something doesn't make sense or is inaccurate. All documents will be signed this way.

After all the paperwork has been signed, the receipts or original documents required by the mortgage company collected, IDs gathered, and the buyer's check handed over, the escrow officer leaves the table for a few minutes. The documents are reviewed, IDs checked, and copies made of everything. The escrow agent then cuts a check for the seller, and the two real estate offices. These three checks are dispersed as well as the payoff of the seller's current money.

If any documents need signed between the buyer and seller or the seller owes the buyer money from the inspection this can be handled while the escrow agent is making copies and cutting checks.

Power of Attorney for Long-Distance Purchases

Power of attorney is one person granting power or privilege to another to sign their name to a legal document in their absence. If a spouse cannot be at a closing they can grant power of attorney to the other spouse to sign all documents for them. Realtors also can be given power of attorney by a client to sign documents and close a deal.

Mortgage companies and banks have power of attorney forms they provide when scheduling conflicts arise. Lawyers also can draw up the necessary forms. Make sure to have the paperwork filled out in advance, not the day of closing. If the documentation is not filled out correctly or in time power of attorney will not be granted and the deal will not close.

Gaining Power of Attorney

Power of attorney must be granted. The person giving power of attorney must be of sound mind, and not be coerced in any way to grant it. Your mortgage company can provide the form to use. They prefer their form over a lawyer's. The document must be notarized. The cost is about $40 to $50.

The Least You Need to Know

➤ Make sure all parties have signed the contract and counteroffers and earnest money has been delivered to the listing agent within forty-eight hours of acceptance.

➤ Meet with your loan officer as fast as possible after the contract is accepted and bring whatever he requests. Work with your lender to move things along quickly.

➤ Contact your home inspector immediately to set up a time and date to conduct the home inspection.

➤ Obtain homeowner's insurance a week or two prior to closing and do the final walk through a few days to a week prior to closing. Make sure the home is in the same condition as when you bought it and all repairs have been done correctly.

➤ The title company oversees all aspects of the closing and acts as the closing agent for the lender. The seller and listing agent select the title company.

➤ Buyers must bring a certified or cashier's check to closing along with picture ID, proof of homeowner's insurance, and a clear termite report if applicable. Sellers must bring photo ID and keys to the home and any receipts of work done if applicable.

➤ The escrow agent explains all charges and credits on the settlement statement, collects signatures, money and verifications, and disperses checks to the seller and the Realtors.

➤ Power of attorney consent can be granted when one person cannot be at a closing so another person can sign documents for them.

Chapter 16

Tying Up
Loose Ends

In This Chapter

➤ Changing your address and selecting a moving company online

➤ Coordinating possession at closing

➤ Coordinating a delayed possession

➤ Searching online for short term housing, storage facilities, and home improvement sites

➤ Canceling memberships, subscriptions, and affiliations

Congratulations! You are now a proud (and massively in debt) homeowner. Closing wasn't that bad, was it? After a second celebration, it's time to start coordinating the move into the new home. Lots of little details have to be done to ensure a smooth, low-hassle move. If the sayings "success is in the details" and "it's the little things that matter most" are accurate (and they are), then this chapter can make or break a happy, convenient move.

Changing Your Address Online

To change your address online, go to www.usps.gov (the United States Postal Service's Web site) and click the change of address option. Type in your information and proceed from screen to screen. Currently you can type your information in and print out the forms but you can't submit or email your form to the post office (leave it to the post office to make changing your address complicated).

You must drop the completed form in your mailbox or take it to your local post office. After it is received, the post office will process the address change in a few days to a week. You can see the change of address form from the United States Postal Service in Figure 16.01.

Figure 16.1

Fill out this form and the Post Office will forward your mail to your new address.

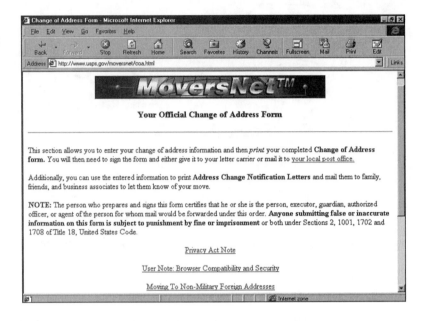

Packing for the Move/Selecting a Moving Company Online

One way to facilitate packing is visiting local businesses and emailing friends to obtain boxes for the move (and strong backs if you're moving yourself). Grocery stores, liquor stores, manufacturers, and factories that ship appliances and other large items are terrific sources. Other items needed to pack include tape, box cutters, plastic wrap, tissue paper or newspaper, markers to label boxes, trash bags, and hangers. These supplies can be bought at Wal-Mart, Sam's Club, Meijer, Office Depot, Copy Max, Staples, Menards, Target, and many other stores. Contact Uhaul or Ryder online at www.uhaul.com and www.ryder.com to reserve a moving truck. They also sell boxes and supplies.

Start packing as soon as your offer is accepted, but really pick up the pace after the home inspection process is negotiated. Don't put it off or wait until right before closing and possession. You'll have enough to deal with then. Your financing should not be a problem because you got pre-qualified, so after the inspection is negotiated start packing. Have a packing plan even if you are a fly-by-the-seat-of-your-pants person. Contact friends and family members for help ahead of time.

To find out how to dispose of hazardous waste materials like paint, motor oil, dye, ink, asbestos, and so on, visit "Earth's 911" Web site: www.1800cleanup.org.

What Does Tenant's Rights for Possession Mean?

Tenant's rights means that if you buy a property that someone else rents, the tenant can stay in the home until the term of the lease expires, even if the lease period ends months after the sale and closing of the home. If a landlord sells a home, the tenant leasing the home can stay in the house until the lease time period is up, regardless of when the new owner wants them out. The tenant's lease survives the closing.

Moving companies also can be found online either through their Web site directly, or by using a search engine like www.yahoo.com. If you want to use a big, reputable company like Mayflower movers, go directly to their Web site. To view Mayflower's home page, see Figure 16.02.

Figure 16.2

A moving company such as Mayflower will try to attract your business online.

See Table 16.1 for an alphabetical list of national and international moving companies and their Web addresses.

Table 16.1   Moving Companies on the Web

Company Name	Web Site
Allied Van Lines	www.alliedvanlines.com
Atlas Moving Company	www.atlasvanlines.com
Bekins	www.bekins.com
Budget Moving Company	www.budget.com
Mayflower Moving Company.	www.mayflower.com
North American	www.northamerican.com
Ryder	www.ryder.com
Uhaul	www.uhaul.com
United Van Lines	www.unitedvanlines.com
Wheaton Van Lines	www.wheatonvanlines.com

If you don't know which moving company you want to use or want to shop for price go to www.yahoo.com and search under **moving company**, **movers**, or **moving**. I recommend you contact three moving companies to compare prices. Service is compromised the lower you go in price. Make sure the moving company is bonded and insured in case they break or damage any valuables. Smaller outfits might offer a lower price, but their service will reflect this. Decide if you want to save money or get reliable, quality service from your mover.

Get written estimates from all the companies you contact and ask if the estimates are binding, non-binding, and guaranteed not to exceed a certain amount. Obtain each company's assigned Motor Carrier number and contact the Department of Transportation online (www.fhwa.dot.gov) or (202) 358-7000 to see if they are registered and have the proper insurance.

If your schedule permits moving during the week, you will probably save money, as opposed to moving on the weekend when movers are busier. Many moving companies require a minimum number of hours worked, or people moved, and charge a mileage fee for extra long distances. Notify the movers in advance if you have extremely large, bulky, or unique items to be moved. They need to be prepared with the proper equipment and personnel. Examples of these items are pianos, safes, basketball goals and backboards, and animals.

Ask your prospective mover for a copy of the booklet titled "Your Rights and Responsibilities When You Move." The Department of Transportation Web site can give additional tips for moving successfully.

Possession at Closing

Common practice years ago dictated buyers taking possession 15 to 30 days after closing. This has slowly changed because buyers want to move into their newly purchased homes as soon as possible and sellers are able to find new homes quicker with the help of Realtors and technology (everything in real estate moves faster nowadays). More homes than ever are vacant because many financially strong sellers are able to find their next home without selling their current one.

Normal possession times in today's real estate market are either at closing to 15 or 20 days after closing. Local customs differ from city to city, but possession at closing is probably the most common possession time frame across the country.

Passing the Keys, Manuals, and Warranties to the Buyer

Sellers have few responsibilities at the closing. If possession is given the day of closing, the list increases. The home must be entirely vacated and left in "broom clean" condition. The seller must also bring a set of keys or all the keys to the closing site. This includes keys to all doors in the house and garage, and mailbox or mini-barn keys if applicable. Garage door openers also should be handed over at the closing table.

The seller can bring one complete set of keys to the closing and leave the rest locked inside the home. A good place to leave additional keys and garage openers is a cabinet or drawer in the kitchen.

Manuals and warranty plans can be brought to the closing or left inside the home. If something needs to be explained in a manual or with a warranty the seller should bring the material to the closing and give it to the buyer after explaining the item.

Check This Out

What Items Do Sellers Leave Behind?

Sellers should remove all personal items from a home and garage and dispose of all trash and debris in the dwelling and the yard. The home should be left in "broom clean" condition (a middle of the road cleaning). Sellers should leave behind all items that pertain to the home such as keys, garage door or fence openers, manuals, warranty plans, and leftover supplies that were used on the home. Examples of leftover supplies are paint materials, carpet, vinyl or tile flooring, roofing shingles, and so on. Items left behind that are worth $100 or less are generally considered to be the new owner's property a week after possession. Larger, more valuable items left behind may be considered the new owner's property after a month or two has passed.

Examples of manuals and warranty plans that can be difficult or confusing are alarm systems, association memberships, appliances, and mechanical or housing contract work such as roofs, windows, or termite treatment.

Switching the Utilities into the Buyer's Name

The major utility companies (gas, electric, water, phone, and cable) are just catching up to the rest of the world and offering online services to change utilities. Contact the utility companies by searching an engine like www.yahoo.com with the utilities' name (Consolidated Edison, for example), or by inserting www in front of, and .com after, the name in your browser's location text box.

The traditional way to switch utilities is for the buyer and seller to get the utility company phone numbers from their agents and call a few days to a week prior to closing. The seller should call first and have a final reading done instead of having the service disconnected. When a final reading is done the service is read out in the seller's name through the date of closing.

After the seller has called and ordered a final reading for the date of closing, the buyer can order new service starting the day after closing. New installation and hookup charges are avoided with the final reading.

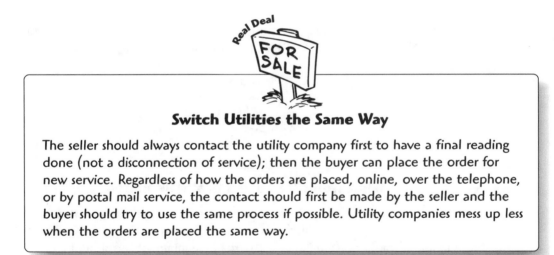

Switch Utilities the Same Way

The seller should always contact the utility company first to have a final reading done (not a disconnection of service); then the buyer can place the order for new service. Regardless of how the orders are placed, online, over the telephone, or by postal mail service, the contact should first be made by the seller and the buyer should try to use the same process if possible. Utility companies mess up less when the orders are placed the same way.

Making a House File with All Documents

One of the more important yet simpler things to do when closing on a home and moving in is creating a house file to organize, store, and preserve all documents relating to the purchase and the home itself. Do this online *and* keep a hard copy file with documents and receipts. If you don't already have a filing system, ask your agent for a folder with his company name and logo on it to easily distinguish the file.

Everything you do in the future that is house related, make an improvement or repair, refinance the mortgage, appeal your property taxes, and so on, add the documents to the paper file and electronically amend your online records.

Try to organize the house file into sections if possible. Keep all mortgage and financial documents together. Any documents related to legal issues, title and deed, should be kept separate. The last category is home improvement or repairs. File all documents, receipts, invoices, bids, photos, and canceled checks together.

Storing House Files Safely

Store either a paper folder file or a floppy disk file off the premises in case a fire or tornado destroys the entire house. You can keep a copy of the paper file or disk at your place of employment, in a safety deposit box at the bank, or at a relative's home. Have copies of everything in a second place to prevent loss of all real estate records.

Delayed Possession

If you do not get possession of the home until after closing, the dynamics of the transaction are slightly different. The seller will not have to be packed and out of the home at closing. Keys and manuals will not be passed and the utilities won't be transferred the day of closing.

Establishing Time and Planning to Move

The best time to begin coordinating the exchange of keys for a delayed possession is at the closing. At the end of the closing proceedings the escrow officer will leave the room to make copies of all paperwork and cut checks. This is an excellent time (the work is done and everybody's happy) for the buyer and seller to exchange phone numbers and email addresses.

The idea is to decide as much as possible the day of closing so the process of exchanging keys is convenient for both parties. If time or scheduling appears to be a problem, have the agents assist. There is usually a great deal of flexibility in a Realtor's schedule.

When Sellers Rent Back the Home from Buyers

Renting back is a term to describe sellers who stay in the home after closing and possession. The sellers pay the buyers—the new homeowners—rent to remain in the property for an agreed-upon amount of time. Renting back usually occurs when the sellers are building a new construction home that isn't ready yet or when they haven't begun looking for their next home. The purchase agreement contains a rent back clause or it can be written on an addendum to the purchase agreement. The rent amount should cover the buyer's new mortgage payment and possibly a bit more to compensate the buyers for their inconvenience.

Coordinating Exchange of Keys, Utilities, Manuals, and Warranties

Buyer and seller should work out a tentative plan at the closing table to determine who will contact the other and when. There will be an agreed upon possession date in the purchase agreement but sellers often vacate homes hours or days ahead of schedule. As the date for possession approaches the buyer and seller can get in touch to decide exactly what time the seller will hand over the keys.

Buyers should avoid having keys left under the welcome mat or on the back porch for security reasons and because it's better to see the home when the seller is still there. If something was broken, or removed from the home that should not have been (unintentionally or otherwise), or the house was not cleaned, the buyer can address the issue immediately. After a seller has left it's incredibly hard to get them to come back and address a problem.

Also decide at the closing table when the seller will contact the utility companies. Make sure the seller knows to do a final reading, not a disconnection of service. The buyer can plan to contact the utilities later that day or the day after the seller has ordered the final reading.

The seller should tell the buyer at closing where additional keys, manuals, and warranties will be left inside the home. The seller also should explain or describe at closing as many nuances or problems in the home as possible so the buyer can prepare or make plans to have work done.

Understanding the Transfer of Warranties

Warranty transfers depend on the item under warranty, the company the warranty is with, and the terms of the warranty plan. For instance, the 10-year warranty on a new construction home will be different from the warranty on a washer and dryer, or termite treatment and mitigation. Many warranties are for a specific period of time. Others do no not transfer when a home is sold or only transfer to the next buyer, not subsequent buyers down the road. Be sure to get all warranty plans and company information from the seller and review the terms carefully.

Home Warranty Plans: Good Investment or Marketing Ploy?

Home warranty plans can be both good investments and marketing ploys of sellers. Plans cost approximately $350 for one year coverage and include a $100 deductible. All mechanical systems and appliances are covered under the plan. Each time an item malfunctions the deductible has to be satisfied. If a home is older, needs repairs, or the appliances and major systems are at the end of their useful life home warranties makes sense. If these conditions do not exist the plan is simply an insurance policy for peace of mind and probably not worth the money.

Searching Online for Short-Term Housing if Applicable

This section applies to those of you who have to make a double move or stay somewhere temporarily until you can move into your new home. Ask your agent for recommendations and consider asking a friend or family member to put you up.

If you are building a new-construction home ask the builder or developer if they will pay for you to stay at an apartment or short-term housing community. Builders and developers often own apartment complexes or other types of housing communities so housing clients is good business practice. If the builder agrees to pay your rent or a portion of it they will pick where you stay. Another option is to ask the builder if you can stay in one of their vacant model homes or spec homes. If the builder is behind schedule on your home and caused you to need short-term housing he should be extremely accommodating.

If you are not able to secure lodging through your personal contacts jump online to search apartments, extended stay hotels, and communities that specialize in short term housing. If you are aware of a short-term housing community (business travelers and short-term corporate transfers need this service), or an apartment complex that specializes in short leases contact them directly by going to their Web site (*www.* plus *the name* plus *.com*).

To research all available listings online, go to a search engine (refer to Chapter 1, "Preparing Yourself: This Is One of the Biggest Investments of Your Life") and search the key words **short term housing**, **housing**, **temporary housing**, **short leases**, **temporary stay**, and **extended stay**.

To view an example of a search for short term housing on Lycos, see Figure 16.3.

Figure 16.3

Search sites such as Lycos often list available short-term housing.

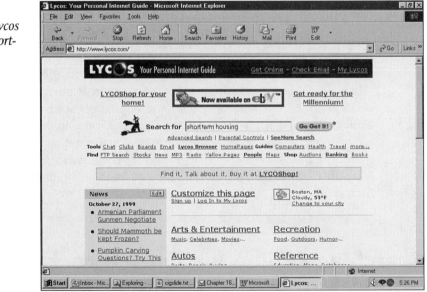

Searching Online for Storage Sites and Home Improvement Companies

Check first with your Realtor, relatives, and friends to see if they have storage space available. If not, to hunt online for information on storage sites go to a search engine (see the list in Chapter 1). Search under **storage**, **storage sites**, **storage facilities**, and **storage companies**.

If you are building a new-construction home ask the builder if you can store your furnishings in one of the builder's unfinished spec homes. Many builders have communities all over town and loads of storage space exists in unfinished homes and spec homes. The big draw back to this is the safety and security of your possessions. Many contractors, laborers, and sub-contractors have access to spec homes and unfinished homes at new-construction home sites.

There are a number of ways to search online for home improvement companies. One Web site to try is www.remodel.com, shown in Figure 16.4. This site gives information and tips on all facets of the remodeling and renovating processes. Besides being user-friendly and easy to navigate, remodel.com lists vendors that specialize in various aspects of home improvement.

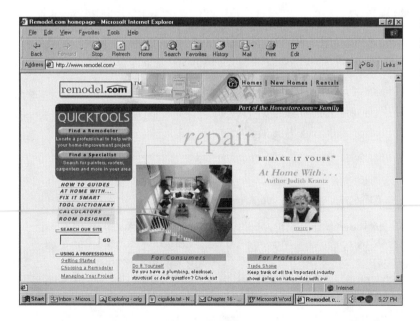

Figure 16.4

remodel.com can put you in touch with home improvement experts in your area.

If you have a favorite home improvement store like Lowes Hardware, Wal-Mart, Sears, Menards, Target, Meijer, and so on you can go directly to their Web site. For instance, to access Wal-Mart's site type www.walmart.com. Most major retailers, home improvement stores, and hardware stores can be visited online.

To generate a list of home improvement companies, contractors, and firms go to a search engine. Key words to search under are **home**, **home improvement**, **repair**, **remodel**, **fix**, and **renovate**. Be sure to check the reputation and credibility of unknown companies or small, fledgling outfits.

Canceling All Applicable Memberships, Subscriptions, and So On

Unfortunately, turning in a change of address card is not the only housekeeping task involved with moving. When you are moving a fair distance, or far away from your old place of residence some memberships in clubs, organizations, and societies will have to be terminated (due to email and the Internet this is changing). Contact these groups in advance so they will know how to correspond with you (you'll have more time for these tasks before the move than after).

Subscriptions also must be canceled or transferred. Newspaper subscriptions, landscaping services, baby sitting and day care services, and any delivery services should be canceled prior to closing if possession occurs at closing, or prior to possession if it is after closing.

Some subscriptions like magazines and books don't have to be canceled, but should be changed to reflect the new address. The Web address of these companies should be on the magazine or product. Visit their Web site to change the address or write the new address on the form the next time you receive a bill.

Obtain a Free Moving Guide

Ask your postal carrier or leave a note in your mail box for your postman to give you the United States Postal Service's Mover's Guide. This guide contains an official mail-forwarding change-of-address form, resources on selecting moving companies, boxes for packing, and address labels and stamps, and tips on making your move as smooth and convenient as possible.

The Least You Need to Know

➤ Visit the U.S. Post Office's Web site to download change of address forms and the Department of Transportation's site to get information on moving companies and moving guides.

➤ Search engines are the best places to generate detailed lists of moving companies, short-term housing communities, storage facilities, and home improvement stores.

➤ When possession occurs at closing the seller must be moved out of the home, have all repairs done, utilities switched over, and be able to deliver all keys, openers, documents, receipts, manuals, and warranties to the buyer at the closing table.

➤ If possession takes place days or weeks after closing the seller and buyer should agree at the closing table on times and dates to exchange keys, and transfer utilities and all documents, manuals, and warranties.

➤ Memberships and subscriptions should be canceled or changed prior to moving.

Part 6
Selling Your Home

To sell or not to sell: That is the question. You must know reasons and circumstances for doing one or the other. In some cases, buying your dream home will be contingent on selling the home you currently own.

After you've decided to place your home on the market, you must decide whether to choose an agent to represent you or to sell your home on your own. What steps must you take to prepare for these endeavors? What secrets can help your home appear more attractive to buyers? How do you decide what the fair market value of your home is, and make sure you get that price? In this section, you'll learn what it takes to become a successful seller.

THAT IS THE QUESTION...

Chapter 17

To Sell or Not to Sell

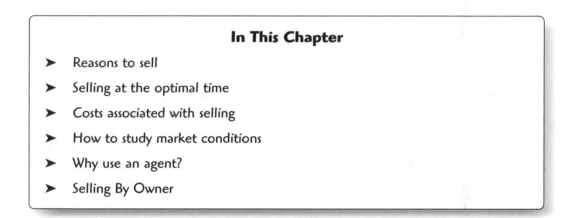

In This Chapter

➤ Reasons to sell

➤ Selling at the optimal time

➤ Costs associated with selling

➤ How to study market conditions

➤ Why use an agent?

➤ Selling By Owner

If you are reading this chapter because you're selling a home, you've probably been through the process of buying a home and know the joys of ownership. However, this might be your first experience selling a home. You're in for an adventure. Selling a home has consistently been rated one of the top five most stressful experiences in people's lives in national surveys. The process can be extremely difficult, confusing, and time-consuming. This chapter arms you with information and knowledge to make the adventure a good one.

Why Sell?

Before you plant that sign in your yard, call a real estate agent, and start mailing out flyers, ask yourself why you want to move. If there is a compelling reason you are most likely justified in your decision. If you are moving just because you want to move, you might be heading for trouble.

Selling for the wrong reasons does nothing but put you through the grind of selling, and then moving your problems to a new address. Selling a home will not fix relationships, make a career better, or improve a person's self-image. These and other reasons are not good reasons to sell. Sometimes redecorating, refurnishing, or building an addition corrects a problem. Make sure you have exhausted all possibilities before you commit to selling your home.

Reasons Owners Must Sell

There are numerous reasons to sell a home. See the following list for some of the more common reasons owners must sell:

➤ Job transfer to different city or state

➤ Family outgrows home because of new baby

➤ House becomes too small because kids are growing up

➤ Commute to work is too long after changing jobs

➤ Divorce

➤ Death

➤ House and yard upkeep is too demanding

➤ Owner is getting married and moving in with spouse

➤ House is too large and children are grown up so retired age couple wants to downsize

➤ Medical problems or age prevent owner from maintaining home

➤ Owner must re-finance mortgage or sell and interest rates are extremely high

In these situations, owners don't have much of a choice. They are forced to sell by factors out of their control.

There are other reasons owners sell their homes. These situations are different because the owner has options. Owners should be careful to ask themselves if their reasons for selling are worth the headaches and aggravation that come with putting your home on the market.

Reasons Owners Want to Sell

These scenarios present options to the homeowner:

➤ Income increases and bigger, more expensive home is now attainable

➤ Area is depreciating, or the homeowner doesn't feel safe anymore

➤ Horrible neighbors

➤ Owner wants different style of home or different amenities in a home

➤ Real estate market is hot in area and owner wants to make money

➤ Owner wants to live in a different area

➤ Owner wants to live closer to work, family, or friends

Not much reflection is needed when an owner must sell their home because of factors beyond his or her control. Owners should take their time to consider whether selling really is the best thing or if they are selling simply because they want to.

Organizing Your Thoughts

A good way to organize your thoughts is to write down all the things you like and don't like about the home. When you're done with that list, make a second list with the things that can be changed from a dislike to a like.

For instance, if you hate the lack of storage space and want a larger garage, can you add on to the current garage or build a two-car garage in the side yard? If you can't stand the crowded, closed-off feel of the kitchen, can you add a skylight, paint the room a light color, build a sun room or breakfast nook off the back that opens the kitchen up, or exercise some combination of these options?

You might find that you can effectively remove some or all the things you don't like about the home. If so, great! You just avoided a major headache and probably saved thousands of dollars. On the other hand, sometimes the likes and dislikes exercise shows you even more clearly that the problems cannot be overcome and you really do need to sell.

Fishing for Buyers or Testing the Market

These terms describe a seller who is not motivated to sell unless the right buyer comes along and writes the perfect offer. Sellers usually list homes at extremely high prices when they're fishing in hopes a buyer will pay it. If a buyer bites on the high price, the seller will try to hook them and reel them in. If no one bites, the seller takes the home off the market.

Another question to ask yourself is what are you trying to gain from selling your home. If you can verbalize this you stand a much better chance of making the right decision.

There is a lot at stake when selling your home. The total expenses for selling are usually around 8% of the sales price. That's $12,000 on a $150,000 house.

Selling your home takes hundreds of hours of time and labor for these things among others:

➤ Preparing the home to be put on the market

➤ Leaving so it can be shown

➤ Maintaining the cleanliness and condition

➤ Working with your agent during the process

➤ Making repairs and improvements

➤ Closing the deal

➤ Finding and buying your next home

➤ Packing and moving

Selling By Owner takes two to three times more work, effort, and time. Make sure selling is the wise decision and you are truly committed before you put yourself through the ordeal.

Timing the Sale Correctly

Timing the sale of a home depends on many factors. Some are within your control, others are not. The key to timing a sale properly is knowing what factors matter and effectively controlling the things you can and not letting the factors out of your control bother you.

There are two things to consider when preparing to sell your home. The right time for you and your family is the first. The right time in the real estate market is the second. Sometimes the right time for you dominates all other considerations and prevents you from considering market conditions completely.

For example, if you are promoted to a much better job earning substantially more money, but have to sell in the middle of the winter during the down time in real estate, do you really care? Odds are most of you will rejoice in the promotion, put your home on the market, and not look back.

If you are able to time the sale correctly in regard to both your personal needs and the best market conditions, good for you. Remember: Some things simply can't be controlled so don't let those factors get you down.

One of the biggest factors when considering your personal needs is coordinating the purchase of your next home with the sale of your current one. Before I discuss how this can be done, let's explore the dynamics of selling at the right time for your personal needs and at the right time to maximize market conditions.

Elements to Consider When Timing a Sale

Sellers must consider three factors when attempting to time a sale correctly. The first is their personal needs and wants (and their family's). The second is the coordination of selling their present home and buying the next one. The third is balancing these personal goals with real estate market conditions to find the peak time to sell.

Your personal needs might include considerations about your job and career. For instance, accountants probably don't want to sell their home and look for a new one during tax season—they'll be too busy. If you're offered an excellent new job but have to move immediately, you might not be ready to sell but will because you don't want to lose the terrific opportunity. If you have health considerations, or your spouse or children would be adversely affected by selling and moving during a particular time of the year, you might have to postpone selling. For example, your wife teaches and can't move until the summer months.

Negotiating Relocation Packages with Your Employer

Selling your current home and buying a new home are factors to consider when deciding to take a promotion or relocate to another city. Immediately research the market you live in and the real estate market you are potentially moving to. If market conditions are average to poor in either place, or in both markets, use this to negotiate a more attractive relocation package for you and your family. This might include your moving costs being paid for, the real estate commissions covered for you when selling, a partial down payment or closing costs paid on your new home, a moving bonus or a guaranteed buyout of your current home if it doesn't sell within three to six months.

There are personal issues that have to be taken into account when selling. Sometimes they can't be avoided. These are factors out of your control that shouldn't upset you or get you down. It's part of living.

Market conditions are sometimes within your control and other times out of our control. No one can control the interest rates and the strength of the economy (except Federal Reserve Board Chairman Alan Greenspan). You can control to some extent when you capitalize on the market conditions. Do you want to sell your home in a seller's market when you'll get more for your home in a shorter time on the market, but pay more when you buy? Do you want to sell during a buyer's market, when you'll get less for your current home, but have additional leverage when you buy the next home and pay less?

Things to Consider

Consider several other factors when selling your home: What time of year is it? What are interest rates? Is the market strong right now? Is it a seller's market or buyer's market? Are there lots of buyers looking for homes or just a few? Is there lots of competition from other seller's homes or not much? Will you have time to find your next home after selling this one? Will market conditions be the same when you buy the next home? Will conditions be better or worse?

These factors can make a huge difference in how fast your home sells, what you sell it for, or if you're even able to sell your home at all. I recommend selling your home at the optimal time and getting as much money as you can in the fastest time period possible. You might pay a bit more for your next home because you are buying in a seller's market, but I like those odds better.

Buyers have lots of control over what they want to buy and where they do it. Sellers have very little to no control over selling. The harder part of the sell and buy combination is selling (unless you're selling in a fantastic area or trying to buy in a down time when few homes are on the market).

Many people can't buy another home unless they sell their current house. Because you have more control over what you buy and can't make someone buy your home, I suggest selling during the peak time and taking your chances on possibly paying more for the next home. The upside is you'll have lots of homes to look at and a larger down payment to put down.

Timing the sale of your present home with the purchase of your next one can be difficult. Is it best to sell first then buy? Should you buy first then sell? Or should you attempt to sell and buy simultaneously? There are advantages and disadvantages to all these scenarios.

The Peak Time to Sell

Peak times can vary slightly from region to region. Late spring and the summer months are generally considered the best time of the year to sell. Many factors influence this with weather being the biggest. Sellers don't like to put their homes on the market during the holidays or in bad weather months. Homes look better in the spring and summer and have less mechanical and structural problems. Parents prefer to move during the summer months when kids are not in school. People are more active and energetic during warm weather months.

Selling First

As I mentioned earlier, selling is the hardest part of the equation. If you sell first, you are past the biggest hurdle, plus you have more leverage when you buy because the offer to purchase won't be contingent upon your current home selling. You also have the added knowledge of knowing what your home sold for, which helps in making financing decisions on the next home.

The downside with this strategy is you might sell your home and have to make a hasty decision to buy a home. You might have to stay in an apartment or with friends or relatives until you can find the right home. Worse still, some people in this situation are rushed into making a poor decision concerning the home they buy. This is a mistake that can haunt you for years to come or cost thousands of dollars.

Buying First

This is the best option if you can afford to buy a second home and still pay for the first. You have the most control in this scenario. You can take your time and make wise decisions on the buying end. You also have peace of mind in knowing you won't be without a place to live or won't have to make a double move into an apartment, and then into a new home.

If you aren't financially able to make two mortgage payments this strategy is much riskier. You could be stuck paying two mortgages for awhile, or be forced into taking a lot less than what your current home is worth.

One way to avoid this is to make the purchase of your next home contingent upon the sale of your present home (a first right contingency offer). This protects you but makes your offer much weaker. Many sellers won't accept an offer like this. Another downside to this is if the seller limits your contingency by showing the home to other buyers. If a second buyer makes an offer on the home that is accepted you have one to two days to sell your home, find financing for the new home, or withdraw your offer.

One final downside to a first right offer is the buyer usually loses leverage by coming in with a contingency offer. To make up for this the buyer might have to make the offer close to or at the seller's asking price. Buyers typically end up paying more when they write first right offers because they have less leverage to negotiate.

This is an incredibly stressful situation that often causes people to sell their home at a drastically reduced price or back out of the deal. Many times they end up buying a home that wasn't as nice as the first one or spend a lot more money.

What's a First-Right Contingency Offer?

A *first-right contingency* is buying a home subject to your current home selling. A time period to do this is set forth (usually 30–90 days) and the seller continues showing the home to other buyers. If another buyer writes an offer that is accepted, the listing agent immediately contacts the buyer's agent and activates the drop-dead clause. The first buyer has 24 to 48 hours to sell their home, find financing to buy the home without selling their home, or withdraw their offer and lose the home.

Buying and Selling Together

Another excellent option is to put your home on the market and begin looking to buy at the same time. Simultaneously buying and selling offers the smallest downside. You could sell your home and already have researched areas and be ready to buy. This scenario allows you to close the sale of your current home, then hours or days later close on your new home. Done the right way you could move directly into your new home without having to do a double move.

If you sell your home too fast you might not have a place to go. On the other hand, if you find and buy your dream home quickly you might struggle to sell your current home. Buying and selling is an ideal way to start but issues frequently come up that change the situation to selling first or buying first.

Time Frames in a First-Right Contingency Offer

The drop-dead clause in a first-right offer is the time frame in which the first buyer can execute the purchase agreement or withdraw it. Buyers can execute the purchase agreement by selling their current home or securing financing for the next home without selling the old one. Buyers should request the longest drop-dead clause possible (48–72 hours) and the longest first-right period possible (60–90 days). Sellers should limit the drop-dead period to 24 to 48 hours and the first-right period to 30 days.

Costs Involved in Selling a Home

When selling a home it's important to not focus solely on what you will make, but also on what you will spend. The money you spend directly affects your net proceeds check. Your expenses are deducted from the gross sales price to give you a net proceeds amount. Good agents understand the way to maximize your net total is limit your expenses while increasing the sales price of your home.

Mandatory Seller Costs

There are some costs that sellers must pay. Mandatory seller costs can vary slightly from city to city but for the most part they remain fixed nation wide. The biggest mandatory cost is the payoff of the current mortgage. Many sellers have mortgages on the home when they sell. This absolutely has to be paid off and is usually the largest expense.

Real estate commissions are typically the next largest expense. Sellers that list their home with a real estate agency pay the entire commission (5% to 7% of the gross sales price depending on local custom).

Sellers also are responsible for the buyer's title insurance policy, or attorney's fees in states that don't use title companies. This is based off the gross sales price (title insurance rates go up as the sales price increases).

Nearly all states pro-rate property taxes through the date of closing so the seller is responsible for these taxes at the time of closing.

There are a few smaller closing costs sellers must pay. There are the courier fee to overnight the loan payoff (at $25), attorney fees to review the closing documents (at

$50), the release of the current mortgage (at $10), and roughly $350–700 in additional closing fees if the buyer uses FHA or VA financing to buy the home.

Repair costs are sometimes mandatory if they are called for on an appraisal or if they violate health codes. The final mandatory seller cost is moving expenses.

Paying Agents Consulting Fees at a Reduced Commission Rate

When money is extremely tight but selling your home without an agent will be difficult or you don't want to sell yourself, consider paying a consulting fee to an agent. For a commission 2–5% of the gross sales price the agent can manage the transaction for you and the buyer. Commissions should be based on how much time, work, advertising, and negotiating the agent does. You save money but still get the services of a professional real estate agent.

Optional Seller Costs

Optional seller costs are items the seller does not have to pay, but might choose to pay to entice a buyer. Repairs made to the home to make it more attractive for buyers are optional seller costs. Repairs made during the home inspection process also can be optional. Sellers can always lower the price of the home instead of repairing or replacing items. Home warranty plans may be purchased by the seller as a marketing tool, or requested by the buyer for peace of mind, but they aren't mandatory.

Many closing costs like the settlement fee paid to the title company and the survey are optional, although the buyer typically pays them. Sellers might pay some initial inspection fees like the termite or water reports.

Any or all the buyer's closing costs can be paid by the seller if he elects to do so. For a complete breakdown of buyer's closing costs, refer to Chapter 2, "Can You Afford Your Dream of Owning?"

Researching Market Prices and Conditions

Research is just as important when selling a home as when buying. The asking price of a home is the number one factor that determines success or failure when selling. Location plays the biggest role in determining price, but how do you know what price to ask? How do you compare your home to the other homes in your area?

FHA and VA Mandated Costs Sellers Must Pay

Per government guidelines, sellers must pay the document preparation fee (at $150), the underwriting fee (at $150), and the tax service fee (at $75) for buyers obtaining an FHA mortgage. Fee prices vary from lender to lender. Sellers must pay these same fees plus the settlement fee to close the transaction (at $300) and the initial termite inspection (at $75) for buyers obtaining a VA mortgage. These fees are *in addition to* any money towards closing costs the seller agrees to pay the buyer.

The answer is research. Your agent should research as many comparable homes as can be found in the multiple listings service. All the data needed to accurately price homes is available. Finding the data and interpreting it is a little bit trickier.

What if you aren't using an agent? What if your agent isn't competent or isn't doing his job the right way and you want to do research on your own? You can get online and access much of the same information that Realtors do (the MLS is by far the most detailed, thorough compilation of sales price statistics).

Before we dive into Web sites that enable you to research prices and market conditions, let's discuss what factors are most relevant:

Comparable Sales   Sale prices of related homes (similar in number of bedrooms, baths, square footage, garages, and so on) in the immediate vicinity or same locale in the past year.

Area Conditions   Selling statistics for homes in the immediate vicinity. Statistics include the average days on the market, percentage off list price homes sold for (a home listed at $100,000 that sold for $97,000 went for 97% of the list price), average and highest list price and average and highest sales price in the area, number of homes currently for sale, number of homes sold in the last year, and the number of homes that did not sell or were withdrawn.

Current Trends   What time of year is it? Is it a seller's market or a buyer's market? What are the appreciation rates for the area? Are there any new factors influencing the area in a positive or negative way (grammar school being built, crowded strip mall going in, run-down apartments being leveled)?

All the statistics in the world are helpful but if you don't know how to interpret the data, you might be in for a long, painful selling experience (this is where Realtors are extremely valuable).

For instance, if your home has the same number of bedrooms and baths as ten other homes that have sold in your area are they similar in price? You have to take a closer look at the amenities to determine value. What if some of these other homes had fireplaces, larger lots, better locations in the subdivision, much larger square-footage dimensions, basements, a two-car garage or an attached garage, extra storage space, vaulted ceilings, brick exteriors, gas heat, neutral decors, were in better condition, and sold during the peak summer months?

You might mistakenly believe your home will sell for a comparable price as these other homes when in fact your home is worth $10,000 to $25,000 less. If you don't find this out until your home has sat on the market for six months, you will really be inconvenienced. On the other hand, if your home has these amenities and other homes don't, you want to be sure you don't sell the house for less than it's worth just because other homes in the neighborhood sold for a given price.

This is an exaggerated example, but the point is subdivisions and locales can have huge swings in value. The factors causing these swings can differ from subdivision to subdivision, or area to area. Sometimes the relevant factor is being on a lake, other times it's having a finished basement or a two-story home. Understanding the nuances of your area and interpreting the statistical data is vital to picking an asking price that is accurate and reasonable, yet still gives you the opportunity to make a healthy profit from your investment.

Tracking Sales in Your Area

Other than hiring a strong Realtor, the best way to become competent about your area and learn how to interpret data is to track sales over a period of time. If you haven't done it in the past and are now preparing to sell your home, gather as much data as you can from the past two to three years. Look for trends or patterns in sale prices. Study any upward or downward swings. Try to locate common factors in the highest selling homes and the lowest. After you identify common themes you will have a better understanding of what drives the market in your area.

Sites to Research Sales Prices and Market Conditions

Whether you use a Realtor to sell your home or not, your first task should be researching sales prices to figure out an estimate of what your home is worth. Some agents try to win sellers over with inflated listing prices just to get the business. Know the range of value your home falls within before you start contacting agents. Sites to search include:

www.dataquick.com

www.experian.com

www.homeadvisor.msn.com

www.iown.com

www.realtor.com

DataQuick, shown in Figure 17.1, is a good place to start your research. For $10, you can get as many as 30 comparable sales in your area. Type your address and watch as numerous comps are generated.

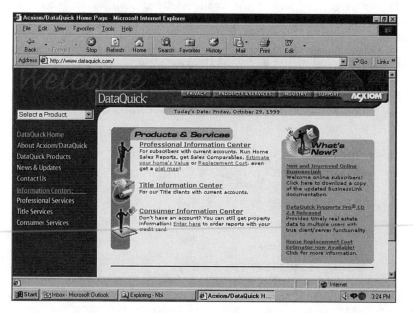

Figure 17.1

DataQuick can provide data on up to 30 comparable homes in your area for a $10 fee.

If DataQuick doesn't have your address in its database, type your next door neighbor's address or an address in your subdivision (make sure the home is comparable in age, size, bedrooms, baths, and so on).

If DataQuick doesn't work, go to www.experian.com. Click **real estate reports** in the left column. For a $10 fee, Experian will generate five comparable sales in side-by-side format for convenient comparison. Once again, make sure the homes are as similar as possible in age, size, bedrooms, and baths.

Trends in home sales can change suddenly or be all over the map. Research current listings to check how asking prices are different or the same as the sold prices you found.

The best Web sites to check current market conditions are www.iown.com (has the most extensive demographic data), www.realtor.com (has the largest number of listings and is tied to MLS systems around the U.S.), and homeadvisor.msn.com (the easiest site to navigate and has great mapping function).

Remember, the best way to do research and become an expert in your area is to list your home with a Realtor and gain the knowledge and information they have spent years gathering and testing.

Reasons to Use an Agent

Exposure to the multiple listing service is one of the premier reasons to list your home with an agent. Eighty percent of buyers use Realtors and the MLS system to find their home. If your home is not listed with a real estate office, these buyers will never know it's for sale.

Another commonly cited reason sellers use agents is the expertise, knowledge, and competence of real estate professionals. Earlier in this chapter I mentioned the problems that arise when sellers don't know how to interpret data regarding home sales. Activities sellers might struggle with are basic, everyday tasks Realtors do in their sleep.

Check This Out

Being A Realtor Isn't Easy

Only one out of every five people that gets into real estate sales stays in the business longer than five years. Agents are independent contractors and do not get health insurance benefits, life insurance, or a retirement/pension plan. Because they are independent contractors, they have to pay an additional self-employment tax on their income taxes. Agents do not earn a salary; their pay is 100% commission based. They get paid only when deals close.

If a real estate agent came to your office and tried to do your job, how successful would they be? The opposite is also true. Many people think they can sell their own home, but find out the hard way the process is much more complicated and difficult than it appears. Good agents make things seem simple or easy. Don't be fooled by this. Selling a home is continually listed as one of the top five most difficult and stressful experiences in life for a reason.

You're Hiring Expertise

Agents get paid to know the ins and outs of the business. Both the big things and the little things must be done for a transaction to be successful and for it to be a good experience for you. The big tasks make the deal get done; the little ones give you a good or bad feeling about the transaction. Selling without an agent puts you behind the eight ball in both these areas before you even start the process.

Another reason to use an agent is the time, work, and trouble it saves you. Realtors can usually accomplish things in half to one third the time sellers could. If your time is valuable and better spent with family and friends, or working on your career or other projects, an agent can protect your time and still help accomplish your goal of selling the home.

Good agents earn their commissions by pricing homes accurately and negotiating the terms of the sale. Thousands of dollars can be made or lost by pricing a home correctly or incorrectly. Negotiating is one of the most important functions agents do. Sometimes deals get done simply because agents negotiate well.

Unfortunately, the opposite also can be true. Most people's largest investment is their home. Having a professional negotiator work for you can make a world of difference.

Often sellers make thousands of dollars more on a sale because of their agent's advice or negotiating skills.

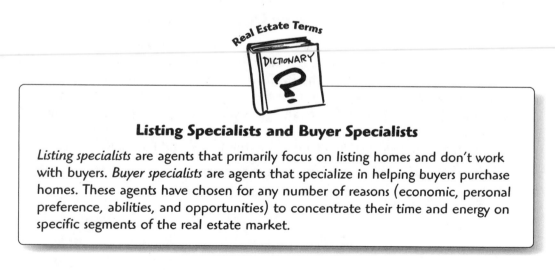

Listing Specialists and Buyer Specialists

Listing specialists are agents that primarily focus on listing homes and don't work with buyers. *Buyer specialists* are agents that specialize in helping buyers purchase homes. These agents have chosen for any number of reasons (economic, personal preference, abilities, and opportunities) to concentrate their time and energy on specific segments of the real estate market.

Realtors provide efficiency and safety from litigation. Many sellers are not aware of or don't understand contract law or the numerous environmental and ecological laws that must be followed. Agents protect sellers from lawsuits and promote smoother, more convenient transactions.

Many buyers won't look at a For Sale By Owner home. They feel it is unfair for a seller to ask them to pay a real estate commission (sellers pay commissions). By refusing to pay the buyers agent's commission, buyers feel the seller is denying them representation. Listing your home with a real estate office will give you the widest possible exposure to all buyers.

Agents are valuable because of the knowledge and counsel they provide in all areas of real estate. Agents handle questions on everything from income tax and financing issues to decorating and yard maintenance. The contacts agents have and their team of experts in related fields are invaluable. Need an inspector, a plumber, electrician, or roofer? Agents are typically the best source for information on tradesmen and real estate related professionals because they face these problems time and again.

Reasons to Sell By Owner

Far and away the number one reason to sell a home without using an agent is to save money. Sellers can save $6,000 to $7,000 in commissions on a $100,000 home sale. Saving that kind of money is tempting to just about anyone.

For Sale By Owners Trial Run

If you think you might be qualified to sell By Owner or want to take a stab at saving the commission money, try selling By Owner for two or three weeks. If you get serious interest, prolong the By Owner period for another few weeks. If you get little interest or get fed up with the process contact a broker and list your home. Be aware of time frames and goals when doing this. You don't want to try to sell By Owner too long and have interest rates shoot up, the time of year change, or put yourself in a bind selling this home, and buying the next one.

Some sellers want complete autonomy and control. They don't want to deal with another person's opinion, personality, or viewpoint. They could have had a bad experience in the past with agents and don't want to work with one. These people choose to sell themselves because they don't want input or interference from an agent. This type of individual might be the hardest person for a buyer to work with. No matter how great a home is, sellers need buyers. Buyers can always buy another house. Sellers have only one home that they must sell.

Another reason to sell By Owner is if the seller already has a buyer for the home. Maybe a relative, friend, or co-worker who has previously seen the home many times has expressed serious interest in the home. If the person gets approved for a mortgage and wants to write an offer, there isn't a reason for the seller to hire an agent to market the home. If both seller and buyer feel comfortable, they should proceed forward.

Occasionally, sellers or buyers in this situation will want a Realtor to oversee or manage the transaction (maybe pull comparable sales to verify value or help write and negotiate the terms of the contract) for a small percentage of the gross sales price or a flat fee. Many of the duties an agent performs are not needed if a seller has already secured a buyer. In this situation it makes sense for the owner to sell the home himself or pay a small fee to have an agent handle the details of the transaction.

Full Commission Rates and Discounted Rates

Agents often get asked to cut their commission rate or to manage a FSBO transaction for 2% or 3% of the sales price. Some agents will do this, others won't. Don't get upset at the agent. They might be bound by company policy that doesn't allow them to do this. They might take enormous pride in their work. They might be extremely successful and busy and don't want to take on a partial deal at a discounted commission. They might be that good of a negotiator they don't feel they need to take less money. To provide the service they normally give they might require the full rate. Communicate openly with the agent and see if this person really is the right agent for you. If an agent is willing to give up her own paycheck so easily, what will she do if your money is on the line?

Sellers in or around the real estate business or persons in related fields might have the knowledge, ability, and access to information to sell a home themselves. Once again, the reason to do this comes back to saving money (nearly all reasons to sell FSBO do).

Related fields where people might have the background and qualifications to sell By Owner are attorneys, bankers, accountants, mortgage company employees, title company employees, real estate teachers or professors, and real estate investors. If a close family member is in real estate sales you might be able to sell your home yourself and get excellent advice for free.

Remember, weigh the pros and cons of saving money against the time and work you will commit when selling a home yourself. It's not coincidence or fate there are so many Realtors. Selling a home is hard, complex work.

Appraiser's Role in Determining Value

Another means of determining value is the appraisal. Real estate appraisals figure value of an individual home by comparing it to similar sold homes in the same geographic area. Appraisals done before a seller puts his home on the market do not guarantee that the home will sell for that amount. Appraised values are a "snapshot" in time while market value is a moving, ever-changing value that reflects an area of homes, not an individual home. Realtors have knowledge of both appraised values and market values and therefore add a key element to the selling process.

The Least You Need to Know

➤ Have legitimate, well-thought-out reasons for selling your home. The process is too expensive, difficult, and time consuming to enter into lightly.

➤ Timing the sale correctly involves balancing your personal needs of work, family, and buying your next home against ever changing market conditions in real estate. Control the factors you can and don't let those out of your control bother you.

➤ There are roughly four expensive mandatory seller costs when selling a home (payoff of current mortgage, real estate commissions, property taxes, and title insurance) and a few minor ones. Optional seller costs could include any of the buyer's closing costs and home repairs.

➤ Research market conditions and the sale prices of homes in your area as thoroughly as possible. Interpreting the statistical data accurately is vital.

➤ DataQuick.com and Experian.com are Web sites that offer comparable sales information for a nominal fee. iOwn, REALTOR.COM, and HomeAdvisor are the best sites to review current market trends and listings.

➤ Some of the many and varied reasons to use a Realtor are exposure to the MLS system, expertise and competence, research and legwork, negotiating skills that make sellers more money, convenience, safety, protection from lawsuits, full exposure to all buyers, and the team of experts in related fields agents bring with them.

➤ Reasons not to use an agent are saving money, self-control, and autonomy, (owner already has a qualified buyer, and owner is in related field and is qualified to sell By Owner thereby saving commission money).

Chapter 18

Getting the House Ready to Sell

In This Chapter

➤ How much to repair

➤ Locating receipts and records of improvement

➤ Cleaning and getting rid of clutter

➤ Stage the home to show

➤ Pros and cons of home warranties

Now that you've decided to sell your home, you have to get it ready to go on the market. Homes that are in excellent condition might only need to be cleaned. Most homes will need a little more attention. Carpets need shampooing? Is the home in need of some touch up painting? Do settlement cracks in the ceiling or walls look a lot worse than they really are?

The condition of your home directly affects your asking price. Should you fix things or ask less money for your home? In addition to making repairs and cleaning, do you have a log of all the repairs and improvements done to the home? Buyers will want to know as much about the home as you can provide. This chapter explains how to prepare your home to be shown and helps you get the most money possible.

Fixing a Lot or Just a Little

There are two schools of thought concerning making repairs before selling a home. The first school believes homes should be completely fixed up and made to look as sharp as possible. All repairs should be done and no money should be spared in making the home's condition near perfect.

The advantage in doing this is the message sent to buyers. Sellers with homes in near perfect condition do not have to come off their listing price much or at all. Buyers love homes in move-in condition where unpacking is the only work they have to do. Homes in top-notch condition usually sell extremely fast if they are priced reasonably. Sellers that spend a lot of money to sell are marketing their homes as the best of the best and position themselves to garner top dollar for their home.

The disadvantages to spending a ton of money to sell should be considered. You won't get to enjoy the improvements you made. The awesome tile floor you had installed or the new thermal windows won't lower your energy bills because you're moving out.

Sellers also can over-improve a home and not reap the financial benefits of the repairs. The value of your home will be determined by the homes in your neighborhood. If you improve your home too much, the area will drag your home down in value. No matter how terrific your repairs or improvements are, buyers decide how much the improvements are worth and what the value of your home is.

Sellers usually only get one-third to half their money back in appreciation when they make an improvement (buyers expect items in the home to be functional and work properly). Sellers often struggle with this but buyers typically attach a vastly different price tag to a repair job than what sellers actually paid. That's why it's important to like the improvement yourself and live in the home long enough to enjoy it.

Another problem can occur if buyers don't like the changes that you made. You might love that new tile floor, but buyers might hate it. Result: you've spent $7,000 and made your home less attractive. Many sellers have spent lots of money to make their home more marketable but actually lost buyers because of their repair decisions.

Always Go with Neutral Colors

When making repairs to your home before selling, always go with white or neutral colors and designs. Don't impose your taste and preferences on prospective buyers. When carpeting, painting, or papering, select light, neutral colors. Buyers will add their personal touches to infuse warmth and character to the home (if they even want warmth). Neutral colors enable buyers to be more open-minded about homes and are easier to change if buyers choose to.

The second school of thought when making repairs before selling is to spend money wisely only on items that really need attention. Sellers often do repairs themselves. Work is done correctly but not necessarily to the highest standard or at the highest expense. Make your money go as far as possible is the mindset of these sellers.

Making Money Go a Long Way

Cabinets and floors can be made to shine for very little money. Painting or re-finishing cabinets in the kitchen and bathrooms can brighten the rooms. New knobs also dress up cabinets. Carpets can be steamed or shampooed to look like new. Hardwoods can be buffed to dazzle potential buyers. There's nothing like the smell of fresh paint, floor wax, and lemony-clean counters and sinks to make a house seem like new.

The advantage with this theory is you won't over-improve the home for your neighborhood and lose money. Because you aren't going to live in the home, why make costly improvements? Sellers usually only get 30% to 50% of their repair investment back so why spend a lot? Fixing just a little is a much more conservative approach. Sellers do not open themselves up to the possibility of flushing considerable repair money down the drain.

The disadvantage of not spending as much is the home will not look as dazzling. If you are competing against similar homes in your area condition is often the determining factor in which home sells first. Spending less money might put a tiny bit of doubt in buyers' minds as to the condition and quality of your home.

When deciding whether to spend a lot of money to prepare a home to be sold or just a little, take these factors into consideration. What is the price range your home falls in and what will buyers expect in the way of condition and quality? What is your reason for selling and how motivated are you to sell? Do you plan to put a price tag on your home that is at the high end of the market in your area, or in the middle or at the low end?

After answering these questions you should have a better idea how much or little needs to be repaired. I usually recommend sellers spend less money to make repairs if they can help it. Buyers are fickle. There is no guarantee expensive repairs or improvements will make a home more valuable. Sellers might love the finished look but buyers many times are not willing to pay for the improvements sellers made.

Spend money carefully and wisely when preparing your home to be sold. Consult your Realtor before committing to costly repairs. You can reduce your list price and not make any repairs if you choose to. Leaving the expensive improvements up to the future owner is usually a safer, more prudent route to take. Plus, that's less painful than making your home look better than it's ever looked and having to move out.

Initial Inspections

There are two ways to do initial inspections. You can do it yourself or you can hire a professional home inspector to do a complete inspection. Before we walk through the personal inspection process let me explain why I don't usually recommend having an inspection done prior to selling a home.

If a seller has lived in a home for any length of time, she usually will become acquainted with the deficient items and little nuances of the home. Maybe the water pressure in the shower is great for hot water but lousy for cold water. A door might swell during the summer and be hard to lock. Most sellers know their homes fairly well to extremely well.

Disadvantages of Pre-inspections

Paying for an inspection up front might be a poor use of $250–500. Ninety-nine percent of all buyers who plan to occupy a home as their primary residence will have a home inspection. As long as the seller knows there isn't a long laundry list of defective problems, you might consider saving the money and waiting for the buyer's home inspection to see what comes up. For many sellers living in a home and doing a personal inspection is sufficient in determining the condition of the home.

Most Common Inspection Deal Breakers

The most common items responsible for deals falling apart are termites and wood damage caused by termites, moisture in basements and crawl space, heating and cooling defects, bad roofs, faulty wiring, and plumbing defects.

Buyers will not use your inspection report. Most will want to have their own inspection done by an inspector of their choice. What if your professional inspection misses something the buyer's inspector finds? You'll feel extremely put out for paying for an inspection that didn't find all the problems in the home.

Advantages of a Pre-inspection

The reason to have a professional inspection done is to be extra prepared. You might find problems you didn't know existed before marketing your home to buyers. Sometimes buyers see a list of problems on an inspection report and freak out. You can prevent this from happening by fixing the problems ahead of time. You might be able to sell your home for more money by fixing items up front.

Personally inspecting your home requires you to detach yourself and be as unbiased as possible. Walk outside the home to the street and tell yourself you are going to put yourself in the average buyer's position. Turn around and view your home as objectively as you can. Is everything in place? Does the home look crisp and clean? Are the roof, gutters, and shutters in order? Is paint chipping or peeling off? Does the yard or fence need attention?

First Impressions Are Vital

Buyers usually rule homes out within the first two to three minutes. Their initial impression is extremely hard to change. If they don't like the outside of a home or the first few things they see on the inside, it's nearly impossible to change their minds. Make the home's exterior appealing and everything they see the first minute or two inside the home attractive as well. The condition and décor of the front door, the entry, and the first room in the home has to be strong or buyers might be lost for good.

Take notes on the outside of the home, then proceed inside. Start at the front door just as a buyer would and be as critical as possible. Does the lock on the front door work properly? Is the door in good condition or need repair? What are the sight lines from the entry? Do walls, floors, and ceilings look good in the first room as well as the sight lines into other rooms?

Within the first two to three minutes buyers will have decided if they like your home or if it doesn't work for them. They might not know why it doesn't work, but they'll say it doesn't feel right, it isn't homey, or I can't see myself here. Attract the buyer's attention in those first few minutes and their attitude and outlook will be positive as they tour the rest of the home. Lose their attention or turn them off and the showing has effectively ended even though they might be in the home another twenty or thirty minutes. The first few things buyers see must look great. If buyers get negative thoughts in their heads at the beginning, it is extremely difficult to change their minds the rest of a showing.

Continue walking through your home as if you were a picky buyer. Do rooms look small and cluttered? Does wallpaper or paint need touching up? Does the condition and décor make your home more valuable or less valuable? Use the following list to examine every room in your home while performing a personal inspection:

Examine all flooring   Does carpet need cleaned or repaired? Is tile cracked or missing? Is vinyl flooring deteriorating or is the design a detriment to selling? Are baseboards and molding clean and in good condition?

Examine walls and ceilings   Are paint and wallpaper in good condition? Are there settlement cracks or nail holes that need fixing? Are colors neutral or are they busy and offensive? Would repainting or papering improve the look considerably or make the home appear bigger and cleaner?

Inspect the kitchen   Is the kitchen updated? Do the colors make the kitchen appear light, bright, and big, or smaller and darker? Do all the appliances work? Is the flooring clean, in good condition, and a relatively neutral style? Is the plumbing functional in the sink, garbage disposal, and dishwasher?

Examine the bathrooms   Does the toilet flush properly, the sink drain correctly, and the shower and tub work? Is the water pressure adequate? Are there any leaks? Is the flooring clean and in good condition? Do the walls and ceilings need repairs, painting, or papering? Is the bathroom updated? Are the colors neutral? Is the room cluttered? Are there any personal possessions that might offend or turn off buyers?

Favorite Rooms by Gender

Blanket statements about gender preferences cannot and should not be made, but some general impressions follow. Women typically examine the kitchen, bathrooms, and master bedroom most closely because they spend more time there and because of hygiene and decorating issues. Men typically are more concerned with the family room (TV room), the garage, and the location and resale potential. Unquestionably, these areas of the home are most important regardless which gender prefers them.

Examine all doors and windows   Do they open and shut properly? Do all locks work? Do doors and windows shut and seal correctly? Do doors or windows need cleaning and painting? Repair doors and windows that don't function properly or are in disrepair and look shoddy visually.

Inspect the basement, garage, and closets   Check basement and garage for moisture, leaks, and stains. Clean out all three areas, organize and throw away all trash, debris, or junk. Sellers can win extra points with buyers for keeping these three areas clean and well maintained. Make sure basement and garages are sealed properly and secured so intruders and weather elements can't get in. Make these areas as tidy, neat, and clean as possible.

Marketing Yourself as Mr. and Mrs. Clean

Sellers should prepare their homes to be shown as if they are the cleanest home-owners on the block (whether they are or will be just for two months). Buyers want to believe they are buying the cleanest, best-maintained home around. Even if they don't plan on keeping it up the same way they prefer to start there. Marketing your home in this fashion will help you sell to all the super-clean buyers out there and the not-so-conscientious buyers. You give yourself a better chance of selling for more money and faster when your home is in this condition.

Inspect the roof, gutters, exterior housing, and yard   Are the roof, gutters, shutters, siding, and paint in good condition? Are there signs of deterioration, moisture, or wood rot? Does the exterior housing, fence, or shed need painting? Is the landscaping acceptable or does it detract from the home?

Examine heating, cooling, and electrical systems   Are they in proper working condition? Are there any defects? Are energy bills reasonable or extremely high? Do all outlets work? Is all wiring done to code or was it sloppily gerry-rigged?

Locating Records and Proof of Improvements

Buyers want to know as much as they can about a home that they are considering

Defining Move-in Condition

Move-in condition means a home is in immaculate condition. All the buyer has to do is bring in and unpack his belongings. Homes in this condition do not require any repairs, and the décor also is tasteful and neutral enough that changes should not have to be made for a while.

buying. How long has the seller lived there? Why is the seller moving? What improvements and repairs did the current owner make? What additional repairs have been made in the last five to ten years if the seller has only lived in the home a short time? How old are the appliances, furnace, air conditioner, roof, and water heater? How often was the furnace and air conditioning unit serviced and cleaned? If the home is on a well and septic system, how often was the well pumped and how old is the finger system?

Locate all records pertaining to the home dating back to the day you closed on the home. Use these records and receipts to market the home. If you have maintained the home exceptionally well, show this to potential buyers not only with the condition of the home, but with the maintenance log.

Don't be afraid to show buyers all the repairs and improvements. They won't think the home is plagued by lots of problems. They'll think you are a responsible homeowner who kept up the home extremely well. All homes have problems, deficiencies, and flaws. Not all homeowners fix them.

Information Requested by Buyers

When you're showing a house, be prepared to provide the following information:

➤ All maintenance records detailing what work was done, when it was done, who did it, and the cost of the job.

➤ Yearly utility bill averages and month-by-month costs.

➤ Warranties on appliances, work done on the home (such as roof, garage door, or termite repairs), and records of a home warranty plan if applicable.

➤ All manuals and service guides to operating equipment, appliances, or mechanical systems.

➤ Property tax information on rates and exemptions.

Making Repairs

After you have thoroughly inspected your home, it's time to objectively determine what repairs need to be made. Prioritize the items by importance and cost. You might want to fix all the items on your list but can only fix a few because of time and money constraints. Decide up front if you want to spend a lot of money on repairs or just a little. Don't get half way through projects then call it off.

Try to do all the jobs that only require time or inexpensive repairs. Start at the top of your priority list and work your way down. Ask yourself if each item is feasible to repair. Maybe there is one large item that has to be repaired or the home simply won't sell. Fix that item and then address a lot of the smaller issues.

Online Repair Resources

www.remodel.com is a great site to visit for making home repairs and renovations. Most major home improvement stores advertise online now. Contact hardware stores, retailers, and contractors online by typing www. plus the store name plus .com. Search engines also can be surfed for information about online repair sites and companies.

Know all your options. If your roof needs major repairs or is completely shot, consider fixing the roof, putting on a new roof, or making no repairs but lowering your price to reflect the bad roof. Get two or three estimates for a new roof or a roof repair and lower your asking price accordingly (make sure buyers are aware you did this).

If you are making repairs yourself, proceed through your priority list. If the work is going well, keep doing additional items. If you grow to hate the work you're doing and/or the home, stop making repairs. Consider hiring someone else to do the work. Selling a home is stressful enough. Don't make yourself miserable or ruin your personal life preparing the home to be sold. You can always adjust your asking price down if you don't want to make additional repairs.

If you hire people to do work for you ask your agent and family members, trusted friends, and co-workers for referrals for contractors or handymen. Get two or three bids on projects if time allows. Be careful not to spend too much money on up front repairs.

Make sure you are capable of doing repair work yourself. Most people can paint, fix a leaky faucet, and clean. Conversely, most people can't fix complicated electrical problems or repair a furnace. Know what you can do and what you can't. Sellers sometimes take on projects too big or dangerous. You might cost yourself lots of money. Even worse, you might endanger yourself or make your home a health hazard.

> **Using Repairs to Market Your Home**
>
> Have all repairs done in a timely manner. If you're doing repairs, set time goals and meet them. If you're hiring professionals to do work, set the appointments up and get starting and completion dates in writing. Market conditions can change rapidly. You don't want to miss the optimal time to sell because you didn't have the house ready to show.

Cleaning

Many people don't like to clean. Unfortunately, it is a vital part of the selling process. Unless you are willing to lower your asking price considerably, you will have to thoroughly clean your home. You can do it yourself or you can hire a professional cleaning service to do the initial thorough cleaning (this is money well spent).

A lot depends on how you live year round. People that clean regularly and keep a home in immaculate condition will not have much to do. The rest of us have our work cut out for us.

> **Dressing Up a Home's Exterior**
>
> Splash a lot of color on the outside of your home with flowers, plants, and a paint job. Shutters, doors, and fences can be touched up with paint or completely changed. Keep the driveway, walk ways, steps, porches, and front door in sharp condition.

The first cleaning should be as thorough, detailed, and intensive as possible. Do this cleaning *after* all repairs have been made and all clutter is removed (see "Eliminate Clutter" later in this chapter) so you're not cleaning the same areas twice or cleaning unnecessarily. This might be the time to consider using professional cleaners. Little things like sparkling sinks, toilets, bathtubs, floors, windows, appliances, and lights go a long way. If buyers see an ultra clean home they automatically perceive the home to be extremely well cared for and maintained.

Clean the outside and the high traffic areas inside first. Once again, first impressions are crucial. Make sure sight lines when buyers first walk into the home and each subsequent room are extremely clean. Work your way from the front of the house to the back. Finish with the rarely seen spots and the hard to see areas.

After you have given the home a deep cleaning, it will be much easier to maintain the clean, crisp look as the weeks progress and you show the home. Maintaining a super clean home is one of the biggest inconveniences of selling a home. The faster you can sell your home the less cleaning and maintenance you will have to do.

Focusing on Kitchen and Bathrooms

There's an old real estate saying concerning men and women's roles in house hunting. The saying is "the woman decides which house to buy and the man pays for it." This might or might not be true. What is factual are the rooms that buyers focus on when they tour homes.

Two of the most important rooms, particularly to women, are the kitchen and bathrooms. These also happen to be the two areas that are extremely expensive to renovate. Typically women spend more time than men in these two rooms, so they are much more critical of the condition and décor.

These also are areas of great importance because of the functions they serve. These are the most important areas to keep clean. If you were to only clean two rooms in your home, make them the kitchen and baths.

All homes have a kitchen and bathroom. Other than a place to sleep, no other area of the house is an absolute necessity. If your kitchen and bathrooms are clean, a positive tone will be set for the rest of the home.

Which Appliances Stay and Which Ones Go

The seller decides which appliances remain in the home and which will be taken. The number of appliances in the seller's next home usually dictates what appliances stay and leave. Normally the refrigerator and oven stay in the home and the seller takes the washer and dryer. Every situation is different though. Buyers can offer more money in the purchase agreement and ask for all the appliances to stay. A new washer and dryer will cost around $800. Refrigerators and ovens each start around $500 and go as high as you want.

Start with the kitchen and focus on the big things first: flooring, appliances, counter-tops, and sinks. Work your way to the pantry, windows, and furnishings next. Make the kitchen immaculate. There is a reason for the saying "these floors are so clean you could eat off them." People like to eat in clean, tidy environments. If your kitchen isn't clean, you might lose some buyers immediately. If it is ultra clean, you will turn buyer's heads and attract their attention.

Bathrooms also should be spotless. This is the area of the home where people clean up so it stands to reason buyers expect this room to shine. Start with the sink, mirror, toilet, and bathtub. Make these areas sparkle. Hit the floor, fixtures, and walls next. Try to clean the kitchen and bathrooms to meet the standards of the cleanest, pickiest buyer. If you accomplish this, imagine how much everyone else will like it.

Organizing Closets and Garage

Sellers can make a home stand out to buyers by giving the closets and garage thorough cleanings. Closets should be organized so they look as big as possible. Buyers understand these areas are designed for storage. Just make sure items aren't tossed randomly in closets with no rhyme or reason. Give everything a place. Stack, store, and organize so shelves appear structured and uniform.

Empty junk and debris from closets. Store the items in the basement or attic, or consider renting a storage facility for a few months. Closets look much bigger when they are organized and junk is removed from them.

Garages are expected to be dirtier than the interior of houses but they should still be organized. Hang items on the walls or from the rafters. Store excessive equipment in sheds or attics. Utilize space effectively and give work benches and shelves a nice cleaning. Put stuff away or in proper places. Whether you live this way or not doesn't matter. Give the appearance that you do.

Closets and garages are down the list of priority areas to clean but when a buyer has to decide between two evenly matched homes, cleanliness and organization in these areas can be extremely important. Don't give off the impression your home has little or inadequate storage space when really you just didn't organize the right way.

Master Bedroom and TV Room

The other two rooms in a home that are extremely important are the master bedroom and the TV room (family room, recreation room, and so on). These living areas are inhabited the majority of the time owners are home. Buyers are wise to view these rooms critically. Comfort and cleanliness in these areas is essential.

The master bedroom should be a sanctuary of comfort, privacy, and harmony. Clean this bedroom better than all the others. Make sure the flooring and walls glow. Dust furniture and always have the bed made. Even though your personal furnishings won't stay in the home, failure to clean these items detracts from the overall perception of cleanliness.

The TV room is generally the room where people spend their time relaxing, entertaining, and unwinding. This room also has to be as clean as possible. Give the flooring, walls, and ceilings a thorough cleaning. Get rid of all cobwebs, dust, and lint. Clean light fixtures, high traffic areas, and molding or trim. Furniture in this room should be as presentable as possible (don't buy new furniture to sell your home).

Handling Pet and Smoke Odor

Many buyers rule out homes because of pet or smoke odors. Sellers shouldn't take it personally. Sellers need to understand the odor is probably much stronger and more prevalent than they realize—they're used to it. Remove the smells by shampooing carpet, furniture, and curtains. Wipe down walls and floors thoroughly to remove stains and odor. Open windows, utilize ceiling fans and candles, potpourri, and fresh-smelling cleaning materials. Regulate the smell to one or two locations in the home or keep it outside. Smell is a huge determining factor. Don't let it prevent your home from selling. (If you're showing the house in winter, a crockpot of warm cider can make a favorable impression that goes beyond just the buyer's nose.)

Buyers can mistake a lack of cleanliness in any of these key rooms as dislike or rejection of the room itself. And if a buyer rejects the kitchen, bathrooms, master bedroom, or main living area, chances are they will reject the whole house.

Don't let the state of cleanliness in your home be a negative or a drawback. Cleanliness is a controllable factor. Use it as a positive and market your home more effectively because of it.

Eliminating Clutter

One of the easiest, most inexpensive yet important chores sellers can do is remove clutter in all areas of their home. Clutter is anything that makes the home look smaller, dirtier or shows who the seller is. In other words, clutter is your personal items.

You want a buyer to view the house, not your possessions. Your belongings can subconsciously or subtly add charm or warmth, but buyers aren't there to buy your furniture or see family photos. They're there to mentally picture *their belongings* in your home. Get your stuff out of the way so they can do this. If the buyer mentally and emotionally moves in during a showing, they will soon be writing an offer so they can physically move in.

Removing clutter also makes your home look more spacious, cleaner, and better maintained. Start with the kitchen and store everything or put it away. Take everything off the appliances, countertops, desks, shelves, tables, and so on. Make the entire kitchen look as "unlived in" as possible.

Large Furniture and Busy Designs

Over-sized furniture can make a room appear much smaller than it actually is. Busy carpet or wallpaper designs also make a room look small. Take the focus off the furniture and the decorating by removing big furniture and repainting, papering, or redoing busy walls and floors. Make rooms look as spacious as possible. Crowded and stifled rooms will make people feel crowded and stifled.

People sometimes think a home would be impersonal or cold if everything is cleared away or removed. Buyers are viewing your home to see if their stuff would be warm and cozy in it. Some buyers even buy new furniture to fit the home they just bought. Emphasize the structure, layout, floor plan design, style, floors, walls, windows, and amenities in your home, not your belongings. Make your home look ready to be lived in for potential buyers, not lived in by you.

Go through every room of your home and remove all or as many personal items as possible. Take down all family photos, trinkets, and collectibles. Decorating touches like paintings on walls, plants, towels, and so on can stay. Books, magazines, coasters, posters, magnets, phone number rosters, supplies, and so on should be removed.

Have your agent or a kind, yet honest friend or family member walk through your home and point out items that should be removed. When in doubt, put the item away. Make the home look almost bare other than your furniture.

Store clutter neatly in the attic, basement, at a friend's house, or in a short-term storage facility. You can get a head start on packing this way and make your home look better. Remember to remove clutter before you clean the home. There's no need to clean items you're going to store or put away.

Consider donating some of your clutter to charities. There are dozens of organizations that will come to your home and haul away items. Garage sales and Goodwill stores also are excellent ways to eliminate clutter and make a little bit of money.

Staging the Home to Show

You will know in advance when your home will be shown (and have weeks to prepare). Whether another agent is showing your home in the middle of the week or you are having an open house on Sunday afternoon, you can stage your home to look its very best. Think of an open house or showing like it's a blind date. Most people spend hours getting ready; preparing themselves for likely questions and answers in case the date is an amazing person. They leave nothing to chance because they want to make the best impression possible.

The same can and should be done when owners are selling their home. Staging the home means playing up all the home's strengths and diminishing the weaknesses. Turn every light on in the home and open the blinds (maybe some windows for a nice breeze). Light makes the home appear larger, cleaner, and more cheerful. Plus, light affects most people in a positive way.

Control the odor and smell you want buyers to experience. Bake cookies or bread that day, put cinnamon in the kitchen, or light candles or incense. Don't make the smell or fragrance overpowering because your plan can backfire and buyers can be completely turned off. Any subtle smell that makes the house feel warm, cozy, and homey adds a nice touch.

Consider lighting a fire if the season and house is appropriate (make sure someone is there at all times). Sometimes soft music adds ambiance. Be careful to not overdo it though. If you play music during a showing, make sure the station plays easy listening songs exclusively and turn the music down so low it can barely be heard.

If certain rooms are small, move furniture out of those rooms to make them appear larger. Think of your home as a model home at a new construction home site (you might even want to visit one to view how to stage your home). If you have a screened-in porch or deck, you might want to set plates and glasses out to give the feel of dining outside on a warm summer evening.

Prime the flowers, cut the grass, and give the home a super cleaning. Just like a blind date you only get one chance to make a first impression. Make it a good one.

When Homes Show the Best

Homes show the best when they are semi-vacant but still have some furniture in them. A somewhat bare, Spartan-decorated look makes a home appear spacious, clean, and roomy. Buyers can easily picture themselves and their furniture in this type of home. Too much furniture makes a home appear small and cramped. No furniture at all shows off every flaw in the flooring, walls, and baseboards. Completely vacant homes also can suffer from being cold and possessing weird smells.

Repair Allowances

When you can't clean or make repairs due to time, money, or a combination of both, sellers should consider lowering their asking price or offering a repair allowance. A *repair allowance* is money given by a seller to a buyer in lieu of making repairs. Sellers admit there is a problem or an issue and offer money for the buyer to fix the problem instead of fixing it himself.

For example, if a roof needs repairs or carpet is old and outdated, a seller might offer $1,000 instead of repairing the damaged roof or replacing the orange shag carpet. Buyers often like repair allowances because they give the buyer more control over the quality of work done. Also, buyers are able to shop around for better pricing. If a buyer gets that roof repaired for $700, they pocket the $300 difference.

Some sellers use repair allowances as an incentive to purchase. They might offer a repair allowance of $500 for carpet if a buyer presents a full price offer or one close to it. Specifying an amount up front shows the buyer you're serious and quantifies the assistance so buyers know what they're dealing with. The downside is you're committed to that amount and you might have been able to spend less and still get a strong offer.

Repair allowances save time and trouble for a seller. They also can be used during the inspection process, especially if closing is a few days or a week away.

The downside to repair allowances is the buyer's knowledge of a defect or problem. It's always better to fix a problem so buyers never knew it existed. Sometimes buyers can be turned off by a house with problems even though a repair allowance is being offered. When time and money prevent sellers from getting a home in tip-top shape, allowances are great ways to overcome the defective item and make a home more attractive to buyers.

> ### Wording Repair Allowances Properly in the Contract
>
> Repair allowances should be written in the following manner: "Seller to give buyer $1,000 in lieu of making any repairs to the roof. After money is received it is understood no repairs will be made and the roof shall not be used as a reason to terminate the transaction." Some lenders don't like repair allowances to be written in the purchase agreement. They can be written in an addendum to the purchase agreement that is included to the purchase agreement but won't be given to the lender.

Home Warranty Plans

Home warranty plans are insurance policies taken out to protect a new homeowner from costly repairs to appliances or the major mechanical systems. Sellers can purchase home warranty plans as a marketing tool to make their home more appealing to prospective buyers. A one-year plan costs around $350 and has a $100 deductible the buyer (new homeowner) pays if something breaks and the plan is used.

Home warranties are most effectively used by sellers when they are selling an older home or their appliances and mechanical systems are near the end of their useful life. Sellers with newer homes should not purchase home warranty plans for buyers because it would have the opposite effect. Buyers would wonder what was wrong with the home and be turned off.

Home warranties cover all the appliances, heating and cooling systems, plumbing, electrical wiring, water heater, central vacuum system, fans, and well and septic systems. Used the right way, home warranties can make buyers feel better about an older home and save them money in the first year or two living there. They also provide more peace of mind for sellers. If something breaks or doesn't work, the new homeowners won't bother calling the old owner. They'll simply call the home warranty company and say fix this.

The Least You Need to Know

➤ Decide up front if you are going to fix a little or a lot, if you're going to do the work yourself or hire a professional, and set time frames for when the work must be done. Get multiple bids if you hire the work out.

➤ When doing a personal inspection be as critical and unbiased as possible. View every room like a buyer would and have your agent or a trusted friend critique your home to find problems.

➤ Collect all records and receipts to show the improvements and repairs you have made to the home over the years.

➤ Give the home a super deep cleaning focusing on the kitchen, baths, master bedroom, and TV room.

➤ Remove all items that clutter up the home and depersonalize the house so buyers can mentally envision their belongings in the home.

➤ Stage the home to look its very best when buyers are coming in.

➤ Repair allowances should be considered when sellers don't have the time or money to make lots of repairs.

Chapter 19

Selling Your Home Through a Realtor

In This Chapter

➤ Locating a good Realtor

➤ Explaining commissions and agency representation

➤ Interviewing agents

➤ Understanding the listing presentation, the list contract, and disclosure forms

➤ How seller and agent work together to achieve a common goal

All the things you learned and did while buying a home now have to be reversed when you sell your home. Selling a home isn't a simple task. You don't just call an agent, stick a sign in the yard, and throw an open house. Many intricate steps must be taken to position your home at the right price in the market place. This chapter explains how to select a good Realtor and how to work with that agent to sell your home for the most money possible in the shortest time frame.

Finding a Good Realtor

There are plenty of agents out there. The problem is finding the right agent for you. Will the agent listen closely and understand your situation? Can you trust the agent to always act in your best interests and be fully committed to sell your home? Will the agent be familiar with your neighborhood and be knowledgeable about current market conditions as a whole and specific market conditions in your area?

Other issues to consider include these: Does the agent have experience in handling a sell-buy double transaction similar to what you need to do? Does the agent work out of a reputable office and have a support staff of professionals backing her up? Will you get along with the agent, communicate comfortably and effectively, and be able to work side by side? What commission rate will the agent charge?

All these questions and more might go through your head as you prepare to select a Realtor. There really are lots of agents. There is no reason you can't find a good one and have a positive experience selling your home. Don't settle for an average or okay agent. You can afford to be picky.

Agents want to work for good clients as much as you want a good agent working for you. After all, selling homes is how they make a living. You are the customer so the agent should give you excellent service. Also remember that the buyer of your home is the customer and they too have high expectations. It's up to you and your agent to satisfy those expectations.

Look for Often-Used Agents

When asking family, friends, or co-workers to refer you the name of a good agent, see how many times they have used the agent. If an agent has been used two or three times by the same person, that is an excellent indication of the agent's service. Agents that are used time and time again have proven their skill, integrity, and service. If you get the names of two or three good agents, pick the one that you feel will work best with you. This might be decided by their age, background, familiarity with your neighborhood, or personality type.

Referrals from Family, Friends, and Co-workers

The first thing to do when searching for an agent is ask trusted family members, friends, and co-workers for the names of a good agent. Only ask people you trust and value their opinion on this matter. For instance, don't ask a trusted cousin who has never bought or sold a home and has no interest whatsoever in real estate.

Consider the source when you ask for this information. Make sure the person isn't giving a name simply to get business or perks from the agent. The trusted friend or family member should have used the agent themselves and be able to speak intelligently about the service they received. If an agent's name comes up repeatedly from different people or someone has used an agent multiple times, you've found your Realtor.

Consider also asking your mortgage originator if you already have one, or your insurance agent. Professionals in or around the real estate business are wonderful resources for information. Typically, they will make good recommendations because their name and credibility are at stake. If they make a bad referral they could lose your business and they won't want to do that.

It's highly unlikely you'll still be looking for an agent after talking to all these people. If you haven't found one yet, consider getting online and searching for agents that do a lot of business in your area. Check available listings to see if one or two agents have sold multiple homes in your subdivision.

Agents to Steer Clear Of

Select an agent that does both listings and works for buyers, or an agent that specializes in listings. You don't want an agent that works for buyers only to try and learn to sell homes with your house as the test case. Stay away from agents that promise they have buyers for your home just to get you to list your home with them. If they really had buyers they would bring you a purchase agreement instead of a listing contract. Be wary of agents that have never sold a home anywhere near your area or your type of home if it's unique (farm house, patio home, multi-family). Be cautious of part-time agents that dabble in real estate. Selling a home is a full-time job and you're paying full-time money for the service. Do not use an agent that doesn't have access to the multiple listing service. If your home isn't listed on the MLS you're essentially selling it By Owner but paying a hefty commission.

Another option is driving around your neighborhood to see if a particular agent or office has more than one home listed. Remember, you are picking an agent first, then their office. Don't pick an office first and settle for any agent in that office if you can help it.

Commission Structure

Commissions vary from city to city. They are based on local custom. Commission structures might range from 5% to 7% of the gross sales price depending on what is standard in that locale. Sellers pay the entire commission for both their listing agent/office and the buyer's agent/office.

Listing agents and buyer's agents usually split the commission in half. If the commission structure is 6% and the sales price is $100,000, the seller would pay a $3,000 commission to the listing agent's office and $3,000 to the buyer's agent's office. The listing agent's office and buyer's agent's office then pay the individual agents according to the contracts they have signed.

Commission structures cannot be set or mandated. It is against the law for offices or agents to collude or conspire to set certain commission rates. Individual real estate offices and what sellers will pay determine commissions. Rates are flexible with some offices and agents, others refuse to change their commission structures. This is something you will have to consider when selecting an agent.

Avoid choosing an agent simply because of commissions if you can help it. There is usually a reason offices or agents discount their commissions and the reasons aren't good. Whether they can't get business the normal way, aren't as qualified, or give inferior service doesn't matter. No one wants to make less than what they deserve for an honest day's work. Take this into consideration when interviewing agents.

If you ask an agent to reduce her commission rate she might say yes if you use her to buy your next home (she'll get a commission when you buy a home). Don't be offended if an agent declines. Her company policy might restrict her from lowering her rate.

What Are Discount Brokers?

Discount brokers are offices that list homes at commission rates lower than the local custom. This is done to entice more sellers to list their homes with the broker. Discount brokers often drop some of the services traditionally provided by agents who receive the full commission rate, or offer different commission pricing depending on what the seller wants to pay for. If local custom dictates commissions are 7% of the gross sales price, discount brokers might charge 5% or 5.5%. Because discount brokers also reduce buyer's agents' commissions, many buyer's agents will not show homes listed by discount brokers to their clients.

If an agent is quick to lower his commission, he might be desperate for business or not a very good negotiator. If an agent is quick to give up his own paycheck, how fast will he give up your money when negotiating for you?

Agency Representation

There are only a few ways agents can represent clients. Agents can represent sellers as listing agents. Agents can also represent buyers as buyer's agents.

The third type of agency representation is *dual* or *limited agency*. This occurs two different ways. When an agent from the same real estate company as the listing agent writes a purchase agreement for a buyer on a property the listing agent is trying to sell, the agency relationships are changed. The listing agent and buyer's agent in this potential transaction are now both limited agents. Because they work out of the same office under the same principal broker, they are considered dual or limited agents. (Limited agency isn't available in all states. Check with your agent for your local conditions.)

The other scenario in which dual or limited agency takes place is when a listing agent finds a buyer and writes an offer for the buyer on a home he has listed. At the point the agent first speaks to the potential buyer about the listed property, he becomes a dual or limited agent for that buyer. When dealing with all other buyers that are represented by buyer's agents, the agent is still a listing agent.

What Is Sub-Agency?

Sub-agency is an outdated form of agency representation where an agent showed buyers homes, did tons of legwork, and helped the buyer write an offer but actually worked for the seller and was paid by the seller. Buyers confided all their thoughts, opinions, and feelings to the sub-agent who turned around and disclosed this confidential information to the seller. Sub-agency was great for sellers (most buyers didn't know the agent helping them was really working for the seller) but lousy for buyers so it was done away with. Now buyers are represented by buyer's agents that act in their best interests but are still paid by the seller.

Agency representation can be described as one person entrusting another to speak and act in his best interests for an agreed upon fee. As in many agency relationships the fee is a percentage of a sales price. When the sales price goes up, the agent's pay check goes up.

When agents sign a listing contract with sellers they agree to work their hardest and do their best to achieve a goal that benefits the seller. If this goal is met, agents receive a commission. If the goal is not met, agents receive no compensation.

Interviewing Realtors

After you have collected the names of two or three good agents (or even just one), contact the agents and set up appointments to have them visit your home.

When the agent comes to your home, have him tour the home and point out any areas that might need attention or could be detriments to selling the home. Don't be insulted by this. In fact, agents show a lot about themselves when they tour your home. Is the agent honest with you or overly nice and tells you what you want to hear? Is the agent competent and skilled in knowing what areas are most important in selling a home and what needs to be done? Is the agent professional in appearance, manners, and speaking ability, or will he embarrass your home and cheapen the product he is trying to sell?

After you have shown your home to the agent, invite him or her to sit down so you can ask questions regarding their company and the agent. The following list is a reference guide of questions to ask agents:

1. How long have you been selling real estate?
2. Why did you get into real estate sales?
3. How long have you been with your current company?
4. How long has your company been in business?
5. What professional organizations do you belong to?
6. How many homes have you listed in the last year?
7. How many homes have you sold in the last year?
8. How many listings do you have right now?
9. How many total clients do you have right now?
10. Are you a full-time agent and do all your listings appear on the MLS system and the Internet?
11. How many of your listings expired in the last year?
12. How many total listings of yours have expired?
13. Where do you advertise your listings?
14. What is the biggest obstacle I will face when selling my home?
15. What are the strongest aspects of your marketing plan?

16. How much of your business comes from the Internet?
17. What do you do differently from other agents?
18. What is your commission rate?
19. What am I going to have to do to sell my home?
20. Why are you the best agent to help me sell my home?

Comparing Your Market Data to the Realtor

All the research you did tracking sale prices in your neighborhood will now come in handy. Pull out your comparable sales data and ask the agent what price your home should be listed at and what it will sell for. Let the agent answer the question thoroughly. She will probably have a comparable market analysis (CMA) with her and refer to the sale prices of properties in your neighborhood.

Real Estate Terms

What Is a CMA?

CMA stands for *comparative market analysis*. CMAs are the tools agents use to gauge the value of homes. List prices are determined by the figures in a market analysis. Agents compare the sold prices of similar homes (similar in number of bedrooms, baths, square footage, garages, basement, lot size, and so on) in the immediate vicinity of the soon-to-be listed home. Only homes that have sold in the last year to eighteen months can be used to compare value with the subject property. The sales price information comes from the multiple listing services database.

Don't share your market data with the agent until she has finished stating her opinion and making her case with the sales data she found. It's important to not ask too many questions yet, or show your market data to the agent. The point of this exercise isn't to ambush the agent, or show her up. You want to give the agent a chance to answer your question fully to see how accurate it is and if it matches the market data you found.

Unfortunately, many agents inflate numbers or lie about the value of homes to get sellers to list their homes with them. It's important to hear the agent's thoughts on the value of your home to see if the agent is competent, understands the market you are in, and is ethical and honest. You also want to know the true range in price in your area and the agent's data should accurately show it.

If your data matches the agent's data or is extremely close you should feel confident those figures are an accurate depiction of the range of value in your neighborhood. You should feel good about this agent's research as well as your own.

If the agent's numbers are drastically higher, you might want to ask her to justify the figures (don't pull your numbers out yet). If she can't substantiate the numbers, or you know for a fact there is other valid data available that she didn't use, you probably won't want to hire this agent. If you want to give her the benefit of the doubt, pull out your data and discuss the difference in figures with the agent.

If the agent's numbers are drastically lower than yours, ask the agent to explain why her proposed list price and sales price are so low. Listen carefully to the agent's response. She might have information you don't or be knowledgeable about the area in a way you aren't.

Active, Pending, Sold, Expired: What Does It All Mean?

Active means a home is on the market for sale. *Pending* means a purchase agreement has been written on a property, but the transaction has not yet been closed. The house is sold pending financing and the inspection going through. *Sold* homes have already closed. *Expired* means the house did not sell during the four or six month listing period. When the contract period is over the home automatically goes off the market unless the seller renews the listing contract. *Withdrawn* means the home was taken off the market, usually by the seller, and is no longer for sale.

Conversely, the agent might not understand the market or be able to gauge prices accurately. She also might have given you a lower price in an attempt to sell the home extremely quickly. Pull out your data and compare with the agents to see what the true range in value is. Agents should have more data then sellers because they have access to the multiple listing service as well as the Internet.

Utilizing All Data in a CMA

Only homes that have sold in the past eighteen months should be used by agents to determine value on a CMA. However, agents should review numbers for homes currently listed and any sales pending. These figures offer a clue to what the current market is like. Be careful not to put too much credence into homes still listed and active. There's no guarantee they'll sell, or at a price near the asking price. Review homes that did not sell as well. Often homes that were withdrawn or the contract expired before the home could be sold say almost as much as those that did sell.

Use the data you collected in your research to gauge the competency, knowledge, and integrity of the agent. You also should have a good feel for the market conditions in your neighborhood after comparing your data with the Realtor.

The Listing Presentation

When agents come to your home to be interviewed, they will give a listing presentation. This presentation is their sales pitch explaining why they are the right agent, to work for you. The presentation should include the following:

➤ Information about the agent and the real estate company he works out of.

➤ Facts about the housing market in that area, such as the average sales price and days on the market.

➤ Information on your home concerning how it compares to other homes in the area, and suggestions on what should be fixed, replaced, or changed to make the home more marketable.

➤ A break down of the agent's complete marketing plan. For instance, how the agent will advertise the home, the role of the Internet in selling your home, national relocation referral networks, open houses, and so on.

➤ A list of comparable sales in your neighborhood with adjustments made for differences in amenities. MLS sheets of these comparable sales are often included.

➤ Questions about your motives. For example, why you are selling your home, and what is your top priority: money, fast sale, convenience, or something else.

Picking a List Price

The agent should recommend an asking price range. Depending on your reasons for selling and your motivation level, you might want to select the high end of the agent's range (this targets a 3-or-4 month sale), the middle of the road price (2-month sale), or the low end of the range (1-month-or-less sale).

By law the agent cannot tell you at what price you should list your home. Ask questions, review the data the agent has presented, and be objective when comparing your home to sold homes on the market analysis sheet. Consider driving by comparable sold homes in your neighborhood to determine how your home stacks up against the other homes. Your reasons for selling and your desired priorities will help you decide what price tag you should put on your home.

Unless you have lots of time on your hands, don't price your home excessively high. Buyers have access to the same comparable sales in the MLS and they will pass on your home. Months later when you decide to lower your price a stigma could plague your home. Buyers will wonder why it's been on the market for three or four months and question if there's something wrong with it.

Don't price your home too low either. Selling your home extremely quickly is desirable but most people want to get as much money out of the sale of their home as possible. Leaving money on the table is not a wise thing for a seller to do.

Strong Price Differential Statistics

Price differential is the statistical difference between the listing price and the average sales price in an area. For example, a home listed at $100,000 that sells for $95,500 has a price differential of 95.5%. This statistic is used by sellers and listing agents to determine an accurate list price. Any price differential above 97% is strong.

Work with your agent to determine a price that is reasonable but high enough to give you room to come down a little (unless you need to sell immediately). Setting a list price is not an exact science. In fact, it is one of the hardest things to do in real estate. Unfortunately, it also happens to be the most important factor in selling your home.

Pick the wrong price and your home might languish on the market for half a year or you might sell it for thousands of dollars less than what it's worth. Pick the right price and you will have a good transaction and a positive experience. Helping set a listing price and negotiating for you might be the two most important tasks a listing agent has.

Commission Percentage and Contract Terms

The commission structure and contract terms should be discussed in detail with the agent if they haven't been already. Ask the agent what commission you will be charged and what the contract length will be. Expect the contract period to be the standard time in your city or town (four to six months is normal).

Allow this time frame because it is fair and reasonable for both the agent and you. Anything too short won't give the agent adequate time to market and sell your home. Anything over six months (except for commercial or multi-family investment listings) is too long and ties you to an agent unnecessarily.

If you feel the commission quoted you is high or want to inquire about a lower rate, this is the time to ask the agent to discount their rate. Politely request a lower rate and explain why you are doing so. Many agents (especially the good ones) will not lower their rate.

Check This Out

Reasons Agents Typically Won't Cut Their Commission

Their company policy doesn't allow it. They're receiving full commissions from all their other clients and would have to shortchange you on time, effort, and service. If they're successful and busy, they don't have to. If your home is difficult to sell, they will spend extra time, effort, and money on your home. If your normal wage is $20 an hour, you expect to make that; they expect to make their normal wage when they give their best.

Discuss the pros and cons of the commission structure. I don't recommend picking an agent solely based on the commission structure because the service you receive will be directly affected.

Marketing the Home

The most powerful marketing tools any Realtor can use are pricing your home accurately and putting your home in the multiple listing service. Over 80% of buyers use agents to help them locate and purchase homes (the Internet is actually driving that number higher). That means over 80% of buyers are finding homes through the MLS system.

Agents pay thousands of dollars every year to have access to the MLS service. There is no better way to market a home. Other marketing tools can be effective but the MLS system is the best way to advertise your home.

Marketing homes online has exploded in the last two years as an excellent way to promote home listings. Buyers can do research and legwork from the comfort of their own homes. Internet listings have given buyers direct access to much of the information agents have in the MLS. Online virtual tours have replaced open houses in many computer-literate families as the way to start the house hunting process.

Sunday open houses are still commonly used by agents to expose homes to as many people as possible. Advertising online (Realtor home pages, real estate Web sites), on radio and TV, and in newspapers, magazines, and real estate trade publications are other avenues to promote homes (and the agents themselves).

Relocation referral networks, broker to broker networking, installation of yard signs, flyers, mass mailings, and word of mouth advertising are all techniques employed by agents.

One final tool agents can use is a reverse prospect search. Agents are able to search the MLS system backwards to see what other Realtors have inputted criteria to locate homes for their buyers. Agents are able to find out which Realtors have buyers that are looking for a home like the one they have listed. Listing agents can then contact the other agent and pass information about the listed house to the buyer's agent.

The agent will also present you a net proceeds sheet. This form itemizes your expected expenses and estimates the amount of the check you will receive after you have paid all charges, including paying off the mortgage. To view an example of a net proceeds sheet, see Figure 19.1.

The List Contract

After you have interviewed each of the agents you were referred to and heard their listing presentations, it's time to sign a listing contract with the agent you like best.

The listing contract should include:

Who the contract is between   The real estate company's name, salesperson's name, and seller's name should be in the contract.

Term of the contract   The time frame the house will be listed.

```
        SELLER'S ESTIMATED CLOSING COST

Property_____Est. Closing Date_____

Sales Price                                      $_____

        First Mortgage              $_____
        Second Mortgage             $_____
        Listing Brokerage Fee       $_____
        Selling Brokerage Fee       $_____
        Title Insurance             $_____
        Deed and Affidavit          $_____
        Pro Rated Taxes             $_____
        Survey                      $_____
        Underwriters Fee            $_____
        Closing Fee                 $_____
        Doc. Prep                   $_____
        Tax Service Fee             $_____
        Messenger Fee               $_____
        Recording Fee               $_____
        Termite Inspection          $_____
        Water Test                  $_____
        Well & Septic Inspection    $_____
        Buyers Cost Paid by Seller  $_____
        Ditch, Barret Assessment    $_____
        Home Warranty               $_____
        Flood Search                $_____
                                    $_____
        _____            $_____
        Misc. Expenses              $_____

        TOTAL DEDUCTIONS            $_____

ESTIMATED NET TO SELLER                  $_____

Seller_____Seller_____

Agent_____Date_____
        PLEASE PLACE COPY IN LISTING AND PENDING FILE
netprocd.wps
```

Figure 19.1

The net proceeds sheet itemizes your expenses and predicts the final proceeds from the sale.

The commission rate   The commission structure the seller will pay.

Condition of the property and attached items seller plans on removing from the home   Any known defects should be listed and the seller's intention of selling as-is if applicable. Any attached items the seller is taking out of the home need to be disclosed—for example, a chandelier or bookshelf.

Marketing plan   The contract should spell out the proposed marketing and advertising techniques that will be used to sell the home.

Listing price   The asking price the seller agrees to sell the home for is written into the contract.

Permissions statement   The contract should seek the seller's permission for a lock box to be used so buyer's agents can gain access to the home, and permission for a sign to be installed in the yard. A clause also should grant the agent permission to give out the seller's mortgage information to a title company to pay off the loan.

Your agent will have you sign an exclusive right to sell listing contract. This grants the agent and her company exclusive rights to sell your property. If your home sells during the listing period to any buyer, the agent and her office will receive a commission. To view an exclusive right to sell listing contract, see Figures 19.2 and 19.3.

Disclosure Laws and Forms

In years past sellers did not have to disclose the condition of the housing structure or the appliances and mechanical systems in it. There was no disclosure system in place. Buyer beware ruled.

Under the buyer beware system many buyers were lied to or problems simply weren't disclosed. Buyers were stuck with huge repair costs soon after moving into new homes. Some buyers defaulted on their new mortgages because they didn't have the money to repair the home and make the loan payments. When they complained to their local legislators, the old system was replaced with a new set of disclosure laws.

Disclosure laws differ from state to state. Most states require disclosure from sellers. The laws were put in place to protect buyers from purchasing homes with known defects and incurring large repair costs. Ask your agent about the disclosure laws in your area. Disclosure should be made as early as possible, ideally the first time a buyer tours your home, but definitely before an offer is written.

The best way to handle the disclosure issue is to fill out a residential sales disclosure form and leave it in the home (kitchen or dining room). Buyers will be more trusting of you and possibly more understanding of the defect if they find out about the problem early in the game.

Issues that should be disclosed are any items that are defective, broken, damaged, or missing. Environmental hazards like asbestos, radon, and lead paint also should be disclosed.

LISTING CONTRACT
(Exclusive Right to Sell)

1. In consideration of services to be performed by _____
2. (Broker/Company, hereinafter referred to as "REALTOR®"), _____ ("Agent") for _____
3. ("SELLER"), Seller hereby appoints REALTOR® as Seller's agent with irrevocable and exclusive right to sell the property known
4. as_____ in _____,
5. Township_____, County,_____, Indiana, _____ Zip Code, which is
6. legally described as: _____.
7. **FAIR HOUSING:** This property shall be offered, shown, and made available to all persons without regard to race, color, religion,
8. sex, handicap, familial status or national origin.
9. **TERM:** This contract begins on _____and expires at midnight
10. on _____ unless extended in writing by all parties hereto. Provided, however, that if the
11. Seller and Buyer sign a Purchase Agreement, Option to Purchase Real Estate, or the closing of the sale of the property will not
12. take place until after the term of this contract, then this contract shall automatically be extended to coincide with the closing date.
13. List Price: $_____ Possession:_____.
14. **ACCEPTABLE FINANCING:** Said property may be sold for cash or any of the following methods indicated below:
15. _____ Conventional Mortgage   _____ Conditional Sales Contract   _____ FHA
16. _____ Assumption of Existing Mortgage Balance   _____ Purchase Money Mortgage   _____ VA
17. _____ Other _____
18. Seller agrees to pay costs associated with financing not to exceed _____.
19. **PROPERTY OFFERED FOR SALE:** The above sale price includes the property and all improvements and fixtures permanently
20. installed and affixed thereto, except _____
21. _____
22. **SELLER DISCLOSURE OF PROPERTY CONDITION:** Seller will provide as required by law, a Seller's Residential Real Estate
23. Sales Disclosure ("S.R.R.E.S.D.") and Lead Based Paint Disclosure form if required. Seller represents to the best of Seller's
24. knowledge and belief, that the property is structurally and mechanically sound and all equipment to be included in the sale is in
25. good operating condition, except as indicated in the S.R.R.E.S.D. as provided. Seller agrees that maintaining the condition of
26. the property and related equipment is Seller's responsibility during the period of the contract and/or until Buyer's time of
27. possession, whichever is later.
28. Seller discloses the following known defects:_____
29. _____
30. _____.
31. **INDEMNITY:** If a dispute arises at any time concerning the condition of the property, the structures, improvements permanently
32. installed and affixed thereto, property defects, or health hazards, Seller agrees to indemnify and hold harmless the REALTOR®,
33. cooperating Broker, and/or Metropolitan Indianapolis Board of REALTORS®, Inc. (MIBOR) and MIBOR Service Corporation
34. (MSC) from and against any liabilities, judgments, damages, expenses, costs, and/or reasonable attorney fees which they may
35. incur as a result of any such dispute.
36. **REALTOR® SERVICES:**
37.   1. REALTOR®, Agent warrants that REALTOR®, Agent holds a valid Indiana real estate license.
38.   2. REALTOR®, Agent will make an earnest and continued effort to sell the property in accordance with the terms and conditions of this contract.
39.   3. REALTOR®, Agent is a member of MIBOR and the Multiple Listing Service (MLS).
40.   4. REALTOR®, Agent will enter detailed information, a photo of the property, if available, and types of financing acceptable to
41.   Seller into the MLS computer system and all available MLS publications.
42.   5. Print-outs of this listing will be readily available to members of MLS by computer and will be provided to other REALTORS®,
43.   Agents and Brokers upon request.
44.   6. REALTOR®, Agent has given Seller a written estimate of selling expenses.
45.   7. REALTOR®, Agent will cooperate with all other REALTORS® and Brokers in an effort to procure a Buyer for the property.
46.   8. REALTOR®, Agent may advertise the property and place a "For Sale" sign upon the premises. REALTOR®, Agent may
47.   provide a lockbox for the keys to the property in order to facilitate showings. REALTOR®, Agent will follow Seller's
48.   instructions for making appointments for property to be shown.
49.   9. REALTOR®, Agent will promptly present all Purchase Agreements received on the property for Seller's consideration. After a Purchase
50.   Agreement has been accepted by Seller, REALTOR®, Agent will continue to present any offers received until the transaction is closed.
51.   10. REALTOR®, Agent may place a "SOLD" or a "SALE PENDING" rider upon the sign after a Purchase Agreement has been
52.   accepted, and will remove all signs after the transaction has been closed.
53.   11. REALTOR®, Agent will assist the Buyer in obtaining financing, if requested.
54.   12. REALTOR®, Agent will make arrangements for closing time and place in cooperation with all parties.
55. **PROFESSIONAL SERVICE FEE:** The Professional Service Fee charged by the listing REALTOR®, Agent for service rendered,
56. with respect to any listing, is solely a matter of negotiation between REALTOR®, Agent and Seller and is not fixed, controlled,
57. suggested, recommended or maintained by MIBOR, the MLS or any person not a party to the contract.
58. Seller agrees to pay REALTOR®, Agent a fee of _____ which
59. shall be paid upon the occurrence of any of the following events:
60.   1. At the time of closing the sale, when title to or an interest in the property is transferred to a Buyer; or
61.   2. At the time of default by Seller if, at that time, Seller and Buyer have entered into a fully executed, written Purchase Agreement; or
62.   3. At the time REALTOR®, Agent procures a written offer to purchase from a Buyer who is ready, willing and able to purchase
63.   the property according to the terms herein, but the Seller refuses to accept the offer; or
64.   4. At the time Seller sells the property to a Buyer procured in whole or in part by the efforts of REALTOR®, Agent, a cooperating Broker
65.   or the Seller during the term of this contract, if such sale occurs within _____ after this contract terminates; however, this
66.   paragraph shall not apply if this contract terminates and the property is listed exclusively with another licensed Broker; or
67.   5. At the time of closing a sale on an Option to Purchase and/or Lease Option entered into during the term of this contract,
68.   even though the closing takes place after the expiration of this contract.
69. Any commission required to be paid under terms (1) and (4) above, shall be due and payable at the closing of the transaction,
70. when title to or any interest in the Property is transferred to a buyer or lessee. Any commission required to be paid under items
71. (2), (3) and (5) above, shall be due and payable upon demand by Broker.
72. **EARNEST MONEY:** Earnest money, tendered with an accepted Purchase Agreement, shall be deposited immediately in listing
73. REALTOR®'s Escrow Account until the sale is closed. In the event the sale is not closed, the earnest money shall be disbursed
74. based on either the mutual agreement of the Seller and Buyer or upon court order. In the event that the Seller is to receive any
75. portion of the earnest money, Seller agrees that REALTOR® shall be entitled to retain any or all of Seller's portion of the earnest
76. money in payment of advertising and/or other expenses. In no event shall the amount retained exceed the amount of the
77. professional service fee had the transaction been closed.
78. **AGENCY DISCLOSURES:**
79.   **a. Office Policy.** Seller acknowledges receipt of a copy of the written office policies of REALTOR® relating to agency.
80.   **b. Agency Relationship.** Seller acknowledges that REALTOR® has advised Seller that the property may be sold with the
81.   assistance of other brokers and salespersons operating buyer's agents and that REALTOR®'s company policy is to
82.   cooperate with both, and (is) (is not) to compensate buyer's agents.

Figure 19.2

This is the listing contract's front page…

Figure 19.3

...and here's what it says on the back.

83. REALTOR® represents the interest of the Seller as his/her agent to sell the property. REALTOR®, Agent owe duties of trust,
84. loyalty, confidentiality, accounting and disclosure to Seller. However, REALTOR® must deal honestly with a buyer and disclose to
85. the buyer information about the property. Such representations are made as the agent of Seller.

86. Buyer's agents are brokers and salespersons who show the property to prospective buyers, but who represent only the interests
87. of the buyer. Buyer's agents owe duties of trust, loyalty, confidentiality, accounting and disclosure to buyers. Representations
88. made by buyer's agents about the property are not made as the agent of Seller.

89.   **c. Informed Consent to Limited Agency.** REALTOR® may represent BUYER as buyer's agent. If such a BUYER wishes to
90.   see the property, REALTOR® has agency duties to both SELLER and BUYER, and those duties may be different or even
91.   adverse. SELLER hereby knowingly consents to REALTOR®'s acting as a limited agent for such showings.

92. If limited agency arises, REALTOR® shall not disclose the following without the consent, in writing, of both SELLER and BUYER:
93. (i)   Any material or confidential information, except adverse material facts or risks actually known by REALTOR® concerning the
94.   physical condition of the Property and facts required by statute, rule, or regulation to be disclosed and that could not be
95.   discovered by a reasonable and timely inspection of the Property by the parties.
96. (ii)   That a BUYER will pay more than the offered purchase price for the Property.
97. (iii)   That SELLER will accept less than the listed price for the Property.
98. (iv)   Other terms that would create a contractual advantage for one party over another party.
99. (v)   What motivates a party to buy or sell the Property.

100. In a limited agency situation, the parties agree that there will be no imputation of knowledge or information between any party
101. and limited agent or among salespersons of REALTOR®.

102. Seller acknowledges that the Limited Agency Disclosure has been read and understood. Seller understands that he/she does not
103. have to consent to REALTOR®'s acting as a limited agent, but hereby gives informed consent voluntarily to REALTOR®'s limited
104. agency and waives any claim Seller may have now or in the future against Broker for acting as a limited agent.

105. **SELLER AUTHORIZATION AND COOPERATION:** Seller agrees to provide REALTOR®, Agent with the required information
106. necessary for entry into the MLS. The Seller will cooperate with REALTOR®, Agent by permitting the property to be shown at
107. reasonable times and authorizes REALTOR®, Agent to place "For Sale" and other signs on the property.
108.   1. Seller hereby authorizes REALTOR®, Agent to conduct or allow cooperating Brokers to conduct key-entry showings of the property.
109.   2. Seller will provide REALTOR®, Agent with key(s) necessary to open the primary door of the property.
110.   3. Seller authorizes REALTOR®, Agent to have duplicate keys made for use in case of an emergency.
111.   4. Seller agrees not to rent or lease the property during the term of this contract without written notification to REALTOR®.
112.   5. Seller agrees that REALTOR®, Agent may appoint or work with sub-agents and Buyer-Agents, to assist in performing
113.   REALTOR'S®, Agent's duties according to the terms of this contract.
114.   6. Seller authorizes REALTOR®, Agent to disseminate price and terms of financing on a closed sale to members of
115.   MIBOR, to other Brokers upon request, and this information shall be published in the MIBOR MLS.
116.   7. Seller authorizes its lending institution to divulge all mortgage information to REALTOR®, Agent and to provide copies of
117.   the note and mortgage, if requested. Seller's lending institution is _____ and
118.   the mortgage loan number is _____. If Seller's mortgage is subject to a pre-payment penalty, Seller
119.   agrees to give timely written notice to Seller's lender that the mortgage is to be pre-paid from the sale proceeds of the
120.   real estate. It is acknowledged that Seller's failure to give said notice may result in a pre-payment penalty.

121. **LOCKBOX AUTHORIZATION/USE:** To facilitate showings of real estate, a lockbox installation (is _____) (is not _____)
122. authorized, subject to the following acknowledgments/conditions:
123.   1. Seller will provide keys.
124.   2. Seller will safeguard valuables.
125.   3. Seller acknowledges REALTOR®, Agent is not an insurer of Seller's real estate and personal property and waives claims
126.   against REALTOR®, Agent and REALTOR'S®, Agent's authorized agents for loss and/or damage to such property
127.   pursuant to showing the property.
128.   4. Seller instructs REALTOR®, Agent to make reasonable efforts to notify Seller of showing requests. If Seller cannot be contacted
129.   to schedule a showing, Seller (wants ___) (does not want ___) REALTOR®, Agent to use the lockbox for access to the property.
130.   5. Where a tenant/lessee occupies the Property, it is Seller's full responsibility to obtain tenant/lessee consent to allow the
131.   use of a lockbox.

132. **ADDITIONAL PROVISIONS:**
133.   1. Seller understands the terms of this contract, and has received a copy hereof.
134.   2. Seller acknowledges receipt of an estimate of selling expenses.
135.   3. Seller represents that Seller has the capacity to convey the property by a general Warranty Deed or by_____.
136.   4. Seller represents and warrants that Seller is not a "Foreign Person" (individual or entity) and therefore is not subject to
137.   the Foreign Investment in Real Estate Property Tax Act.
138.   5. The parties to this contract agree that this contract contains the entire agreement of the parties and cannot be changed
139.   except by their written consent.
140.   6. The parties to this contract agree that this contract is binding upon the parties hereto, their heirs, administrators,
141.   executors, successors and assigns.
142.   7. For purposes of this contract, the parties understand and agree that Broker's commission is deemed to be a share of the
143.   purchase money received by Seller, and Broker shall have a lien on the funds and a lien upon the Property until the
144.   commission is paid. If any action is filed in relation to this Listing Contract, the unsuccessful party shall pay to the
145.   successful party, a reasonable sum for the successful party's attorney's fees and court costs.
146.   8. The parties to this contract agree that if it becomes necessary for the REALTOR®, Agent to retain an attorney or initiate any legal
147.   proceedings in order to secure compliance with this contract, then, in addition to all other sums to which the REALTOR®, Agent
148.   may be entitled to recover, the REALTOR®, Agent shall also be entitled to recover court costs and reasonable attorney fees.
149.   9. Broker(s) may refer Seller to various vendors/providers including but not limited to lender, title insurers, contractors,
150.   inspection/warranty companies. Broker(s) does not guarantee the performance of any service provider. Seller is free to
151.   select providers other than those referred or recommended to them by Broker(s).
152.   10. The parties to this contract further agree that this contract may be executed simultaneously or in two or more
153.   counterparts, each of which shall be deemed an original, but all of which together constitute one and the same
154.   instrument. Delivery of this document may be accomplished by electronic facsimile reproduction (FAX). If FAX delivery
155.   is utilized, the original document shall be promptly executed and/or delivered, if requested.

156. **FURTHER CONDITIONS:** _____
157. _____
158. _____
159. _____
160.
161. SELLER'S SIGNATURE   DATE   SELLER'S SIGNATURE   DATE
162.
163. PRINTED   PRINTED
164.
165. SOCIAL SECURITY # / FED. I.D. #   MAILING ADDRESS   ZIP CODE
166.
167. SALESPERSON/AGENT   REALTOR/BROKER COMPANY NAME
168.
169. INDIANA LICENSE #   INDIANA LICENSE #
170.
171. ACCEPTED BY: NAME AND TITLE   DATE

R
REALTOR®

Approved by and restricted to use by members of the Metropolitan Indianapolis Board Of REALTORS®
This is a legally binding contract, if not understood seek legal advice. ©MIBOR 1994 (Form No. 250-6/99)

EQUAL HOUSING OPPORTUNITY

Filling Out Sales Disclosure Forms

Answer each item honestly and completely. If something needs to be explained, detail the frequency and severity of the problem. For instance, if the basement gets wet, state how often (only during heavy, heavy rain) and how bad (an inch or less of water). If you don't know an answer or are not sure put "Don't Know" or "Unknown." If the seller is taking the washer and dryer with them, they should not address the condition of those items. Knowledge of any future assessments should be disclosed in the additional comments section. Copies of the form should be left in the home so buyers can review it during showings.

If the value of a home is adversely affected by a condition or situation that has not occurred yet but the seller knows about it, the information should be disclosed. Examples are roads being widened, yards that flood in heavy rain, city water and sewers being brought in for $8,000 per homeowner, or a liquor store being built across the street.

Some issues are a bit trickier. For instance, if a murder or serious criminal activity has taken place at a property, sellers should check first with their agent then a real estate attorney to see if this information must be disclosed. Owners of properties believed to be haunted by ghosts or other supernatural phenomenon probably should consult an attorney (or call Ghostbusters).

When filling out the disclosure form, answer the questions as honestly and thoroughly as you can. If your home doesn't have a hot tub or sauna in it, check "Not Included," "Not Applicable," or leave it blank. If you truly don't know if your home has aluminum wiring or aren't sure of the age of the roof, check "Do Not Know." It's better to play it safe than answer incorrectly.

The disclosure form is a vital part of the sales process. If disclosure is required in your state and the seller doesn't comply, the buyer can come back up to one year later and sue to get all their money back if they prove the seller knowingly and intentionally did not disclose a problem.

Disclosure forms are not warranties or guarantees stating appliances, mechanical systems, and the housing structure will always be in good condition. They are simply statements asserting the present known condition of the home and the items in it. Sellers should disclose the condition of the dwelling to the best of their ability. Nothing more or less is required.

An example of a seller's residential sales disclosure form appears in Figures 19.4 and 19.5.

Figure 19.4

The sales disclosure form lists the condition of the property.

SELLER'S RESIDENTIAL REAL ESTATE SALES DISCLOSURE
State Form 46234 (R/1293)

Date *(month, day, year)*

Seller states that the information contained in this Disclosure is correct to the best of Seller's CURRENT ACTUAL KNOWLEDGE as of the above date. The prospective buyer and the owner may wish to obtain professional advice or inspections of the property and provide for appropriate provisions in a contract between them concerning any advice, inspections, defects, or warranties obtained on the property. The representations in this form are the representations of the owner and are not the representations of the agent, if any. This information is for disclosure only and is not intended to be a part of any contract between the buyer and the owner. Indiana law (IC 24-4.6-2) generally requires sellers of 1-4 unit residential property to complete this form regarding the known physical condition of the property. An owner must complete and sign the disclosure form and submit the form to a prospective buyer before an offer is accepted for the sale of the real estate.

Property address *(number and street, city, state, ZIP code)*

1. **The following are in the conditions indicated:**

A. APPLIANCES	None/Not Included	Defective	Not Defective	Do Not Know
Built-In Vacuum System				
Clothes Dryer				
Clothes Washer				
Dishwasher				
Disposal				
Freezer				
Gas Grill				
Hood				
Microwave Oven				
Oven				
Range				
Refrigerator				
Room Air Conditioner(s)				
Trash Compactor				
TV Antenna / Dish				

C. WATER & SEWER SYSTEM	None/Not Included	Defective	Not Defective	Do Not Know
Cistern				
Septic Field / Bed				
Hot Tub				
Plumbing				
Aerator System				
Sump Pump				
Irrigation Systems				
Water Heater / Electric				
Water Heater / Gas				
Water Heater / Solar				
Water Purifier				
Water Softener				
Well				
Other Sewer System *(Explain)*				

	Yes	No	Do Not Know
Are the improvements connected to a public water system?			
Are the improvements connected to a public sewer system?			
Are the improvements connected to a private / community water system?			
Are the improvements connected to a private / community sewer system?			

B. ELECTRICAL SYSTEM	None/Not Included	Defective	Not Defective	Do Not Know
Air Purifier				
Burglar Alarm				
Ceiling Fan(s)				
Garage Door Opener / Controls				
Inside Telephone Wiring and Blocks / Jacks				
Intercom				
Light Fixtures				
Sauna				
Smoke / Fire Alarm(s)				
Switches and Outlets				
Vent Fan(s)				
60 / 100 / 200 Amp Service *(Circle one)*				

D. HEATING & COOLING SYSTEM	None/Not Included	Defective	Not Defective	Do Not Know
Attic Fan				
Central Air Conditioning				
Hot Water Heat				
Furnace Heat / Gas				
Furnace Heat / Electric				
Solar House-Heating				
Woodburning Stove				
Fireplace				
Fireplace Insert				
Air Cleaner				
Humidifier				
Propane Tank				

NOTE: "Defect" means a condition that would have a significant adverse effect on the value of the property that would significantly impair the health or safety of future occupants of the property, or that if not repaired, removed or replaced would significantly shorten or adversely affect the expected normal life of the premises.

2. ROOF	YES	NO	DO NOT KNOW
Age, If known: _____ Years.			
Does the roof leak?			
Is there present damage to the roof?			
Is there more than one roof on the house?			
If so how many? _____ roofs.			

3. HAZARDOUS CONDITIONS	YES	NO	DO NOT KNOW
Are there any existing hazardous conditions on the property, such as methane gas, lead paint, radon gas in house or well, radioactive material, landfill, mineshaft, expansive soil, toxic materials, asbestos insulation or PCB's?			

4. OTHER DISCLOSURES	YES	NO	DO NOT KNOW
Do improvements have aluminum wiring?			
Are there any foundation problems with the improvements?			
Are there any encroachments?			
Are there any violations of zoning, building codes or restrictive covenants?			
Is the present use a non-conforming use? Explain:			
Have you received any notices by any governmental or quasi-governmental agencies affecting this property?			
Are there any structural problems with the buildings?			
Have any substantial additions or alterations been made without a required building permit?			
Are there moisture and/or water problems in the basement or crawl space area?			
Is there any damage due to wind, flood, termites or rodents?			
Are the furnace / woodstove / chimney / flue all in working order?			
Is the property in a flood plain?			
Do you currently pay flood insurance?			
Does the property contain underground storage tank(s)?			
Is the seller a licensed real estate salesperson or broker?			
Is there any threatened or existing litigation regarding the property?			
Is the property subject to covenants, conditions and / or restrictions of a homeowner's association?			
Is the property located within one (1) nautical mile of an airport?			

E. ADDITIONAL COMMENTS AND / OR EXPLANATIONS: *(Use additional pages if necessary.)*

The information contained in this Disclosure has been furnished by the Seller, who certifies to the truth thereof, based on the Seller's CURRENT ACTUAL KNOWLEDGE. A disclosure form is not a warranty by the owner or the owner's agent, if any, and the disclosure form may not be used as a substitute for any inspections or warranties that the prospective buyer or owner may later obtain. At or before settlement, the owner is required to disclose any material change in the physical condition of the property or certify to the purchaser at settlement that the condition of the property is substantially the same as it was when the disclosure form was provided. Seller and Purchaser hereby acknowledge receipt of this Disclosure by signing below:

Signature of Seller	Date	Signature of Buyer	Date
Signature of Seller	Date	Signature of Buyer	Date

The Seller hereby certifies that the condition of the property is substantially the same as it was when the Seller's Disclosure form was originally provided to the Buyer.

Signature of Seller	Date	Signature of Seller	Date

Figure 19.5

Here's the backside of the sales disclosure form.

Communication Is the Key

All the research, preparation, hard work, and good intentions in the world won't make a bit of difference if the seller and the listing agent don't communicate well. Effective communication is an absolutely vital component of the selling process. Few transactions are successful without it.

Listening is an essential element of any selling process. Good agents listen carefully to sellers in an effort to understand the seller's situation. Sellers often communicate clearly their reasons for selling and the goals they want to accomplish. Agents should absorb this information and be able to repeat it at any time during the sales process. Every decision an agent makes should be to achieve the sellers stated goals.

How Good Agents Communicate

Good agents listen carefully before speaking and don't cut off clients or finish sentences. They ask a lot of questions and constantly want questions, comments, or thoughts from the seller. Good agents address problems head on, talk directly to sellers, and don't spare feelings by giving inaccurate information. Information passes freely between good agents and their sellers. Sellers and agents communicate well when both know exactly what the other thinks, wants, and is doing.

Unfortunately, sellers do not always clearly state their goals or aren't always forthright or honest about their current situation. Agents must ask the right questions, probe gently, and uncover the seller's true state of mind. Trying to decipher statements and break codes is not an effective way to sell a home. Sellers and agents need to be open with each other, candid yet courteous, and honest.

Sellers rely on agents for information, updates, and advice. If the seller and agent aren't communicating well the whole process can grind to a halt. If the seller's motives, priorities, or goals change the agent must be notified. Real estate is an ever-changing industry. Conditions are constantly in flux. It's difficult to sell a home when the agent doesn't know what the parameters are and what objectives are being sought.

Communication should flow freely between seller and buyer whether it be via the telephone, email, fax machine, or in person. Agents should be forthright with sellers and not sugar coat or smooth over bad information. Sellers need to be told the truth about their home so they have the best chance possible to sell it. Sellers don't need nice agents. They need sincere, honest, confident agents that can sell homes.

Working Together for a Common Goal

Listing a home with a real estate company should be a win-win situation. The owner has a goal of selling their home and the agent wants to help the seller do that and earn a commission for themselves. Neither person can accomplish their goal without the other.

The process of selling a home is made infinitely easier when the seller and agent are on the same page and are working together. The agent gets a paycheck by helping the seller achieve her goal. The homeowner sells her home (hopefully for a large profit), buys a new home, and moves into the next phase of her life by cooperating with the agent.

Working together the agent and seller can be a powerful team. Working independently of each other or against each other the selling process can be slowed, impeded, or virtually impossible. Differences in politics, personality, personal beliefs, and attitudes should be cast aside. The focus should be on the shared goal of selling the home for as much money as possible in the fastest time frame possible.

Something to remember when things aren't going well is that the seller and listing agent need each other. For the transaction to be completed (let alone go smoothly) both parties must cooperate with each other, work diligently, and be respectful of each other. Done the right way the transaction can be wonderful. Done the wrong way and I could be adding another Realtor horror story to the list in Chapter 9, "Making the Decision Not to Use an Agent."

The Least You Need to Know

➤ Good agents can be found by receiving referrals from trusted friends, family members, co-workers, professionals, or through online searches and neighborhood research.

➤ Sellers pay the commission for both the listing agent and the buyer's agent but buyer's agents work exclusively in the buyer's best interests just as listing agents work solely on the seller's behalf. Limited or dual agency is a special type of agency where buyers and sellers are represented differently.

➤ Ask prospective agents detailed questions to determine whether they are the right agent for you and compare the market data you found with the agent's market information.

➤ Understanding the listing contract and the terms and conditions in it (commissions, list price, marketing plan) are responsibilities of the seller.

➤ Disclosure laws are designed to protect buyers from purchasing problem homes and getting into financial trouble.

➤ Agents and sellers should work together to achieve the common goal of selling a home. Without cooperation and teamwork, the selling process is incredibly difficult.

Chapter 20

Selling Your Home Yourself

In This Chapter

➤ Researching local real estate conditions

➤ Settling on an asking price

➤ Marketing and showing your house

➤ Negotiating the sale

➤ Closing the deal successfully

Have you bought and sold many homes over the years? Are you well versed in real estate matters—marketing, negotiating, and closing a home? Do you understand the market conditions in your neighborhood? Are you a skilled salesperson, and do you enjoy working with people? Do you have the luxury of a little bit of time before you *have* to sell?

If you answered yes to more than one of these questions you might be considering selling your home yourself. If you answered no to all of them, selling your home yourself will be an unbelievably difficult endeavor. You should consider your options carefully before undertaking this challenge because you are at a huge disadvantage. Then again, that's what this guide is for: giving you increased options, opportunities, know-how and experience.

There are a few reasons people sell their homes By Owner, but only one really matters—saving money. Selling your home yourself saves between 5% to 7% of the gross sales price. That's around $5,000 to $10,000 for average home sales in most cities. That's a lot of money to save! Here's the catch—real estate is a results-driven field. You make nothing and save nothing if you don't sell your home. Nearly 75% of all For Sale By Owners (FSBOs) never sell. That's a lot. In this chapter, I will discuss how you can sell your home yourself and be one of the fortunate 25% who make and save money at the same time.

Researching Your Local Housing Market

The first thing to do is research your local market to understand the factors that influence the price and sale of homes. Ideally, you've been doing this casually in the years you've lived there. You have a head start if you have. Don't worry if you haven't. You can get up to speed in no time.

Get online and view any listed homes in your neighborhood at `www.realtor.com`, `www.iown.com`, or `www.homeadvisor.com`. If you know specific homes are listed by a Century 21, Coldwell Banker, or RE/MAX office, visit their Web sites and research those properties (`www.century21.com`, and so on).

Another way to get market data is to drive your neighborhood and jot down the addresses of homes that have recently sold or are currently listed on the market. Call the listing agents or real estate companies and find out how much they're asking and what the size and amenities of the homes are or jump online and specifically search for those homes.

As you gather data look for patterns or trends in the numbers. Do homes on certain streets in your neighborhood sell for more money? Does lot size, finished basements, brick exteriors, or condition of the home push prices up? What key amenities are most desirable? What features hurt the value of homes in your subdivision?

Track sale prices, active listings, and expired and withdrawn listings for as long as possible to understand market conditions in your area. Be mindful that the time of year, interest rates, and the overall economic climate in your city can seriously impact real estate conditions.

Figuring Your Home's Value with Comparable Sales Prices

Now that you have a good feel for the *current* conditions in your local market we have to look at the last year or two to track sales prices and determine the range in value in your neighborhood. There are two ways to do this. The first is the politically correct online way. The second is the more effective way (because I'm not always politically correct and want you to have the best FSBO experience possible, I'll show you both ways).

Log on to your computer and go to `www.dataquick.com`, `www.experian.com`, or `www.homegain.com` to find comparable sale prices in your neighborhood for $10. If possible use the most recent sales (one year or less is great). Make sure the homes are in the same immediate vicinity as yours and are as similar to yours as possible (bedrooms, baths, square footage, and so on).

It's imperative you are objective and unbiased with the sales you select to compare your home to. Every seller wants to make as much money as they can, but if you get dollar signs in your eyes and use the wrong comparable sales you will price your home too high. The result will be a home that sits for months without selling.

Remember, in real estate you only get paid if a home sells and closes. You don't want to put months of hard work into selling your home and receive nothing for it because you got greedy or prideful and used the wrong comparable sales to price your home. Have a knowledgeable, trusted friend, family member, or work colleague review the figures with you if you're having trouble determining which homes really are good comparable sales to use. Two heads can be better than one.

Using CMAs to Determine Your Home's Value

Comparative Market Analyses are only as good as the person doing them. To make the CMA accurate get the most detailed information possible. The more property sales you can draw from the better the CMA will be. Only use homes that have sold in the last year or two. There's no guarantee active homes will sell or at what price. Make sure the homes are as similar to yours as possible and in the immediate geographic locale. Find patterns or trends among the highest selling properties and the lowest, and then critique your home against these trends. Be as honest, objective, and detached as possible. Choosing an inflated asking price does nothing but hurt your cause.

The second way to gather data for a comparative market analysis is to call a Realtor who sells a lot of homes in your neighborhood. Be forthright and explain you are going to attempt to sell By Owner and need to research market conditions. Ask if she, her assistant, or a staff member would be kind enough to mail, email, or fax sale prices from similar homes in your area from the last three years to you. Tell the agent in return for providing the information she will be the first Realtor you call in two or three months if your home hasn't sold.

This is the best method for obtaining market analysis information. Agents have access to the MLS system, which is far and away the most detailed and comprehensive source for sale price data. Agents have knowledge and understanding of your area. Their skill and competence will be infused into the information they send you, which will help you determine what homes are relevant sales and which aren't. (Be careful the agent doesn't send you inflated prices or distort the search so you price your home too high and call her later because your home didn't sell).

For those of you who are politically correct this technique is perfectly ethical. The work will take the agent or their assistant fifteen to thirty minutes to do. In the event your home doesn't sell they have an excellent lead on listing a home without spending any money or very much time.

Now that you have detailed information on the sale prices of homes in your area study the numbers to find a range in value. There is usually a 10–15% swing in value from the average sales price. For instance, if the average price is $150,000 (the MLS data will show this or you can figure it out on a calculator) the swing in value will be approximately $130,000 to $170,000.

Every subdivision in every town is different, but this is a reliable rule of thumb to go by. Home prices are determined by the homes around them. When homes are grouped or clustered together in a subdivision it is difficult for one of them to be significantly higher or lower in price. There are exceptions but they're rare.

Final Determining Factor of Price

No matter what CMA data shows, smart agents tell you, or you believe to be true in your heart, the true value of a home is what a buyer will pay and what the seller will accept. Understanding values of homes is often confusing, frustrating, maddening, and surprising. Buyers determine the value of homes. If no one is willing to buy a home at a price that seems reasonable and fair, the home is simply not worth that price in those market conditions. Everyone say it with me: buyers determine the value of homes.

Choosing Your Asking Price

Take a close look at the range of price in your neighborhood. How does your home stack up against the homes that have sold in the last year or two? Is your home bigger? How does the condition of your home compare to the others? How motivated are you to sell? Does your home have more amenities like a glassed in porch, a den, or a breakfast nook? If it has more amenities what is the value of the extra amenities? Will buyers agree with your assessment? What value will buyers attach to a glassed in porch, den, or breakfast nook?

If you don't have a lot of sold comparables to compare against your home you might want to have an appraisal done. For $350–500 you can have an unbiased, professional appraiser appraise the value of your home. I don't recommend sellers do this when they are listing their home with an agent but it might be worth the money when you are selling By Owner. A word of caution though. Just because your home was appraised for a certain amount doesn't mean you are guaranteed to get that price or more.

After you have objectively (there's that word again) compared your home against the sold homes in your area it's time to set the price.

The most important aspect in the home selling process is price. It's even more important than location. Location is the biggest factor that influences price. Regardless of how terrific or awful a home is the asking price can cause a home to sell or not sell. Price alone can fix all problems with a house or cause a wonderful home to sit for a year without selling.

Price your home too high and buyers will avoid it, not write offers on it, or offer outrageously less for it. When a property sits on the market for a long time it becomes stigmatized (buyers will wonder "what's wrong with it?"), or the target of low ball offers. If you price your home too low you might sell for less than what you could have. Every seller wants to make as much money as possible.

Review your motives for selling one more time and decide if you want to place a high asking price (targeting a 90 day sale), a moderate or middle of the road price (60 day sale), or an aggressive price to sell quickly (30 days or less). Use a 5–10% swing from the average sales price to determine the high end and low end ranges of value. Also review the average days on the market information and the price differential statistics when picking a price. For more information on what these statistics are and how you get them, refer to Chapter 19, "Selling Your Home Through a Realtor."

Factors to keep in mind include the following:

➤ How much cushion or room you want to leave between your asking price and the bottom dollar you will take

➤ How many other homes are being sold in your area

➤ How many homes did not sell in the last year in your area

➤ How soon you need to sell to buy your next home

➤ The time of year

➤ Current interest rates

Reducing Your Asking Price

If you're not sure about what price tag to put on your home you could try a higher price for a few weeks. If you get lots of people to look at your home but no offers or one or two low offers you should consider dropping your price. Don't wait too long to reduce your price. The longer your home sits the less leverage you have. Change flyers and let buyers know you came down in price.

Preparing Your Home to Be Viewed

Chapter 18, "Getting the House Ready to Sell," deals exclusively with preparing your home to be shown to buyers. Refer to it for information on how to get your home ready *before* buyers come through.

It's also important to know what buyers like and dislike when they're touring FSBO'S. Make things as easy as possible for buyers. When they call to set up an appointment, schedule times that are convenient for the buyer, not you. There are sacrifices to be made for all the money you will save. Accommodate the buyers every way possible in the beginning and the transaction will get off to a good start. Inconvenience or offend buyers and they will disappear, or show their displeasure in the amount they offer for your home.

When buyers come through your home greet them at the front door. Briefly introduce yourself or family, invite them to look around, and then *get out of their way*. Step outside or go to the garage or basement while they tour your home. Buyers hate nothing more than to have sellers follow them around pointing out every small detail that might not make a bit of difference to them. Be assured if they have questions they will seek you out and ask them. Leave flyers and information about the home on the kitchen counter or dining room table so the buyer will find them. Store jewelry, money, and other valuables off site, or lock them away.

Don't oversell the buyers. Homeowners don't sell homes. Even good Realtors don't sell homes. Homes sell themselves. The location, condition, amenities, and price will sell your home, not you. Homeowners can stop homes from selling themselves by being pushy, overzealous, rude, or obnoxious. Keep your personality out of the transaction. Don't attempt to make friends with the buyer. Sell and close your home, then be friends.

Marketing Your Home

FSBOs are at a definite disadvantage when it comes to marketing. Not having your home listed in the MLS system severely hurts your marketing effort, but there are other things you can do. Because you are already behind the eight ball when it comes to marketing, pricing your home accurately and marketing the home effectively in other ways is critical.

Marketing actually means making consumers aware of your home and presenting the information in a way that makes buyers interested. You could have the best home in Metropolis, but if no one knows it's for sale, no one will buy it (Superman has X-ray vision, not ESP). Keep reading to see a list of traditional and alternative FSBO marketing techniques that will attract buyer's attention and present in the home in the best possible way.

Marketing Positively, Courteously, and Professionally

Whenever you are sending information about your home into the general public, whether it be online, via newspaper ads, flyers, or talking directly to buyers, be positive, polite, and pleasant. Check the accuracy of the data, the way it is presented, and the manner in which you deliver it. Be careful not to exclude any group of people in your marketing efforts (male, female, young old, black, white, and so on) and play up the strengths of your property.

For Sale By Owner Web Sites: Electronic Open Houses

Want to hold an open house while you watch college football on Saturday afternoons or NFL games on Sunday? Would you like to have an open house where you don't have to clean one room, and you're at the mall shopping for clothes and decorations for your next home?

This can be done by listing your home with a For Sale By Owner Web site. Online listings and virtual tours are replacing weekend open houses as the preferred way to start the house hunting process and do research and legwork. Instead of picking desirable neighborhoods and narrowing choices down by visiting twenty open houses in a month, buyers visit Web sites and look at twenty properties in an hour or two.

FSBO Web sites are the closest thing to the multiple listing service. They also are the most convenient way By Owner sellers can market their homes. There are national sites sellers can advertise on and local sites popping up in cities all over the country. For reasonable fees sellers can list their FSBO home and enjoy the benefits of both worlds: online listing and saving lots of money.

Using the Internet to Find and Sell Homes

Tracking the number of buyers and sellers using online services is a difficult task. The number of people believed to be using the Internet to buy or sell homes is around 20% of all buyers and sellers. Two years ago the number was less than 5%. In two years the number is expected to be 33% to 50%.

Owners.com

The biggest FSBO site is Owners.com (www.owners.com). This is the best site to advertise on because more buyers look for By Owners here than on any other site. There are over 35,000 listings nationwide on owners.com. Another benefit is that the site links directly to E-LOAN's online mortgage assistance program. Buyers can immediately get qualified for a loan and find out how much their down payment and monthly payments will be.

There are three options for advertising your home on Owners.com. The first costs no money and is a simple written description of your home with no photo. You submit the information to the site and they post it. The second option costs $65 and includes one photo with the written description. The third option is the premier package that includes five photos and a customized design layout. All listings are posted for four months, but a three-month extension can be granted.

I recommend the standard one photo listing for $65. You can save a little bit of money by not choosing the premier plan, yet still show the appeal of the home with a sharp picture.

One downside to this site is few sellers pay for the plan with even one photograph. Many buyers will rule out homes with no pictures because they think the seller might be hiding something or is extremely cheap and won't fix any problems in the home. You can distinguish your home from the others and not turn away buyers by spending just $65. I believe it's a good investment. To view the home page of Owners.com, see Figure 20.1.

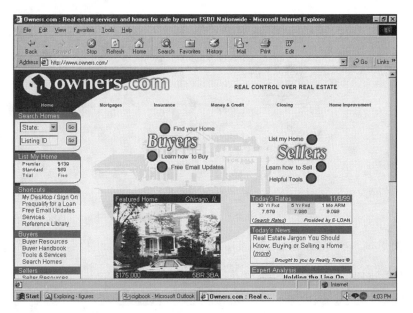

Figure 20.1
The Owners.com Web site is the largest online repository for houses sold by owner.

FSBO.COM

The other national Web site to advertise your home on is FSBO.COM (www.fsbo.com). This site is not as large as owners.com. For $19.95 you can post information about your home and a picture (you provide it) on this site. There are also numerous books and educational manuals available for $20 or less concerning selling By Owner.

FSBO.COM's prices are lower than Owners.com but the site isn't as large and doesn't get as much traffic. There are supplies and products sold on this site (yard signs, books, magazines) as well. To see the home page of FSBO.COM see Figure 20.2.

Interoffice Electronic Bulletins

An alternative marketing technique is posting your home information on your employer's online bulletin board. If you work close to your office or place of employment other employees might be interested in living close to work as well. Someone in your office also might live close to work and have a relative or friend who wants to move closer to them. This is particularly effective in large companies. Check with the human resources department to make sure this is okay and to see how to do it.

Getting the word out to as many people as possible is the key. Your marketing efforts might start a word-of-mouth networking chain that generates a buyer a few weeks later.

Another online marketing resource is list servers. Join a list server group that is interested in real estate. Someone in the group might be seeking a home similar to yours. This is a long shot marketing technique, but once again you might benefit from word-of-mouth advertising and find a buyer from your efforts.

Figure 20.2

At FSBO.COM, you can advertise your house for sale or browse the listings.

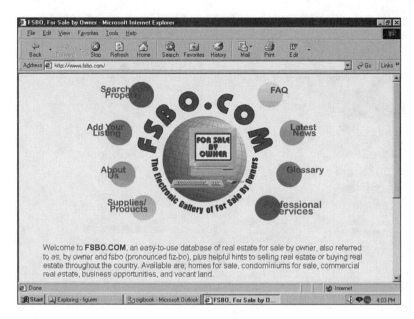

Email Distribution Pools

An excellent way to promote your home through your sphere of influence is email. Email is one of the least expensive, time saving, effective ways to get information about your home to a large number of people.

Email everyone you know (to save time use the copy function instead of mailing people individually) with a tiny bit of information about your home. They shouldn't be offended by this little bit of data. Have them forward the message to any one else they think is appropriate. If you get replies, you can send more complete information about the home.

Word-of-mouth advertising is extremely powerful and emails are a common form of communication in our society (just look at the success of the movie *The Blair Witch Project*). Chances are many of the initial people you email might have already seen your home visiting you. They will pass positive information on to others when they forward your message.

Newspaper Advertising

A traditional form of FSBO marketing is advertising in your town's newspaper. Place an ad in the Sunday real estate section (or whatever day features the most home listings). The ad should be concise, highlight the strongest and most important features of the home (bedrooms, baths, incredible lake view), and have the property address and your phone number and email address.

You can include the asking price if you want or you can leave it out. Including the price weeds out buyers in different price ranges. The bad thing about including the price is you get fewer phone calls and emails.

Track the ad week by week to see the number of buyers who are contacting you. Consider changing the ad or the placement of it in the newspaper if you're not getting good results. Look at other well-written ads or at agents' ads to see examples of strong ads.

Traditional Open Houses

Refer to Chapter 18 for extensive suggestions to prepare your home for a Sunday open house. Getting a large number of people to come to an FSBO open house is determined by two factors: the location of your home, and the marketing you do to promote it. If your home is in a hot location, in an area known for FSBOs, or on or near a busy thoroughfare you will get lots of notice from drive by traffic. The rest of us have to promote the open house the old fashioned way: signs, ads, and flyers.

You should already have an FSBO sign in your yard by the time you are holding your first open house. Get a second or third sign (hardware stores and home improvement stores carry them) and put them up at busy street corners and intersections around your home. These directionals point buyers to your house. Make sure your address is written in large, bold print so buyers can jot down the numbers from their cars.

Flyer tubes also can be purchased and mounted on your yard sign or stuck in the ground. These tubes hold flyers and fact sheets about your home. Don't get overly excited if thirty flyers disappear in the first two days. Nosy neighbors often want to see what you have in your home or what you're asking because they plan on selling in a year or two. Consider putting balloons on your yard sign when you're having an open house, and on the directional signs at street corners to attract people's attention.

Place a special open house ad in the Sunday paper. Make sure you list the time of the open house or buyers might come knock on your door all weekend long. The best time to hold an open house is Sunday afternoon any time between 1 P.M. and 5 P.M. Buyers expect open houses during those hours. Real estate agents hold open houses Sunday afternoons so you should benefit from their marketing efforts as well. If you want to be extra ambitious hang flyers in nearby grocery stores, drug stores, restaurants, and barber shops promoting your open house.

On Sunday stage your home to look its very best. When buyers come, greet them cordially, point out where the fact sheets are, and excuse yourself so they can tour the home by themselves. Step outside if the weather permits (getting cozy on patio or deck furniture shows the buyer how comfortable the home is), or go to the basement or garage. Buyers will appreciate this courtesy. They like to look by themselves with no interference. They will find you wherever you are if they like the home and have questions.

FSBO Newspaper Ads

The cost of newspaper ads are determined by the number of lines in the ad. Place your ad in the FSBO section when you are strictly advertising your home. When you are for advertising an open house your ad should be placed in the open house section. Mention the key features of the home. Use powerful and descriptive words like: elegant, classic, breathtaking, spectacular, stunning, stately, and enormous. Intrigue and tease buyers with short, yet attention-grabbing ads so they will contact you.

Creating Flyers and Fact Sheets

Flyers and fact sheets are much more important to FSBO homes than properties listed by real estate companies. Buyers can call the office or agent almost any time day or night to get information on a listed home. By Owners have to provide literature for buyers to view. If you have an old MLS listing sheet from when you bought the home pull it out and use the agent's information (make sure the data hasn't changed because of a room addition, new garage, and so on).

You can get information on your home regarding the square footage, lot size, year built, and legal description from the assessor's office or treasurer's office in your town. Try to obtain the most accurate information possible. Buyers have been known to sue FSBO sellers because data on square footage or school districts was wrong.

Stick fact sheets in a flyer tube in your front yard so buyers can obtain data when you're not home or without bothering you. Leave some flyers and fact sheets in the kitchen or dining room so you can show the home in a hurry.

Flyers and fact sheets should be professional and attractive in appearance, and loaded with positive information about the home. If your flyers look sloppy or poorly done buyers will assume your home is too. The top of the flyer should contain the key features of the home. List the home's strongest attributes at the top and progress downward.

A sharp color photo of the home dresses up the flyer nicely. Information on how the home is shown (appointment only, drive by, and so on), when it can be shown, and how you can be contacted should be on the flyer. You can put the asking price on the flyer or leave it off. Look at agent's flyers from other homes to get ideas on format, style, and design.

Other documents you might consider leaving in the home or putting in the flyer tube are surveys, residential sales disclosure sheets, and the utility averages. Your flyer and fact sheets are your calling cards. Make them attractive and informational.

Obtaining Proper Documents and Forms

Office supply stores such as Office Depot, Office Max, and Staples have contracts and forms needed to sell your home (any agent, real estate office, real estate attorney, or Board of Realtors office does too). Visit Owners.com and FSBO.COM's Web sites to download some of the basic documents as well. The forms you need when you start are the sellers residential sales disclosure form, the lead based paint disclosure form (for homes built before 1978), the purchase agreement, and the inspection amendment form.

When you get into the transaction you might end up needing counter offer forms, the amendment to the purchase agreement form, an addendum to the purchase agreement form, and an inspection amendment response form. The more negotiating that takes place the more forms you will need. If you get into a complicated transaction and rare or special documents are needed the Board of Realtors in your town will sell you any form you need.

Make these forms available to buyers when they are ready to write an offer. It is your responsibility to provide the documents, not the buyers. If the buyer wants to use their own forms review them carefully to make sure they are standard. You don't want language in a form that will hurt you or give the buyer a huge advantage. If you and the buyer disagree on the forms, use documents from the Board of Realtors. Their documents are the standard that everyone follows in cities across America.

Providing Mortgage Information for Buyers

Another responsibility of By Owner sellers is providing mortgage information to buyers if they need it or request it. Fact sheets with down payment, interest rate, and monthly payment information can be left in the kitchen or dining room. If they don't have financing in place offer the names of two or three good lenders.

Don't push mortgage information on buyers. They are just as qualified as you to research financing and are entitled to use whatever lender they want. Do pre-qualify them to make sure they can afford your home and can get a loan. A problem with many FSBO buyers is they haven't been pre-qualified or pre-approved yet. Ask for information about their lender.

Don't accept an offer until you have spoken to their loan originator or received a pre-qualification or pre-approval letter from their lender (some sellers take the extreme stance to not show their home unless buyers are pre-qualified). It doesn't matter what a buyer will pay for your home if they can't get a loan and close the deal. Be aware of the buyers that are liars.

Questions to ask a loan originator if you contact include the following: Do you know where the buyer's down payment is coming from? Did the credit score come back good? How is the buyer's credit history? How long has the buyer worked at her place of employment? Are the buyer's income and debt ratios in line for a loan of this amount? Is there enough money in reserve accounts if the buyer was unemployed for two or three months to pay the mortgage? Will the buyer be approved for this loan?

Getting Buyers Pre-Qualified

If the buyer doesn't already have a mortgage company or bank they are working with you should offer the names of two or three lenders that you have researched or used in the past. Without pressuring the buyer try to get them to use one of your lenders because you know your lender is good (you'll be using them when you buy your next home). Consider offering two or three different types of lenders; mortgage company, bank, male originator, female originator, big company, small company. You'll have more control over the deal if you know the buyer's financing is going smoothly with your lender.

Negotiating Price and Terms

Without an agent you will do all your negotiating yourself. You must be thick skinned during this process and not take things personally. Buyers usually say as many negative things as possible to try to get a better price on the home. If you let things get to you and are emotional the negotiating process can be extremely difficult.

Try role playing with a friend or neighbor to get used to negative comments about your home. See past the negative comment and counter verbally with a positive response.

For instance, your friend might say the basement has a bit of moisture, the appliances are old, and the paint and wallpaper are horribly outdated in the bedrooms. You could counter by saying the asking price reflects the tiny bit of moisture in the basement, the appliances are covered by a home warranty, and the paint and wallpaper can easily and inexpensively be changed.

Control how information is being passed if you don't negotiate well. Use the email, faxes, or the phone if you don't like talking face to face with buyers while negotiating. For an in-depth discussion on negotiating, refer to Chapter 14, "Writing an Offer and Negotiating the Terms."

Ordering Title Insurance

Congratulations, you accepted an offer! There is still a ways to go before you receive a proceeds check. Your first duty is to order title insurance.

How to Pick a Title Company

The seller gets to pick the title company because you will be paying the larger premium for the buyer (the buyer has to pay for a title insurance policy for their lender). Ask any professionals you know that work in or around the real estate business if they can recommend a good title insurance company. Also, ask your insurance agent, attorney, or accountant. If you have a friend, family member, or co-worker who recently closed on a house inquire about the title company they closed at and how the proceedings went.

A final way to find a title company is to pick one close to your home. Contact them and ask how long they've been in business, how many closings they handle each week, and what their rates are to close a deal. Title policies are based on the gross sales price so most title companies fees are within a few dollars of each other. Contact a couple other companies to make sure your title company's fees are standard.

Role of the Title Company

The title company presides over all aspects of the closing. They do a search on the property address and the buyer and seller's social security numbers to make sure there are no liens or judgments. They order the survey to ensure there are no encroachments like a fence, shed, or garage (easements and right of ways are also listed), and to show where the property lines fall.

What Is Title Insurance and Marketable Title?

Title insurance is insurance protecting a seller and buyer from a lien, judgment, or encumbrance against the deed and title of a property. Sellers pay for a title insurance policy for the buyer so marketable title can be passed without fear of any lien showing up later. *Marketable title* means the title is free and clear of any liens or judgments. If the title company missed a five-year-old tax lien on the property, the new homeowner would not be liable, the title company would.

Sellers should fax or mail copies of the purchase agreement and all additional forms to the title company. They also should give the name of their current mortgage company and the loan account number to the title company so they can order a payoff of your mortgage.

The title company's escrow officer explains all documents to the buyer and seller, collects signatures on the documents, gathers funds from the buyer, verifies both parties' identities, and disperses funds to the seller in the form of a proceeds check.

In essence, the title company serves as an impartial third party that closes all the paperwork and financial and legal matters for the buyer, seller, and mortgage company. If the title company makes a mistake, the seller has purchased title insurance through the closing and the seller would not be liable. Refer to Chapter 15, "Congratulations Mr. & Mrs. Jones, They've Accepted Our Offer: Now What?" for additional comments about the role of title companies.

The Inspection Process

The inspection process is a negotiation just like the negotiation that takes place when seller and buyer agree on a sales price. Inspections can be extremely easy to get through if the home is an excellent condition. On the other hand, if a home is older, in average to poor condition or the buyer is paying top dollar, the inspection process can be long, difficult, and stressful.

Have the inspection done as quickly as possible and ask for a written report immediately. If there are going to be problems with the negotiation you want to know about them right away and you might want to keep showing the house to other buyers (if you are going to accept backup offers let the buyer with the primary accepted offer know).

What Does a Seller Have to Repair?

There are some items the seller will have to fix if you want to close the deal, and there are many others that are not mandatory but the buyer will want you to repair them.

Items sellers usually have to fix are

➤ Furnace/AC that doesn't work

➤ Roof that leaks or has no remaining life

➤ Active termite infestation or other wood destroying infestation (ants, mold, and mildew)

➤ Electrical problems that are known fire hazards

➤ Plumbing that leaks excessively or doesn't work

➤ Excessively high radon gas levels

➤ Asbestos wrapped materials that are loose and sending fibers in the air

➤ Structural problems that compromise home's structural integrity

➤ Water damage and active moisture

These items are generally considered major defects and sellers have to fix them. If the buyer agrees to buy the home in as-is condition or the seller has disclosed one of these defective conditions prior to the buyer writing the offer, the buyer should not be able to use the disclosed defect as a means of getting out of the transaction.

Any problem or deficiency that is not a major defect is negotiable. The buyer can ask for anything to be fixed. The seller can negotiate and say he'll only fix three of the five items the buyer requested. The seller also can say he'll lower the purchase price $500 instead of doing any repairs or give the buyer $500 at closing instead of making the repairs.

The inspection process usually comes down to a negotiation. There might be one major defect the seller has to fix and three smaller, less important and inexpensive items the buyer wants fixed. Whatever the seller and buyer come to agreement on will be what gets fixed. Remember, buyers want to buy homes and sellers want to sell homes so try not to lose a good buyer and good transaction over the inspection process. You'll have to sell your home all over again (maybe for less money the next time) and you might have to go through the same inspection problem again.

Are Attorneys Needed?

Opinions vary on this issue. There is nothing inherently necessary about having an attorney. No laws require it. When in doubt I say FSBO sellers should contact a real estate attorney. If you think you might be doing something erroneously, a buyer might be trying to take advantage of you or you might be hit with a lawsuit.

If the transaction is going smoothly and you feel comfortable with everything that is happening you might consider moving forward without the help of an attorney. There isn't one right way to answer this question so common sense and your gut instinct should guide you. As long as seller and buyer are comfortable and the trans-action is on a healthy, positive level, you might be able to close the deal without spending a few hundred to $500 on an attorney.

For those of you who are extra cautious or don't have stomachs for messy, compli-cated situations you might want to contact an attorney up front and have them review all documents and proceedings. When things are done the right way attorneys are no more than insurance policies that read contracts and say "It's okay. Sign it." Title companies are good places to find real estate attorneys. They have them on staff or on retainer.

Seller's Closing Costs and Responsibilities

If the seller is giving possession the day of closing they should be completely packed and out of the home. Keys are usually handed over at the closing table. All repairs and money for repairs also should be taken care of. Any manuals, garage door openers, and warranty plans should be passed the day of closing as well.

Sellers need to bring photo identification to the closing and any documents verifying completed work (for example, clear termite report after termites are treated or invoice from electrician with license number)

Check This Out

Closing Costs Sellers Are Expected to Pay

➤ The remaining balance of your first mortgage loan and the payoff of a second mortgage or equity line if applicable.

➤ Property taxes through the date of closing (the title company will figure this amount for you).

➤ Title insurance for the buyer. The premium amount is based on the gross sales price of the home.

➤ Title company attorney fees to review all documents (about $50–75).

➤ Courier fee to send the check to pay off your mortgage balance (about $25).

➤ If the buyer's financing is an FHA loan, the document preparation fee, the underwriting fee, and the tax service fee (about $350–400).

➤ If the buyer's financing is a VA loan, the items involved with an FHA loan plus the settlement closing fee (about $300) and the initial termite inspection (about $50–100).

All other closing cost items are negotiable and the seller does not have to pay them. Actually, the other closing cost items are the buyer's responsibility unless they offer a high sales price and entice the seller to pay more closing costs.

The Least You Need to Know

➤ Research market conditions such as the average number of days on the market, average sales prices, and so on, in your neighborhood to know the range in value of similar homes and the market value of your home.

➤ Use sold data from comparable homes in your area that have sold in the last six to 18 months as well as the reasons you are selling to determine an asking price that is neither too high nor too low.

➤ Advertise your home in the newspaper, with street and yard signs, with mass email distribution, by word of mouth networking, on office bulletin boards, through open houses and flyers, and consider using a For Sale By Owner Web site. Accommodate buyers' wishes when showing your home, even if it inconveniences you.

➤ Try to learn as much as possible about the buyer writing an offer on your home; figure out what they want, and gain as much leverage as possible when negotiating. Expect a lot, and you will get a lot—low expectations result in inferior results.

➤ Pick a reputable title/escrow company or attorney to handle the closing; prepare in advance for all the sellers' responsibilities, and have everything done in a timely manner so closing is simply a signing party with no last-minute problems.

Speak Like a Geek: The Complete Archives

A-level credit   Buyers with credit ratings of "A" have the best credit and get the best interest rates from lenders. Conversely, "D" credit is the worst rating and lands buyers the worst interest rates.

ACCs; Architectural Control Committees   Committee of homeowners in a condominium complex or planned unit development (PUD) that determines what changes, modifications, and additions can be made to individual units.

adjustable-rate mortgage   A mortgage that permits the lender to adjust its interest rate periodically on the basis of changes in a specified index.

agent   A person authorized to work on another's behalf. They are obligated to work in the other person's best interest.

appraisal   A determination of the value of an improved property or parcel of land by a licensed, certified, impartial individual.

appreciation   The increase in the value of a property due to changes in market conditions or other causes. Appreciation is the opposite of depreciation.

As Is   Buying a home without a home inspection. The home is purchased in the condition it was viewed.

balloon mortgage   A type of mortgage where the loan amount is amortized over the entire length of the loan (30 years), but the loan comes due in a shorter time (typically 5 or 7 years). The balance of the loan is due in one final installment known as the balloon payment.

blueprints Mechanical scale drawings that lay out the specifications to size of the exact dimensions and measurements of a home, inside and out, level by level.

broker An agent authorized to operate his own agency. A principal broker is the sole individual who runs an office.

budget plan A payment plan where a homeowner pays the same amount each month, regardless of what the actual utility usage was.

building code Local regulations that control design, construction, and materials used in construction. Building codes are based on safety and health standards.

buyer specialists Agents that specialize in helping buyers purchase homes.

buyer's agent A real estate salesperson who works exclusively for the buyer but is paid a commission by the seller.

buyer's market When market conditions favor the buyer. Time of season, interest rates, the number of homes on the market, the economy, and trends within the real estate industry dictate whether a market is a buyer's market, a seller's market, or a level playing field.

cash flow The difference between the monthly mortgage a landlord pays a bank and the monthly rent a tenant pays the landlord for a rental property.

clear title A title that is free of liens or legal questions pertaining to the ownership of the property.

closing The process of finalizing all the dealings associated with the sale and purchase of a home.

closing costs Expenses over and beyond the sales price of the property incurred by the buyer and seller in transferring ownership of real property.

commission The fee an agent earns for the sale of a home, usually a percentage of the gross sales price.

common areas Those portions of a building, land, and amenities owned or managed by a planned unit development (PUD) or condominium project's homeowner's association that are used by all unit owners, who share in the common expense and maintenance.

comparable properties Used for comparative purposes in the appraisal process and in picking a list price of a home. Comparables are properties like the property under consideration. They have reasonably the same size, location, and amenities and have recently been sold. They help determine fair market value.

contingency   A provision included in the purchase agreement that states certain events must occur or conditions be met for the contract to be valid and the transaction closed.

contract   An oral or written agreement to do or not to do a specific thing.

conventional mortgage   A type of mortgage made by lending institutions where the buyer pays at least 5% of the purchase price as a down payment at closing.

counter offer   A counter response or new proposal that makes changes to terms in the original purchase agreement.

credit report   A report of all your debt information compiled by an independent agency. The credit report shows all outstanding debt as well as a record of payment on outstanding debts.

custom built   Homes that are designed and built with a buyer's individual wants and needs in mind. They are typically more expensive, better quality construction, and designed in collaboration between a builder and the buying customer.

default   Failure to make payments on a loan or mortgage.

defect   Any problem, flaw, or deficiency in a home or its improvements. Major defects can make transactions fall apart during the inspection process.

depreciation   A decline in the value of property; the opposite of appreciation.

discount broker   A real estate office that lists homes at commission rates lower than the local custom.

discount points   A lender's tool to lower the interest rate. Buyers can buy down the rate by paying for a discount point (usually 1% of the loan amount).

down payment   Money paid up front for the purchase of a home.

earnest money   Deposit made when an offer to purchase is written. Shows buyers' sincerity and ability to purchase the home.

easement   A right of way giving persons other than the owner access to or over a property. For example, utility poles.

encumbrance   Anything that affects or limits the fee simple title to a property, such as mortgages, leases, easements mechanics liens, or restrictions.

equity   The financial interest or cash value of your home, minus the current loan balance and the costs incurred to sell the home.

escrow account   The account in which a mortgage service holds the borrower's escrow payments prior to paying expenses such as property taxes and homeowner's insurance.

fee simple   The greatest possible interest of ownership a person can have in real estate.

FHA mortgage   A loan guaranteed by the federal government. Stands for Federal Housing Administration. A small down payment is made, but mortgage insurance is required.

fiduciary responsibility   The relationship that exists when an individual or company represents someone else.

first mortgage   A mortgage that is the primary lien or debt against a property.

first-right contingency   Sales contract where buyers stipulate they want to buy a home subject to their current home selling.

fishing for buyers   A seller who is not motivated to sell unless the right buyer comes along and writes the perfect offer. Sellers usually list homes at extremely high prices when they're fishing in hopes a buyer will pay it.

fixed-rate mortgage   A type of mortgage where the interest rate is fixed for the life of the loan.

flood insurance   Insurance that compensates for physical property damages resulting from flooding. It is required by properties located in federally designated flood areas.

foreclosure   The legal process where a mortgaged property is seized because of failure to make payment.

FSBO   For Sale By Owner; A home that is offered for sale without the services of an agent.

Gift Letter   A letter that is required by lenders if you receive a down payment from a family member or friend as a gift.

good-faith negotiating   Two parties engaging in a fair, open negotiation where both parties genuinely seek a resolution that benefits both sides.

hazard insurance   Insurance coverage that compensates for physical damage to a property from fire, wind, vandalism, or other hazards.

home inspection   A thorough examination that evaluates the structural and mechanical condition of a property. It is usually inserted in the sales contract as a contingency by the buyer and performed by a licensed professional.

home warranty   A type of insurance to protect owners from expensive home repairs. Most plans cost around $350 (with a $100 deductible) and cover all the major mechanical systems and appliances for one year. They are especially useful for older homes, or homes in disrepair.

homeowners' association   A nonprofit association of homeowners that manages the common areas of a planned unit development or condominium complex.

house poor   When a buyer has bought a home at the uppermost level of his price range and stretched himself so far financially he can barely make the mortgage payments.

income-debt ratios   The percentages of your monthly income compared to the amount of monthly debt you pay out.

interest rate   The percentage the lender charges you for borrowing money.

investment property   A property not occupied by the owner but leased out to tenants. Investors own these properties strictly to make money.

lien   A legal claim against a property that must be paid when the property is sold.

listing specialists   Agents that primarily focus on listing homes and don't work with buyers. Buyer specialists are agents that specialize in helping buyers purchase homes.

Loan-To-Value ratio; LTV ratio   Used by lenders to describe how much the borrower has financed. For example, if you put 20% down on a $100,000 home, you have financed 80% or $80,000. Your LTV is 80%.

lock-in   Guaranteeing a certain interest rate for a period of time.

low-ball offer   An offer considerably lower in price than the seller's asking price. An offer 15% lower than list price or more is considered a low ball.

maintenance fee   A fee charged by condominium associations, co-ops, or planned unit developments for the upkeep of common areas of property.

MLS; Multiple Listing Service   A computerized database of all the past and current homes for sale in a large area. Homes that are listed with real estate companies are entered in this database system. Agents share the information to help the sale of real estate.

mortgage   A legal document that pledges a property to the lender as security for payment of a debt.

move-in condition   A home in such excellent condition structurally, mechanically, cleanliness-wise, and décor-wise, no work needs to be done.

origination fee   A fee paid to a lender for processing a loan application and originating the loan from start to close. Usually one percent of the loan amount.

PITI; principal interest taxes insurance   The total monthly payment made on a home that includes the principal and interest payments on the mortgage, the property tax escrow payment, and homeowner's insurance escrow payment.

329

power of attorney   A legal document that authorizes another person to act on one's behalf and sign legal documents.

pre-approved   Supplying a lender with all pertinent financial and personal details before you start looking for a home. Lenders give a definite commitment that a borrower will be approved for a loan.

pre-qualified   Supplying a lender with a portion of financial and personal details before you start looking for a home. Lenders give an estimate or educated guess that a borrower will be approved for a loan.

price differential   The statistical difference between the listing price and the average sales price in an area. For example, a home listed at $100,000 that sells for $95,500 has a price differential of 95.5%.

PUD; planned unit development   A project or subdivision that includes common property that is owned and maintained by a homeowners' association for the benefit and use of the individual PUD unit owners.

purchase or sales agreement   A written contract signed by the buyer and seller stating the terms and conditions under which a property will be sold.

proration   A division of fees in an exact manner, usually to a certain date. For example, property taxes are paid according to who lived in the home up to the day of closing.

radon   A naturally occurring radioactive gas found in some homes that in sufficient quantities can be hazardous to a homeowner's health.

recorder   The public official who keeps records of transactions that affect real property in an area. Sometimes referred to as Recorder's Office or County Clerk.

rent back   A term to describe sellers who stay in the home after closing and possession. The sellers pay the buyers, or new homeowners, rent to remain in the property for an agreed upon amount of time.

repair allowance   Money given from the seller to the buyer in lieu of any repairs being made to a property.

sales status; active, pending, sold, expired, withdrawn   Active means a home is on the market for sale. Pending means a purchase agreement has been accepted on a property, but the transaction has not yet been closed. Sold homes have already closed. Expired means the house did not sell during the four- or six-month listing period. Withdrawn means the home was taken off the market, usually by the seller, and is no longer for sale.

second mortgage   A mortgage that has a lien position subordinate or behind the first mortgage. Also known as a credit line or equity line of credit.

seller disclosure   A form required by most states in which the seller must disclose any known defects or problems of the home.

seller's market   When market factors favor home sellers so they have strong leverage when dealing with buyers. Time of season, interest rates, the number of homes on the market, the economy, and trends within the real estate industry dictate whether a market is a buyer's market, a seller's market, or a level playing field.

settlement statement; HUD one closing statement   A document that provides an itemized listing of all funds that are payable at closing from buyer and seller. Determines the closings costs and down-payment dollar amount the buyer needs to bring to closing and the net-proceeds dollar amount the seller receives at closing.

spec homes   Speculation or speculative homes. These homes are built by builders even though there is no buyer under contract to buy the house.

sphere of influence   All the people in your life that influence you and vice versa. Generally this consists of your family and relatives, friends, co-workers, business associates, and sometimes acquaintances.

sub-agency   An outdated form of agency representation where an agent showed buyers homes, did tons of leg work, and helped the buyer write an offer, but actually worked for the seller and was paid by the seller.

subdivision   A large piece of land divided into several plots on which individual homes are built.

survey   An examination of the property boundaries to find out the quantity of land, location of improvements, and other information. The surveyor creates a map or drawing of the legal boundaries of the property.

sweat equity   Contribution to the construction or rehabilitation of a property in the form of labor or services rather than cash.

tenant's rights   A property is rented by a tenant and the tenant can stay in the home until the term of the lease expires, even if the lease period ends months after the sale and closing of the home.

title   A legal document evidencing a person's right to or ownership of a property.

title company   A company that specializes in examining and insuring titles to real estate.

title insurance   Insurance that protects the lender (lender's policy) and the buyer (buyer's policy) against loss arising from disputes over ownership of a property or legal claims against the property.

under appraising   When a home does not appraise for the sales price in the purchase agreement. For example, if a seller and buyer settle on a price of $120,000 with a loan amount of $116,000, but the home appraises for $114,000, the lender will not loan $116,000 for a home deemed to be worth only $114,000.

underwriting   The process of evaluating a loan to determine whether the loan is a good risk.

zoning   Laws that establish how a property can be used and what codes must be followed when constructing new buildings.

Index